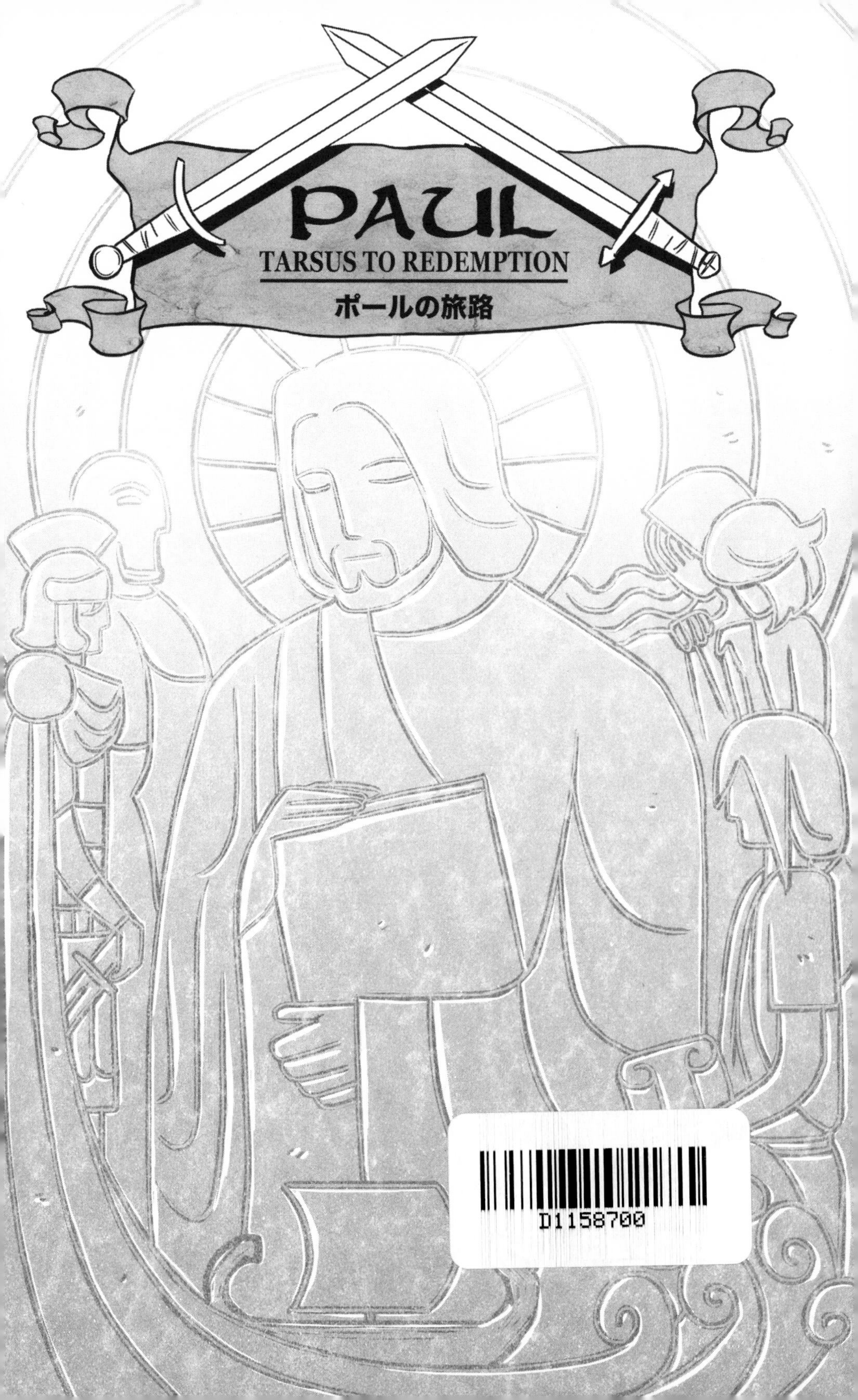
PAUL
TARSUS TO REDEMPTION
ポールの旅路

PAUL
TARSUS TO REDEMPTION

VOLUME 3

Story by Gabrielle Gniewek
Art by Sean Lam

PAUL: TARSUS TO REDEMPTION (VOLUME 3) by Gabrielle GNIEWEK and Sean LAM
© 2010 ATIQTUQ

ISBN 978-0-9826538-4-5

0 9 8 7 6 5 4 3 2 1

Printed in the United States of America

Published by ATIQTUQ
817 Mission Ave., Suite 1A
San Rafael, CA 94901
www.atiqtuq.com

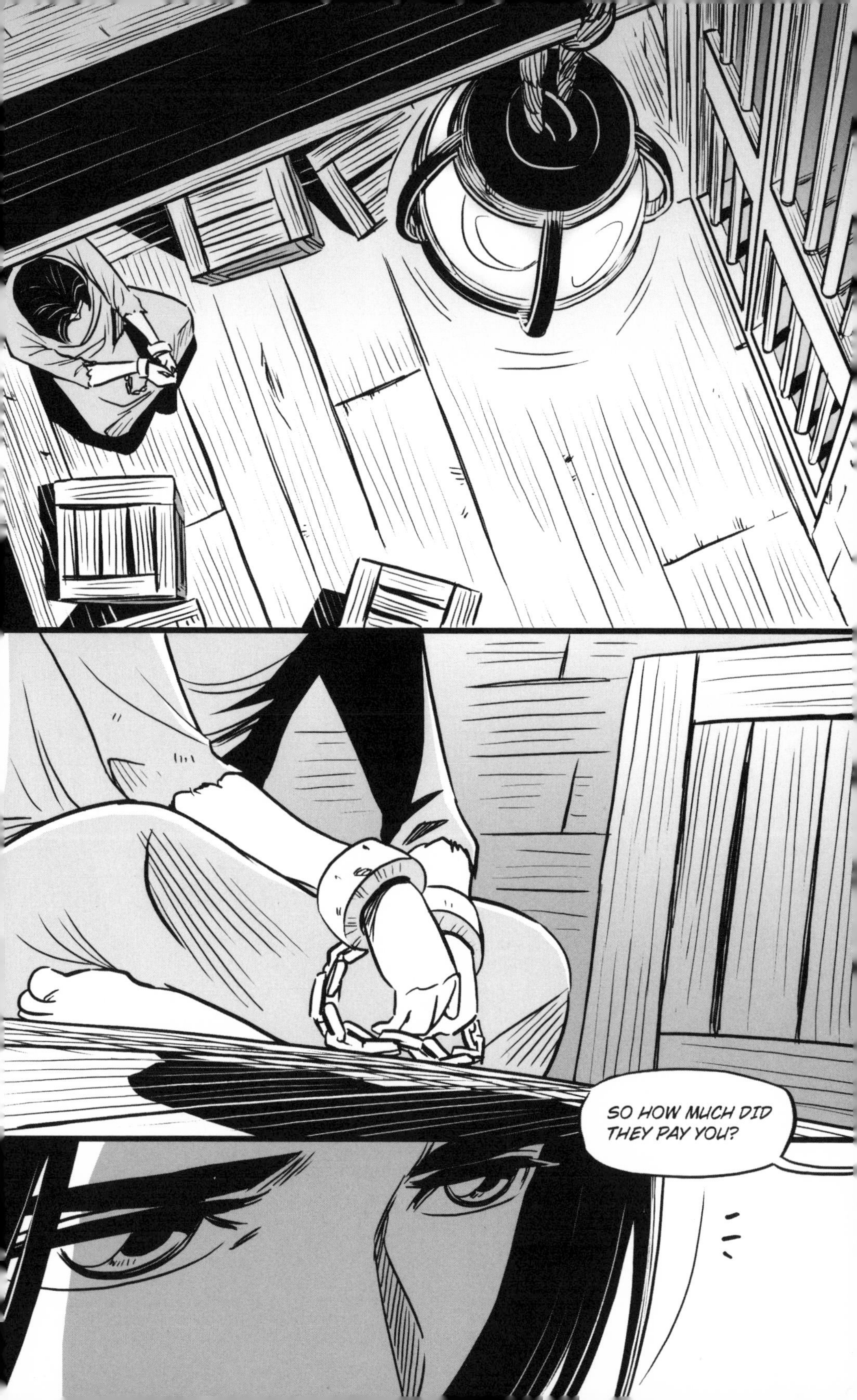
SO HOW MUCH DID THEY PAY YOU?

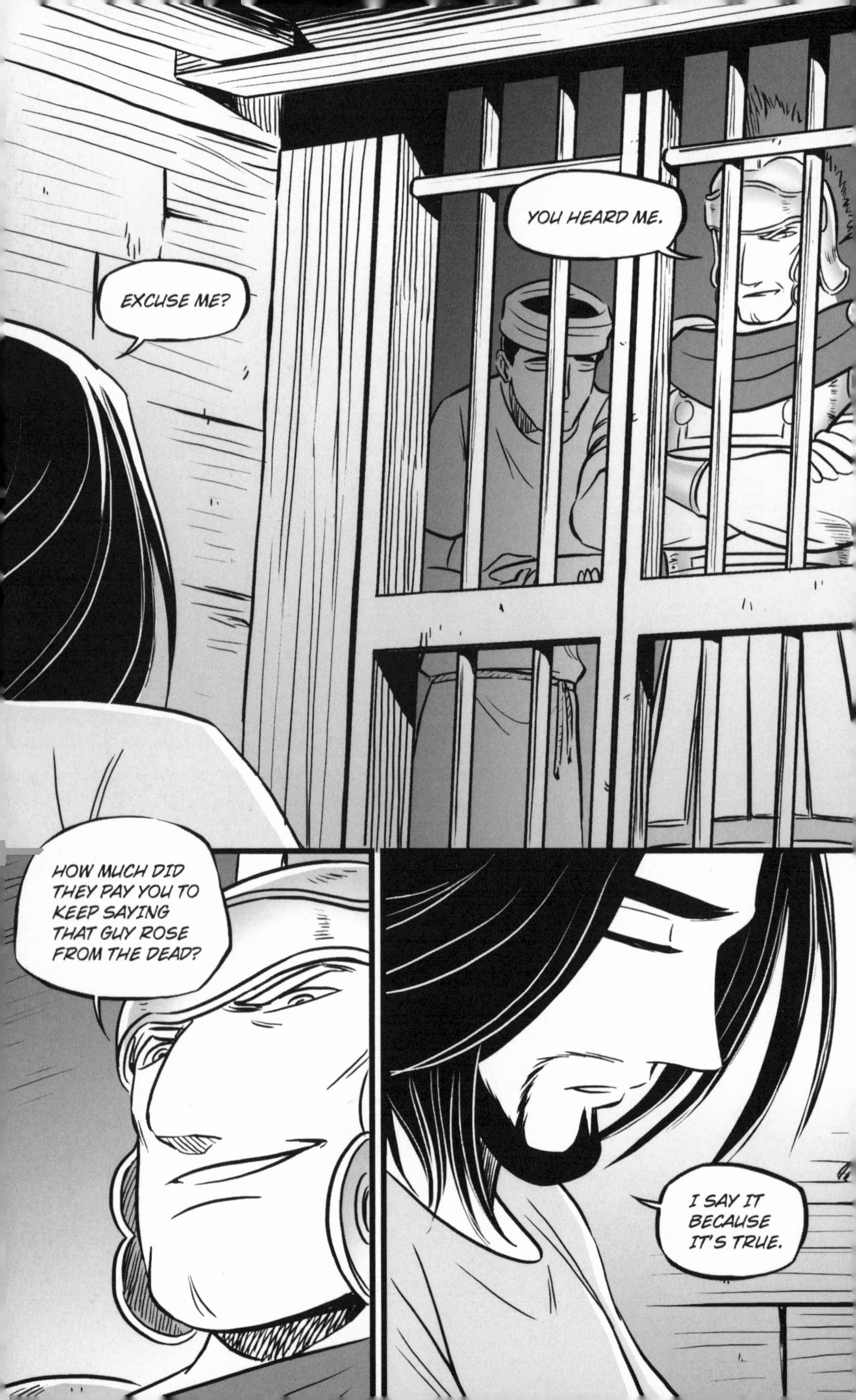
EXCUSE ME?
YOU HEARD ME.
HOW MUCH DID THEY PAY YOU TO KEEP SAYING THAT GUY ROSE FROM THE DEAD?
I SAY IT BECAUSE IT'S TRUE.

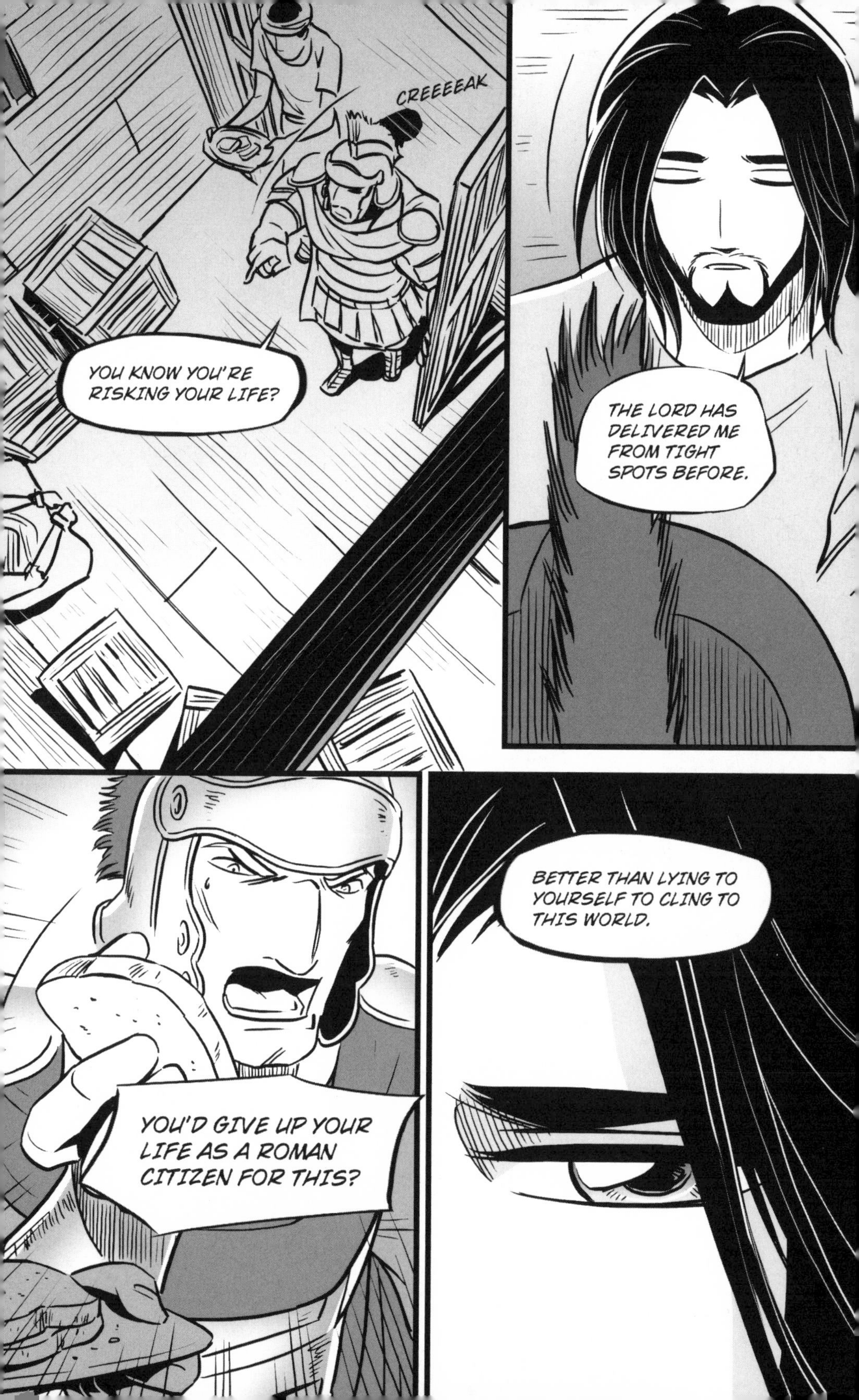
CREEEEAK
YOU KNOW YOU'RE RISKING YOUR LIFE?
THE LORD HAS DELIVERED ME FROM TIGHT SPOTS BEFORE.
YOU'D GIVE UP YOUR LIFE AS A ROMAN CITIZEN FOR THIS?
BETTER THAN LYING TO YOURSELF TO CLING TO THIS WORLD.

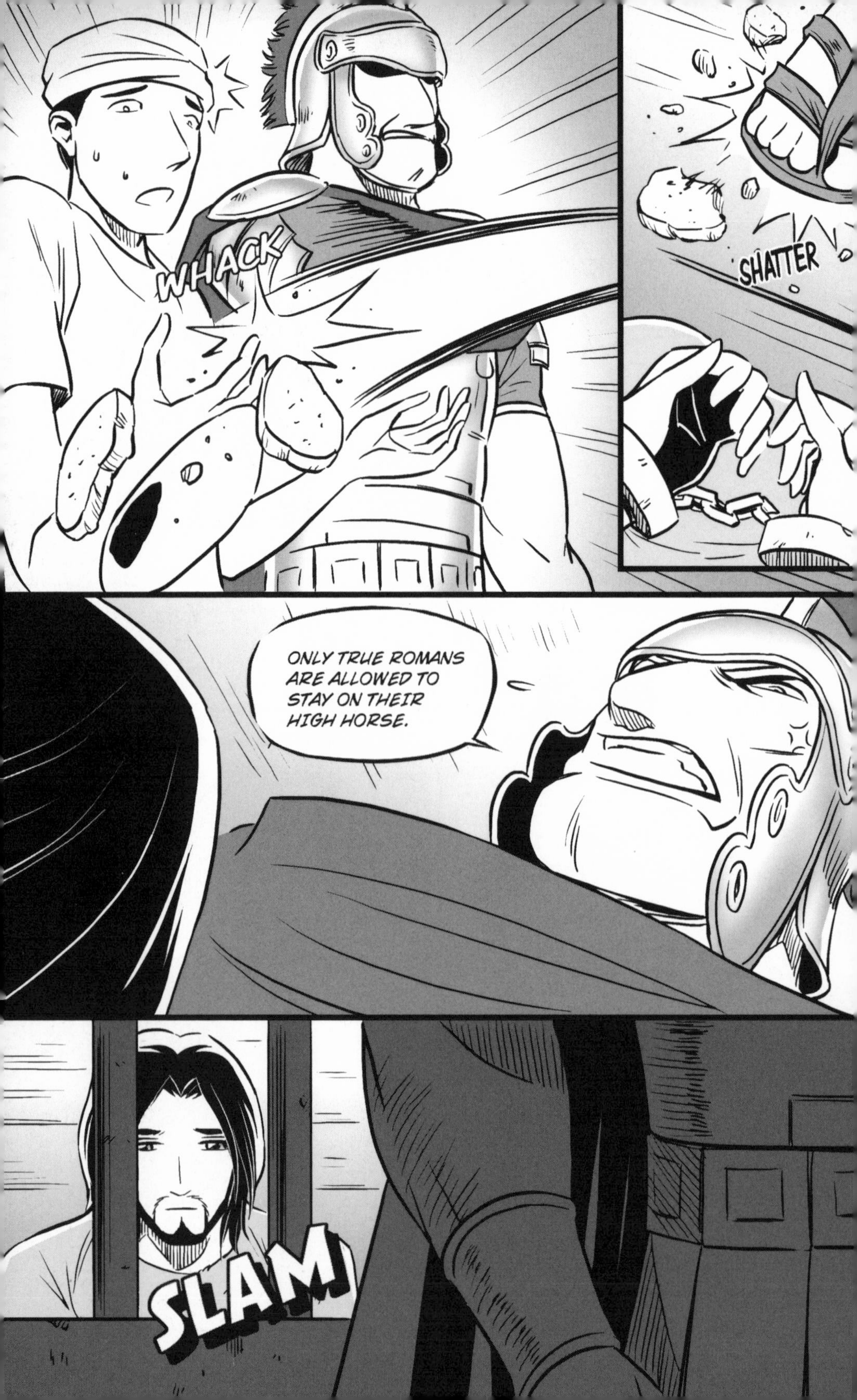
WHACK
SHATTER
ONLY TRUE ROMANS ARE ALLOWED TO STAY ON THEIR HIGH HORSE.
SLAM

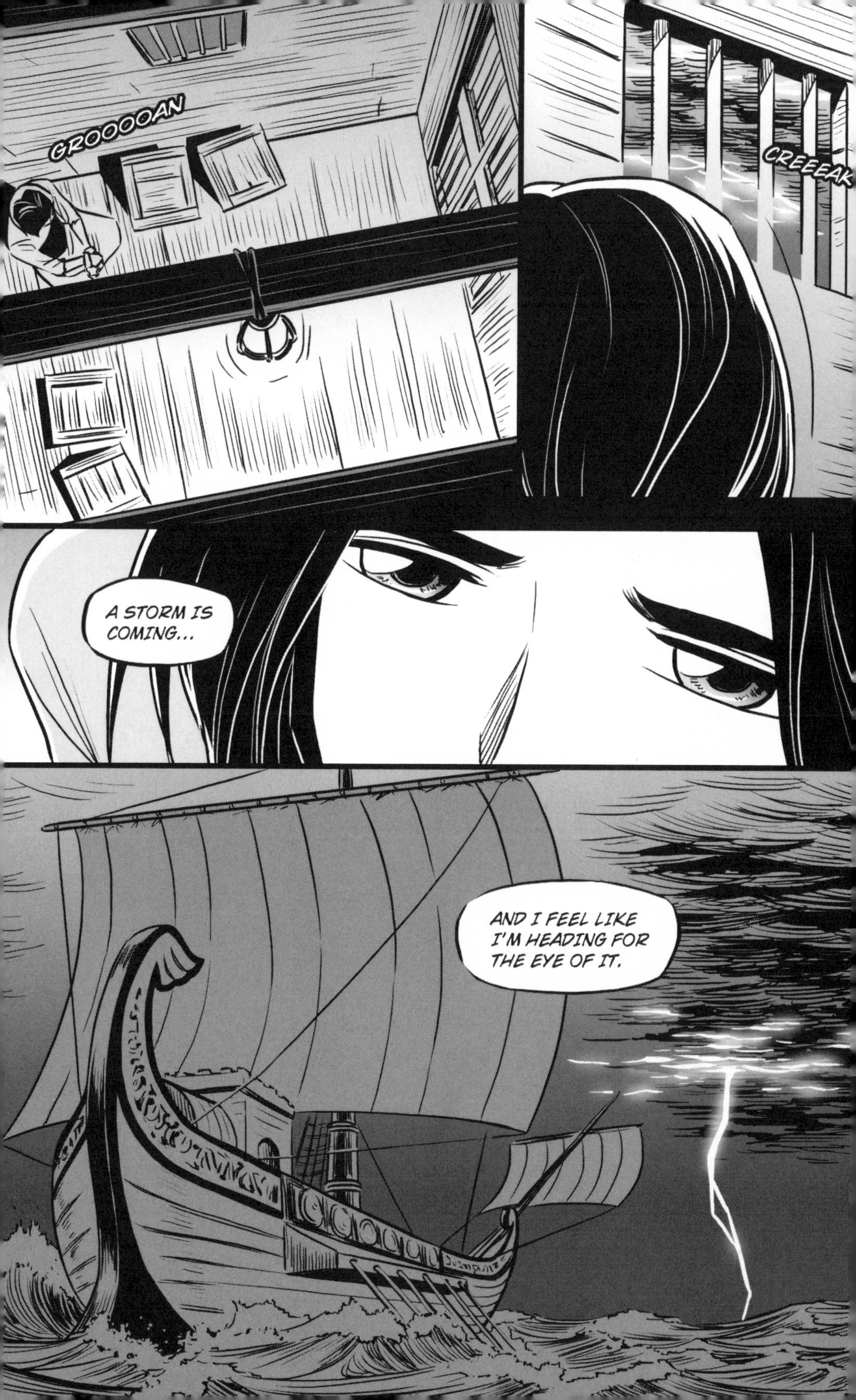
GROOOOAN
CREEEAK
A STORM IS COMING...
AND I FEEL LIKE I'M HEADING FOR THE EYE OF IT.

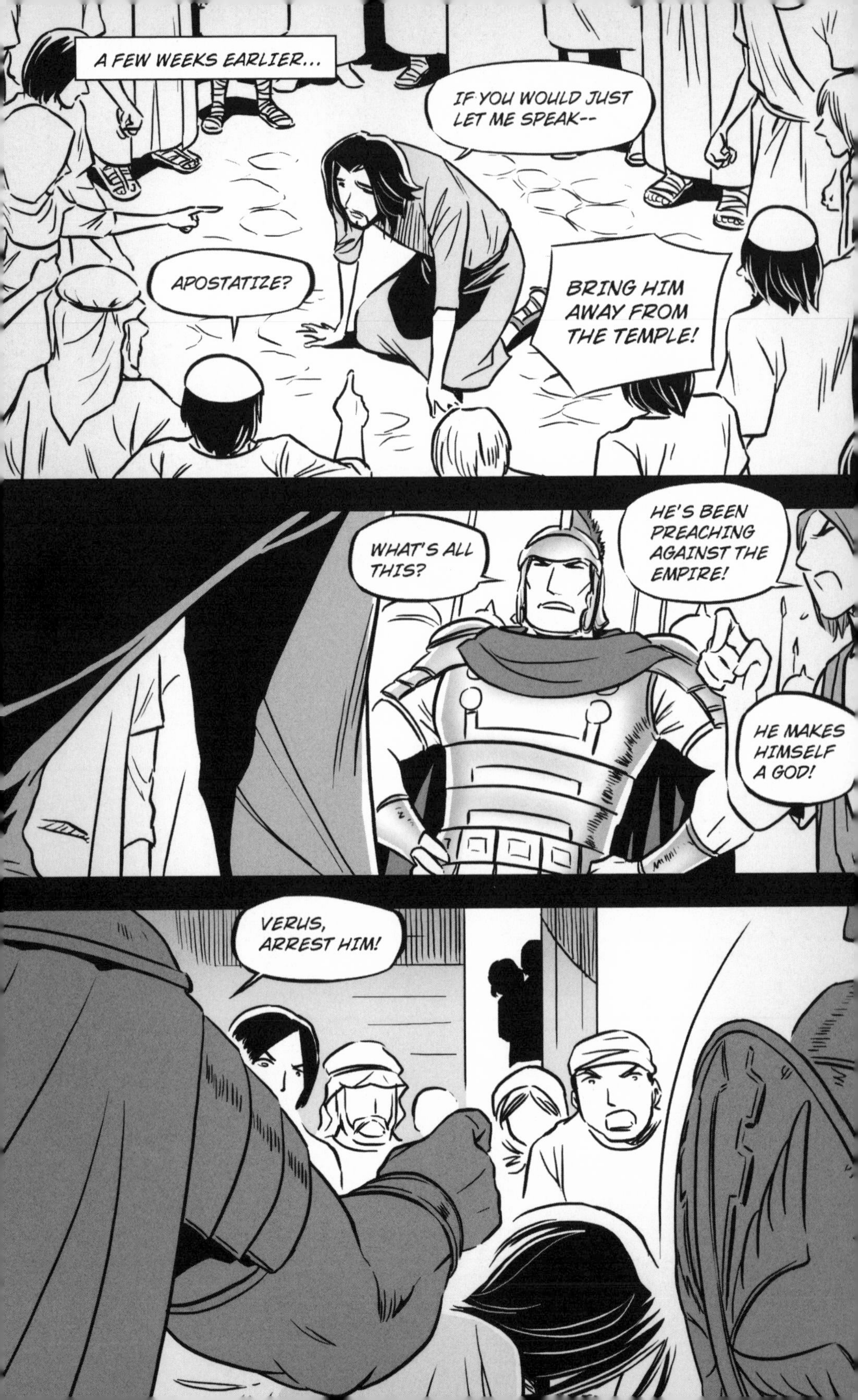
A FEW WEEKS EARLIER...
IF YOU WOULD JUST LET ME SPEAK--
APOSTATIZE?
BRING HIM AWAY FROM THE TEMPLE!
WHAT'S ALL THIS?
HE'S BEEN PREACHING AGAINST THE EMPIRE!
HE MAKES HIMSELF A GOD!
VERUS, ARREST HIM!

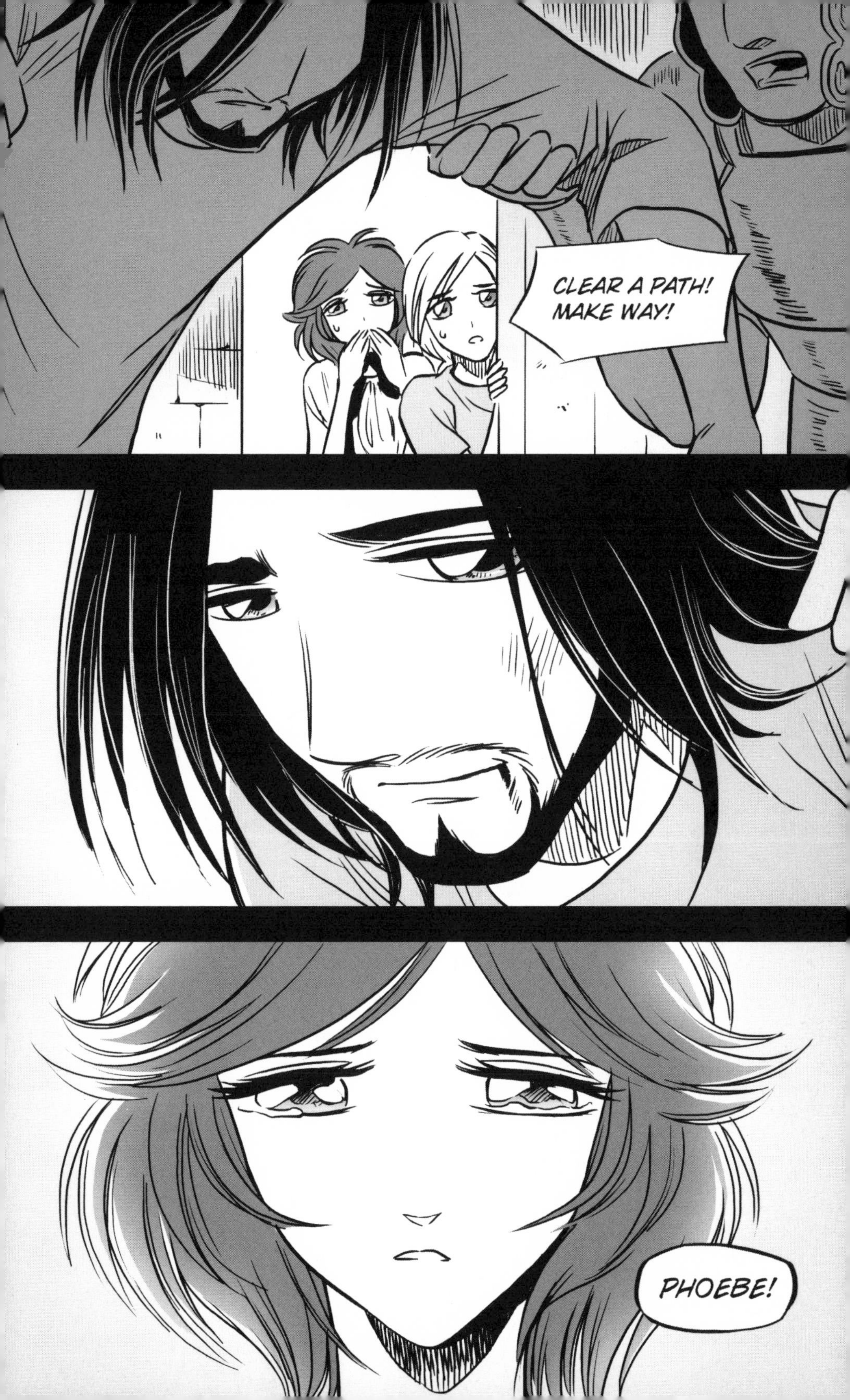
CLEAR A PATH! MAKE WAY!
PHOEBE!

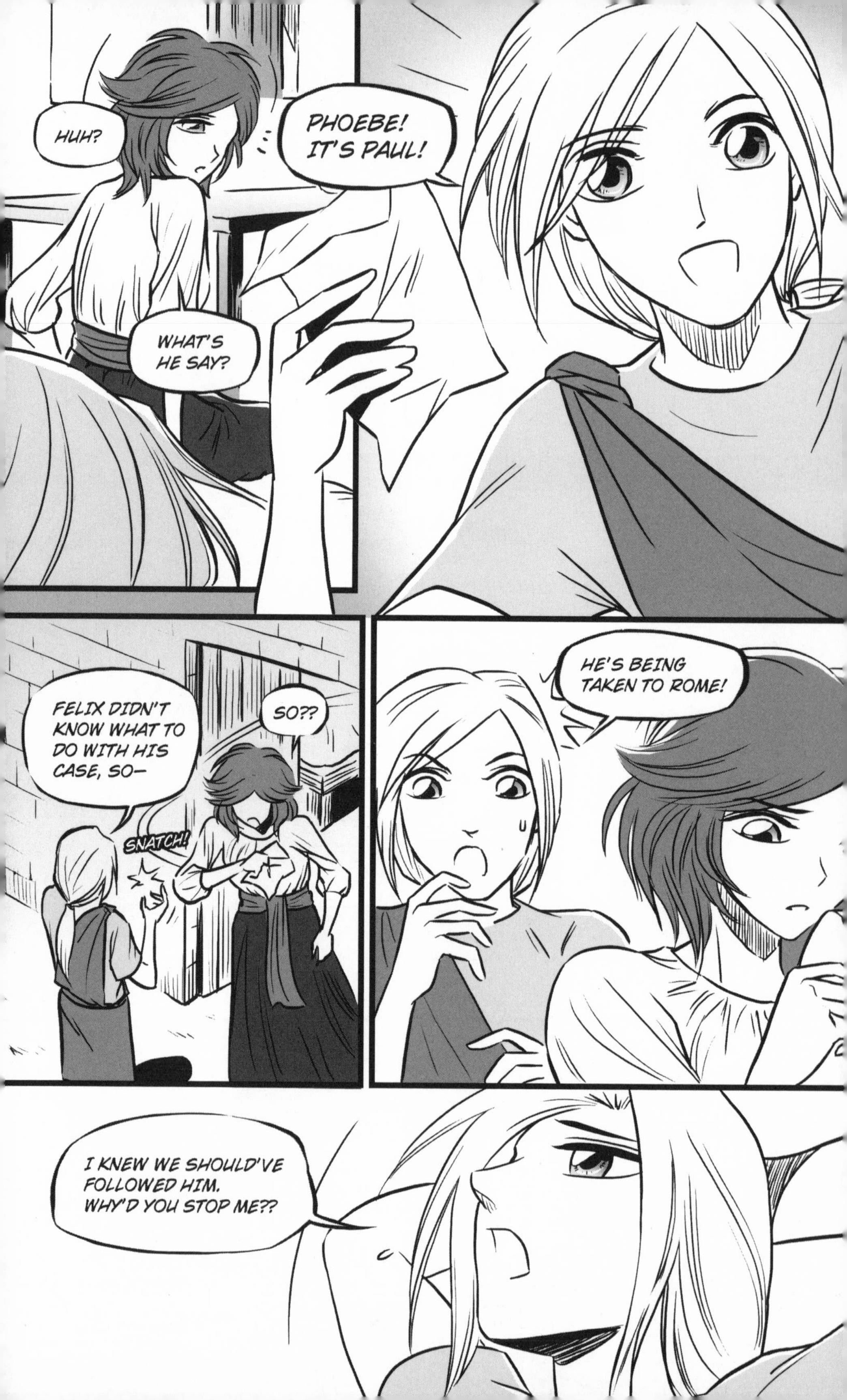
HUH?
PHOEBE! IT'S PAUL!
WHAT'S HE SAY?
FELIX DIDN'T KNOW WHAT TO DO WITH HIS CASE, SO—
SO??
SNATCH!
HE'S BEING TAKEN TO ROME!
I KNEW WE SHOULD'VE FOLLOWED HIM. WHY'D YOU STOP ME??

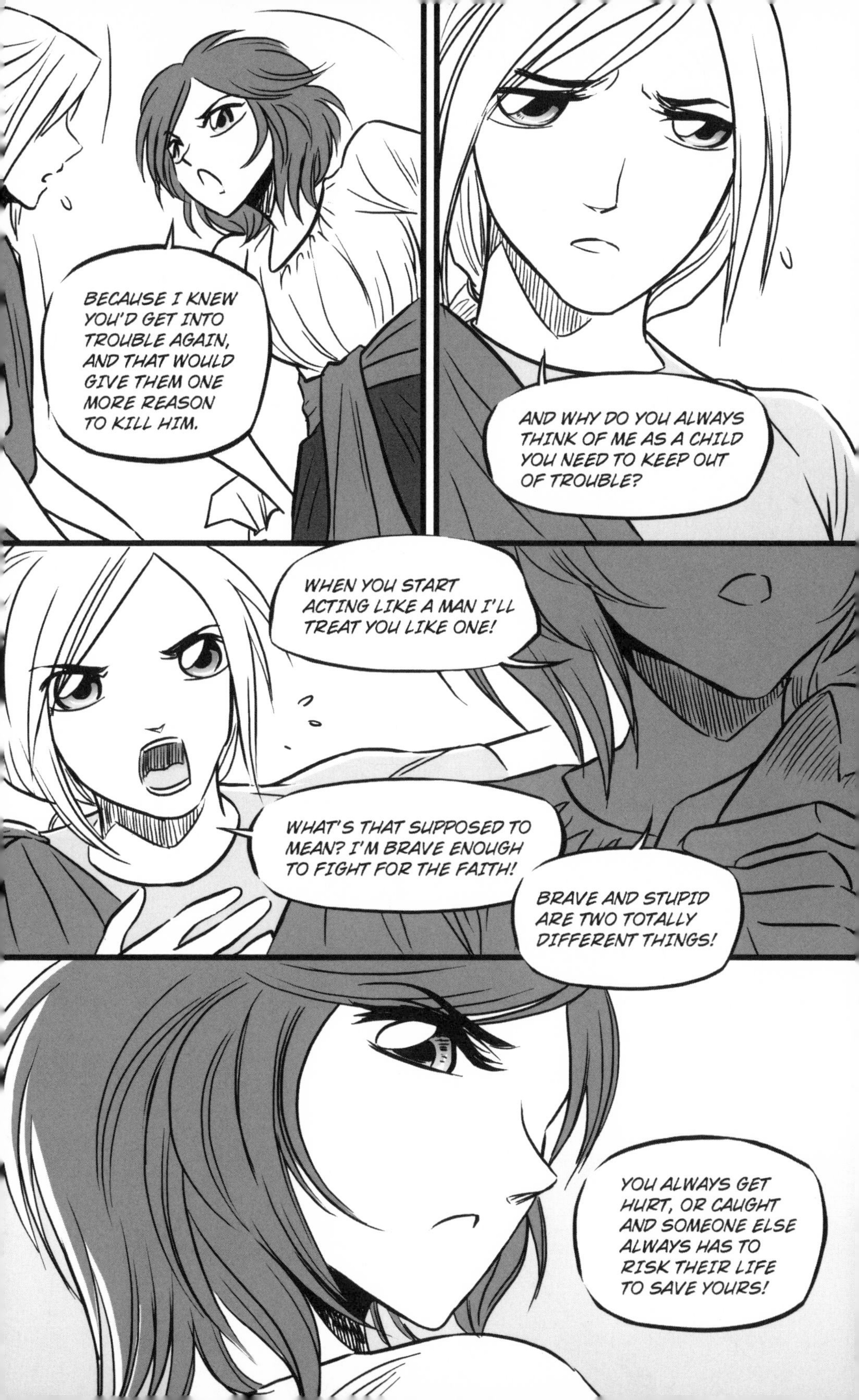
BECAUSE I KNEW YOU'D GET INTO TROUBLE AGAIN, AND THAT WOULD GIVE THEM ONE MORE REASON TO KILL HIM.
AND WHY DO YOU ALWAYS THINK OF ME AS A CHILD YOU NEED TO KEEP OUT OF TROUBLE?
WHEN YOU START ACTING LIKE A MAN I'LL TREAT YOU LIKE ONE!
WHAT'S THAT SUPPOSED TO MEAN? I'M BRAVE ENOUGH TO FIGHT FOR THE FAITH!
BRAVE AND STUPID ARE TWO TOTALLY DIFFERENT THINGS!
YOU ALWAYS GET HURT, OR CAUGHT AND SOMEONE ELSE ALWAYS HAS TO RISK THEIR LIFE TO SAVE YOURS!

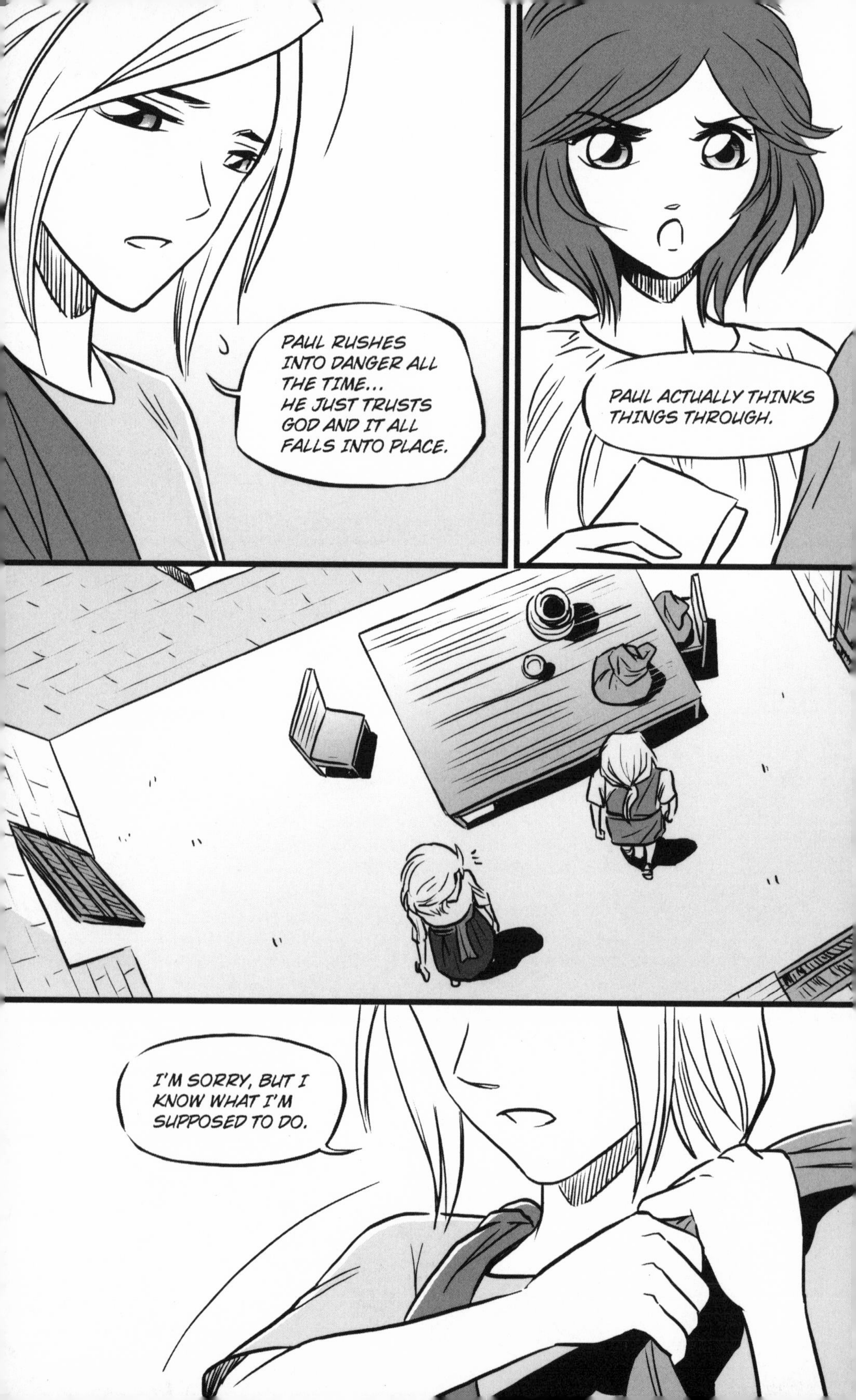
PAUL RUSHES INTO DANGER ALL THE TIME... HE JUST TRUSTS GOD AND IT ALL FALLS INTO PLACE.
PAUL ACTUALLY THINKS THINGS THROUGH.
I'M SORRY, BUT I KNOW WHAT I'M SUPPOSED TO DO.

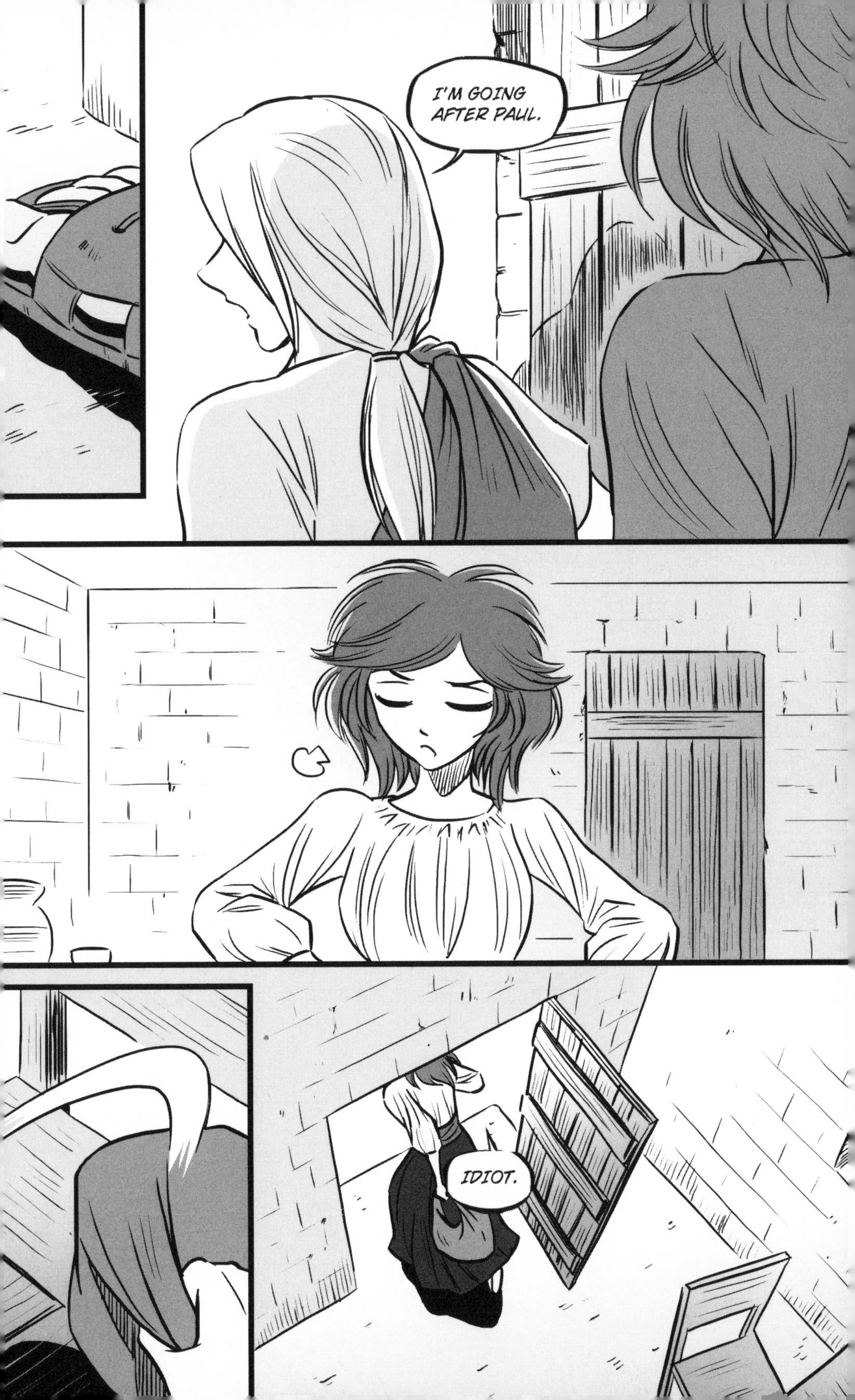
I'M GOING AFTER PAUL.
IDIOT.

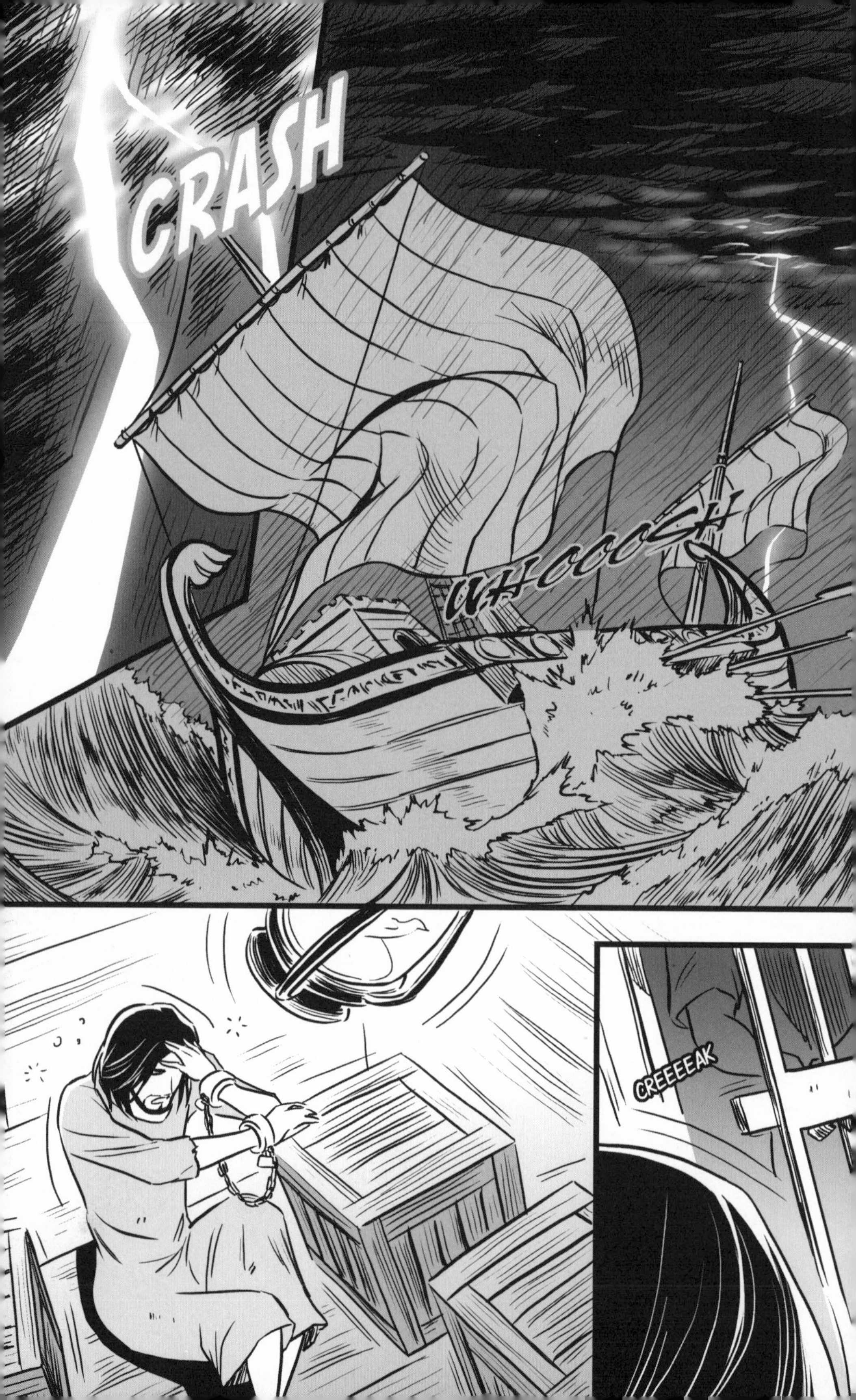
CRASH
WHOOOOSH
CREEEEAK

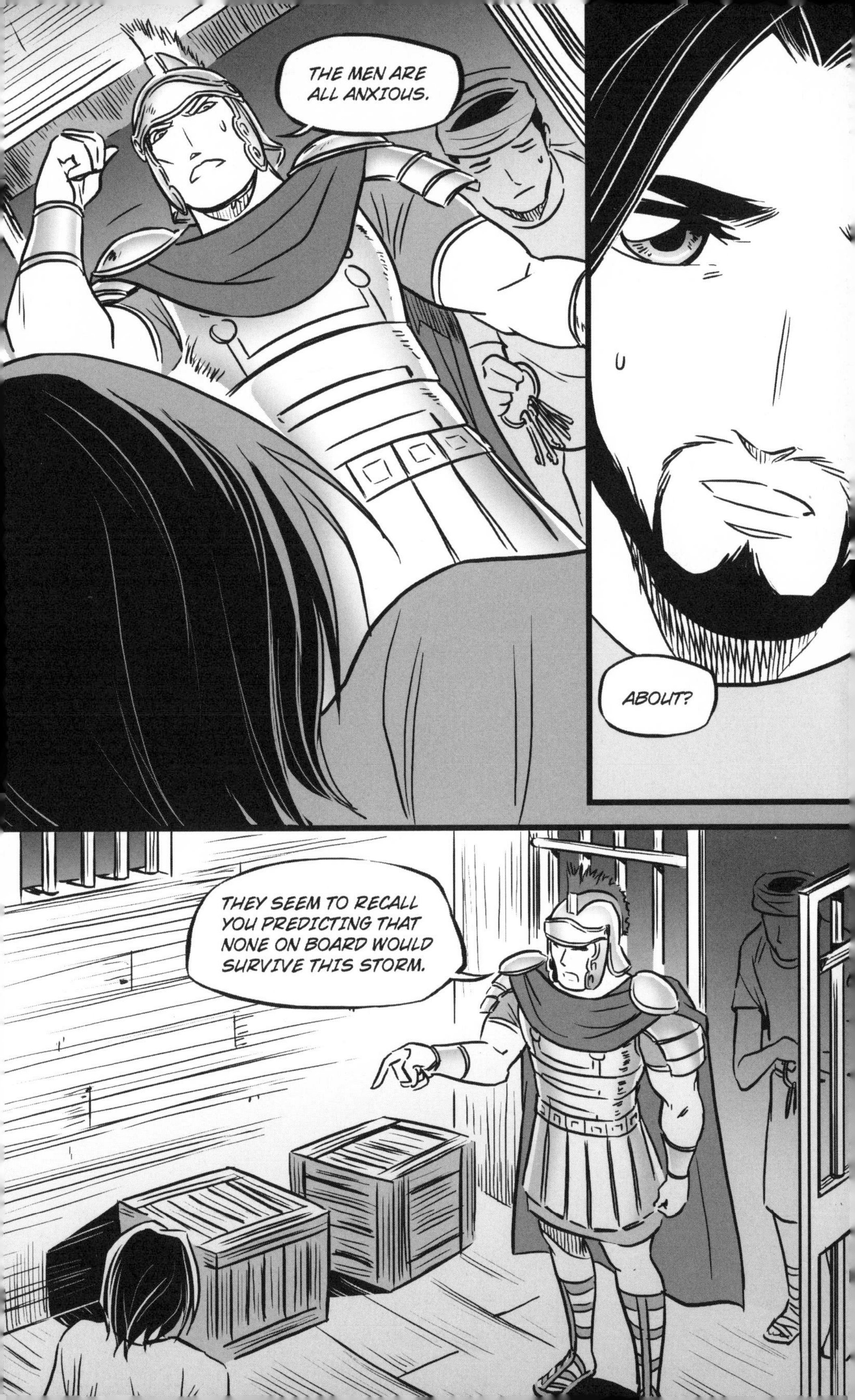
THE MEN ARE ALL ANXIOUS.
ABOUT?
THEY SEEM TO RECALL YOU PREDICTING THAT NONE ON BOARD WOULD SURVIVE THIS STORM.

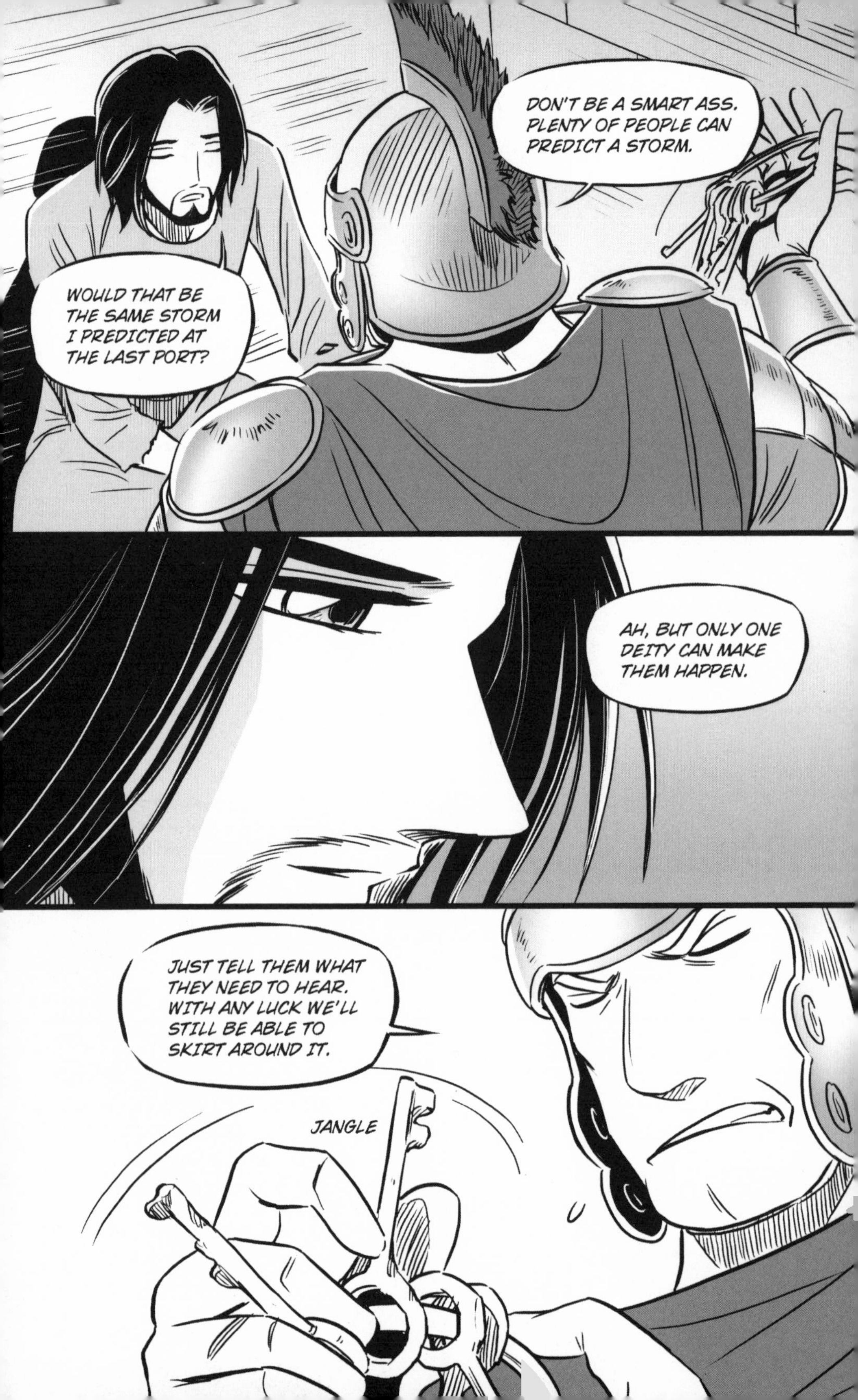
DON'T BE A SMART ASS. PLENTY OF PEOPLE CAN PREDICT A STORM.
WOULD THAT BE THE SAME STORM I PREDICTED AT THE LAST PORT?
AH, BUT ONLY ONE DEITY CAN MAKE THEM HAPPEN.
JUST TELL THEM WHAT THEY NEED TO HEAR. WITH ANY LUCK WE'LL STILL BE ABLE TO SKIRT AROUND IT.
JANGLE

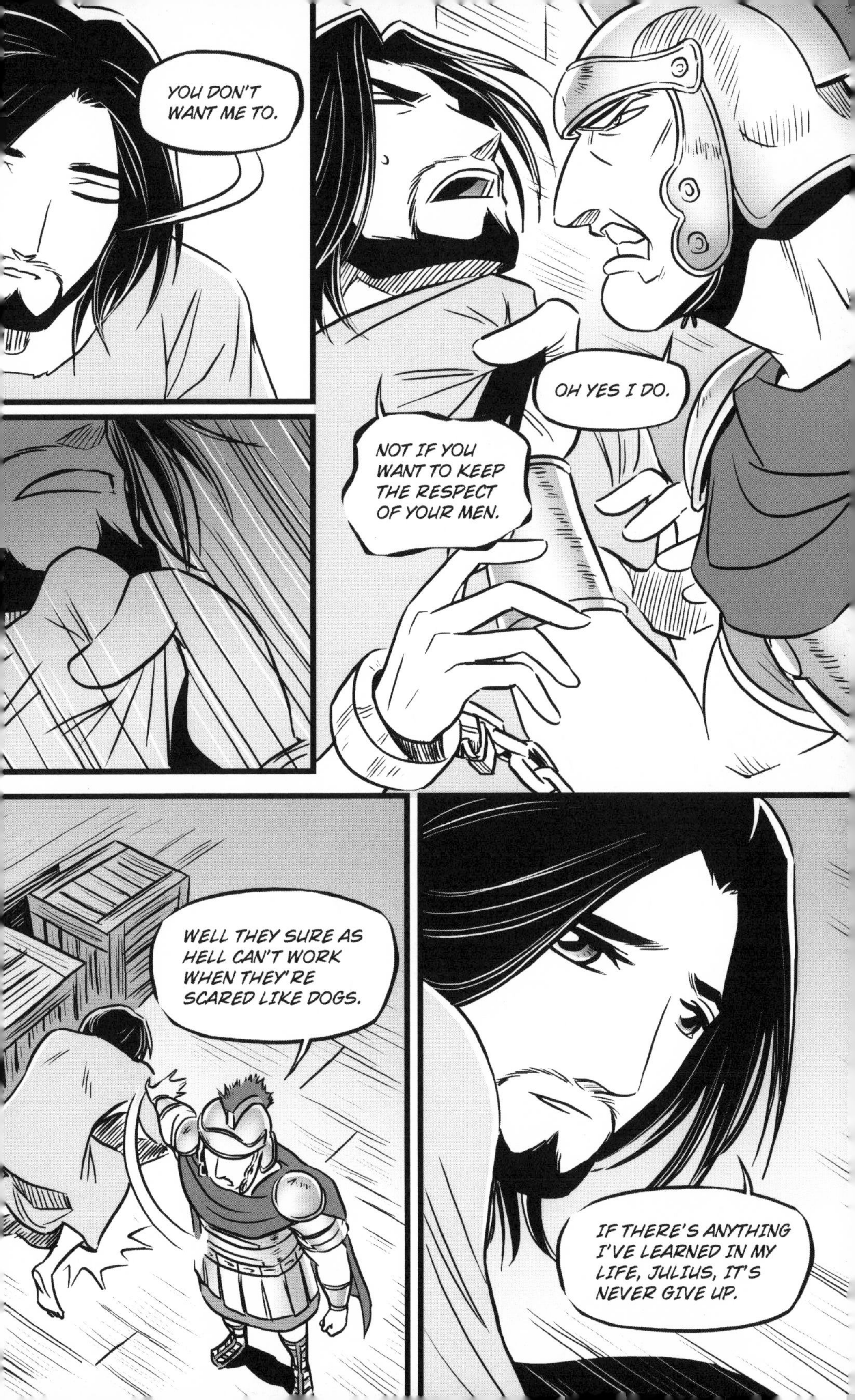

YOU DON'T WANT ME TO.
OH YES I DO.
NOT IF YOU WANT TO KEEP THE RESPECT OF YOUR MEN.
WELL THEY SURE AS HELL CAN'T WORK WHEN THEY'RE SCARED LIKE DOGS.
IF THERE'S ANYTHING I'VE LEARNED IN MY LIFE, JULIUS, IT'S NEVER GIVE UP.

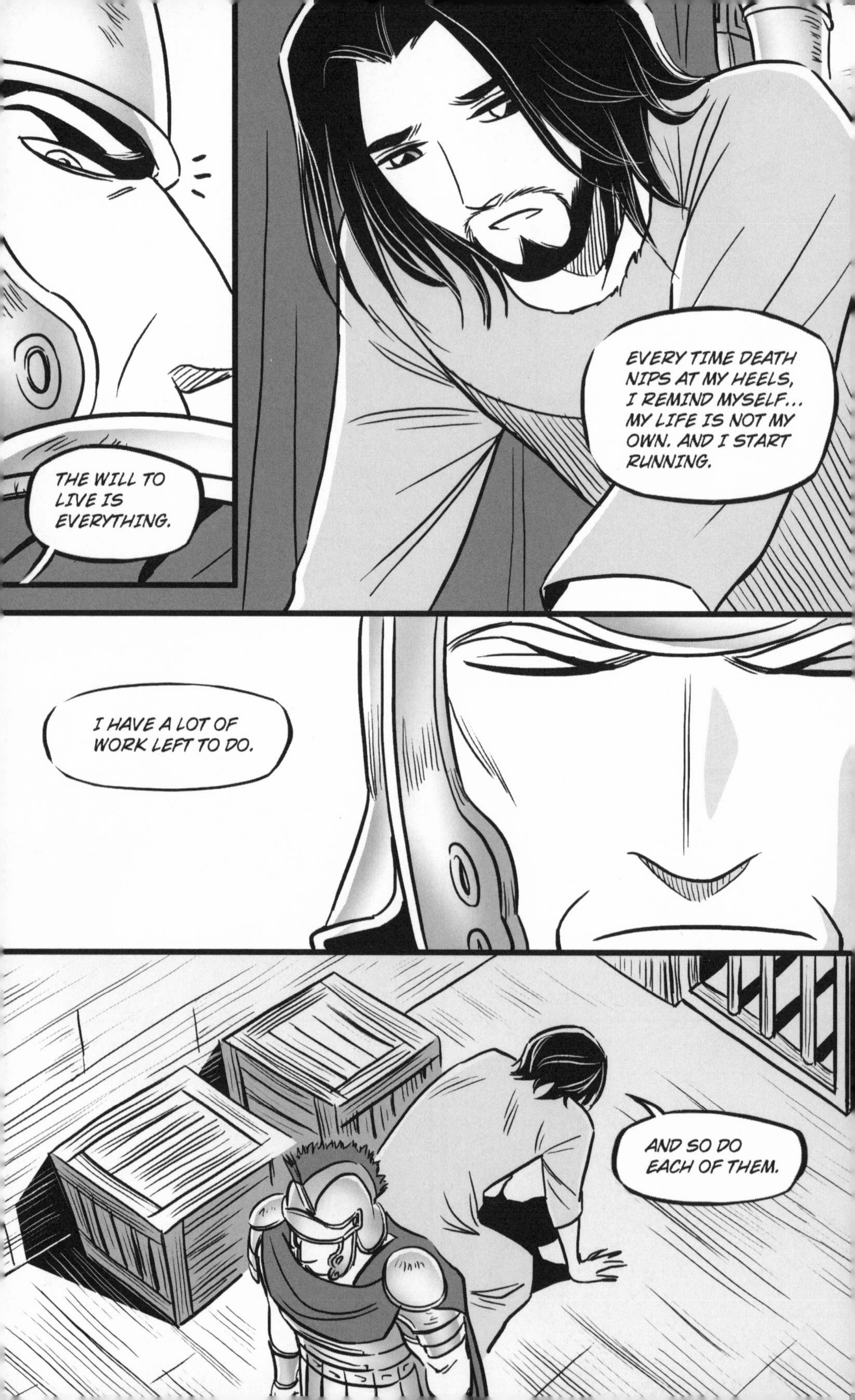
EVERY TIME DEATH NIPS AT MY HEELS, I REMIND MYSELF... MY LIFE IS NOT MY OWN. AND I START RUNNING.
THE WILL TO LIVE IS EVERYTHING.
I HAVE A LOT OF WORK LEFT TO DO.
AND SO DO EACH OF THEM.

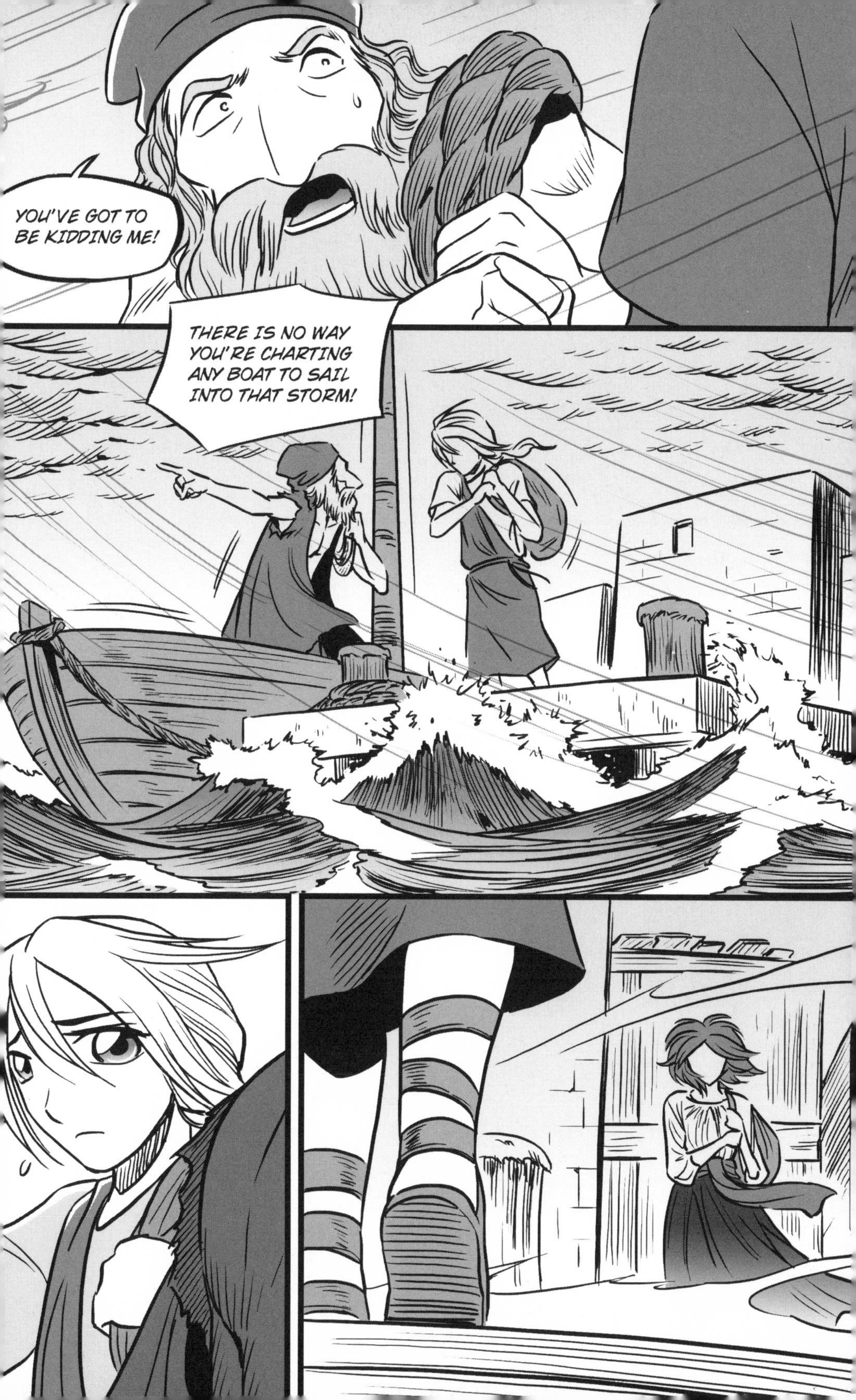
YOU'VE GOT TO BE KIDDING ME!
THERE IS NO WAY YOU'RE CHARTING ANY BOAT TO SAIL INTO THAT STORM!

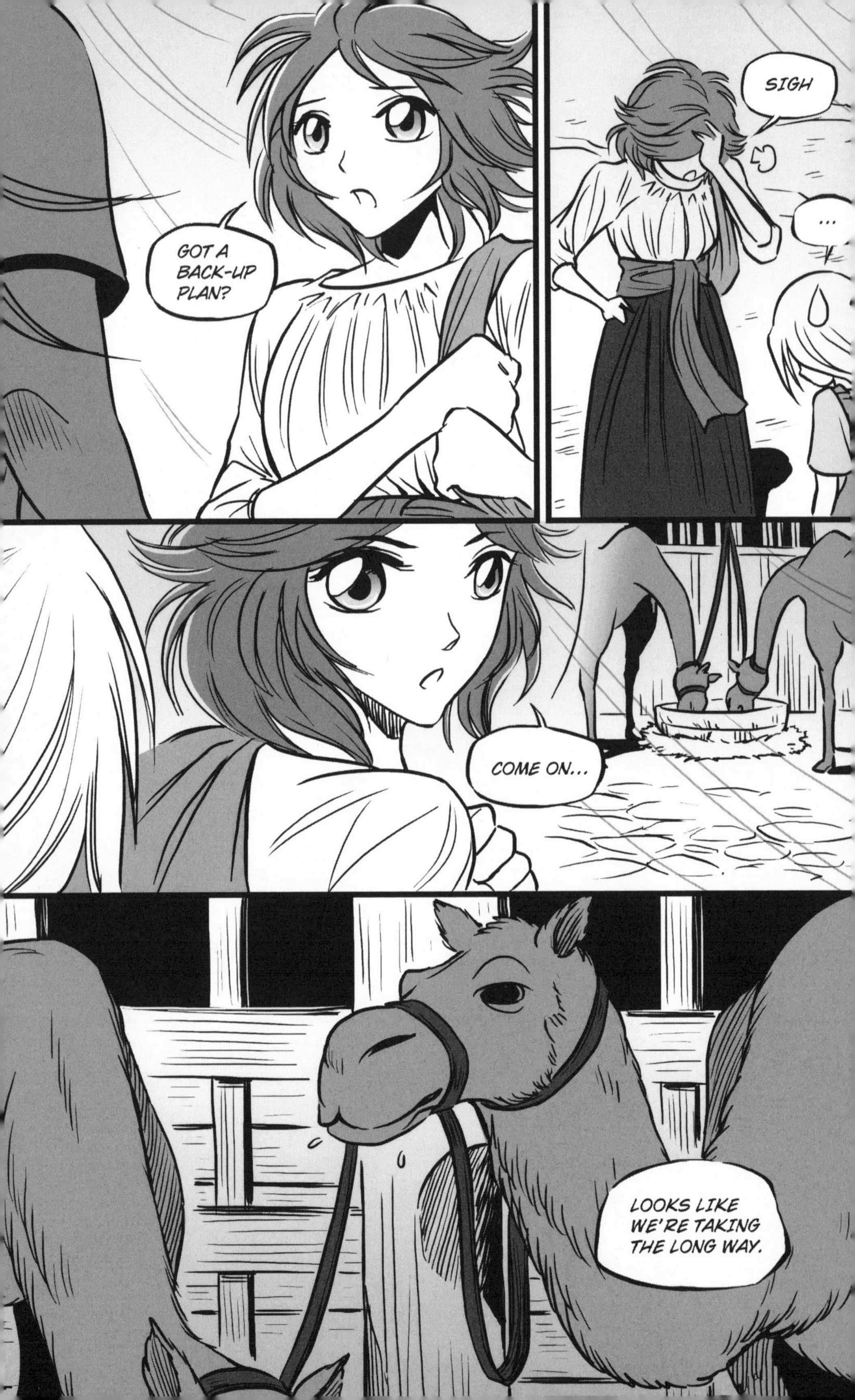
GOT A BACK-UP PLAN?
SIGH
...
COME ON...
LOOKS LIKE WE'RE TAKING THE LONG WAY.

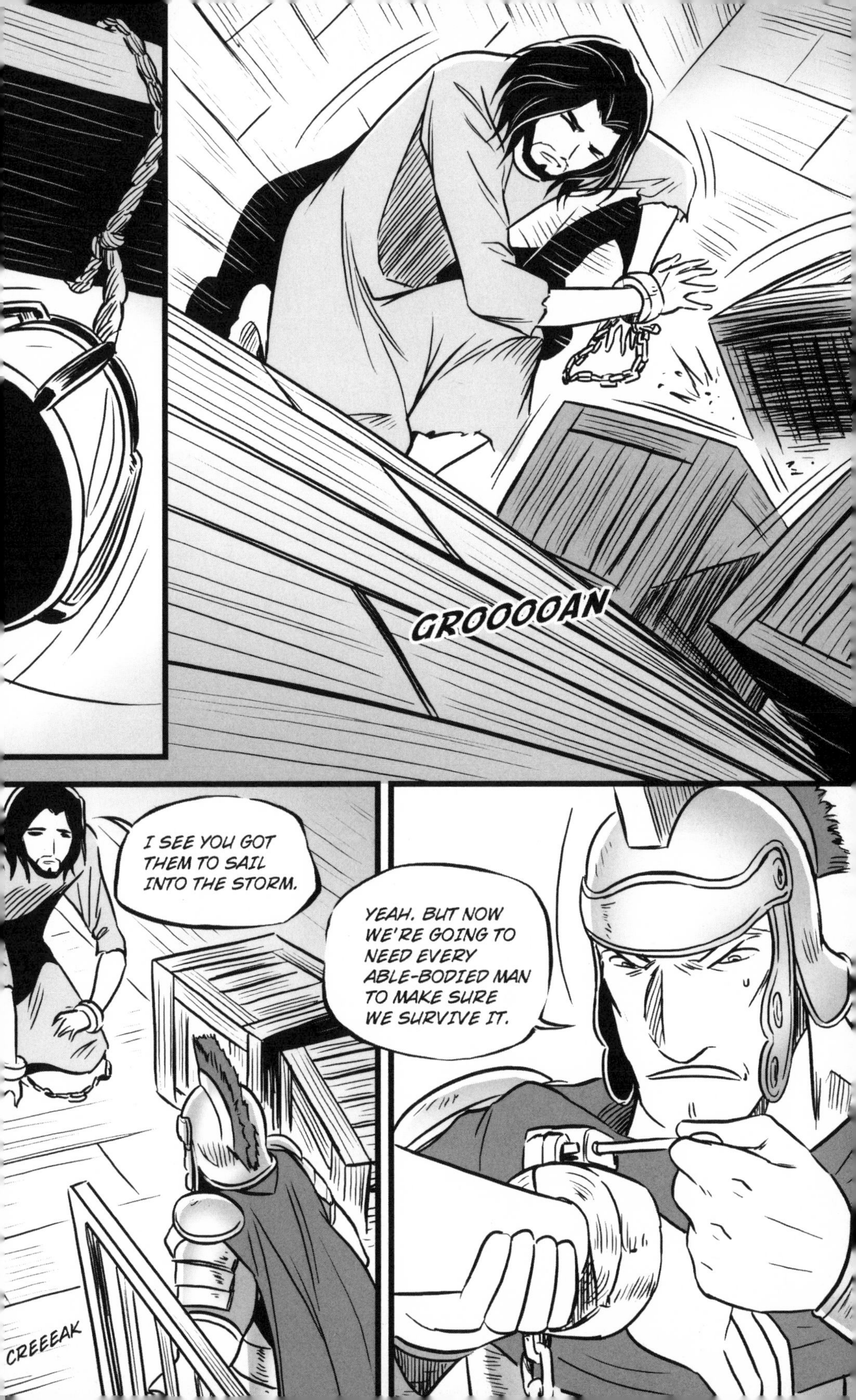
GROOOOAN
I SEE YOU GOT THEM TO SAIL INTO THE STORM.
YEAH. BUT NOW WE'RE GOING TO NEED EVERY ABLE-BODIED MAN TO MAKE SURE WE SURVIVE IT.
CREEEAK

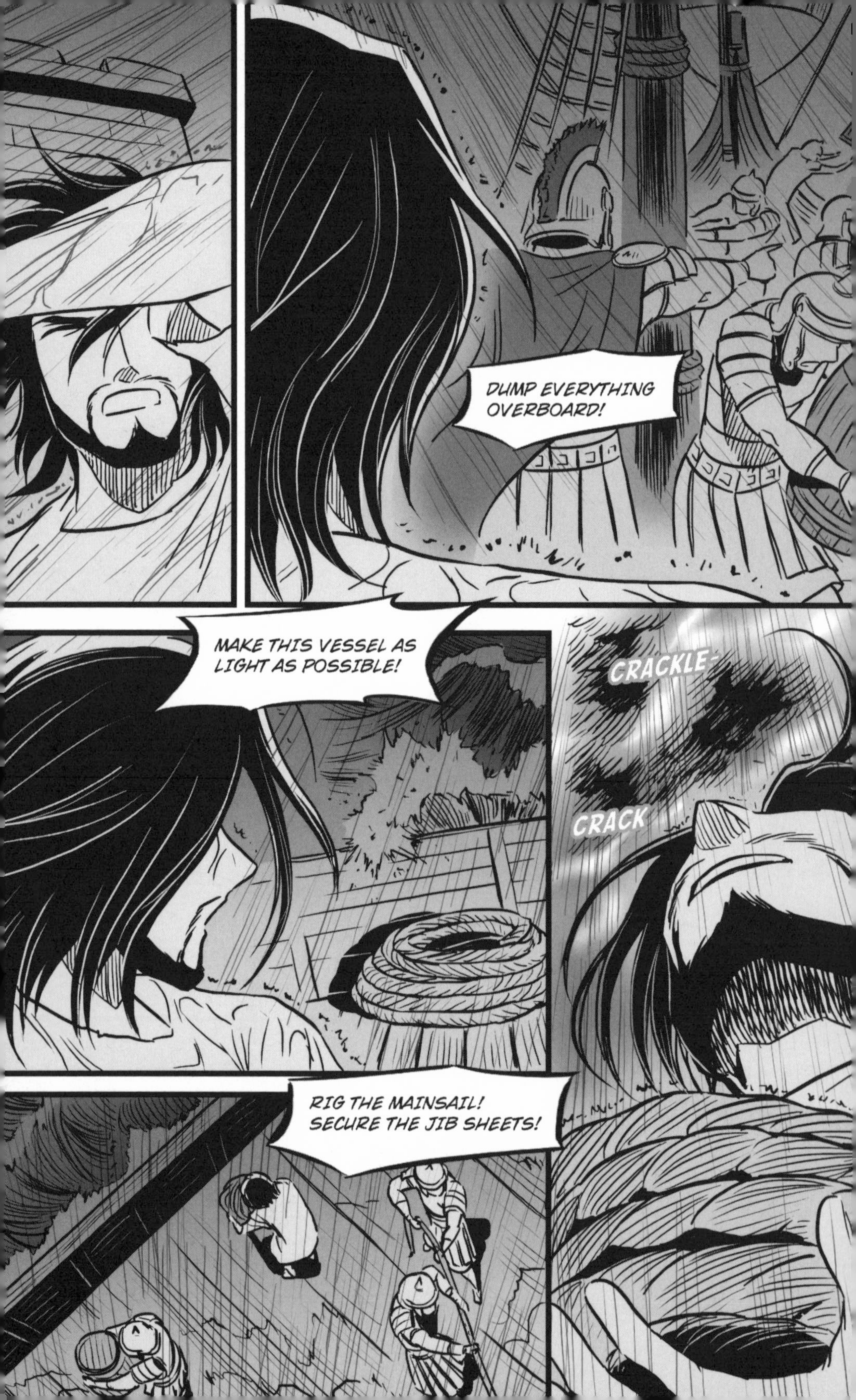
DUMP EVERYTHING OVERBOARD!
MAKE THIS VESSEL AS LIGHT AS POSSIBLE!
CRACKLE-
CRACK
RIG THE MAINSAIL! SECURE THE JIB SHEETS!

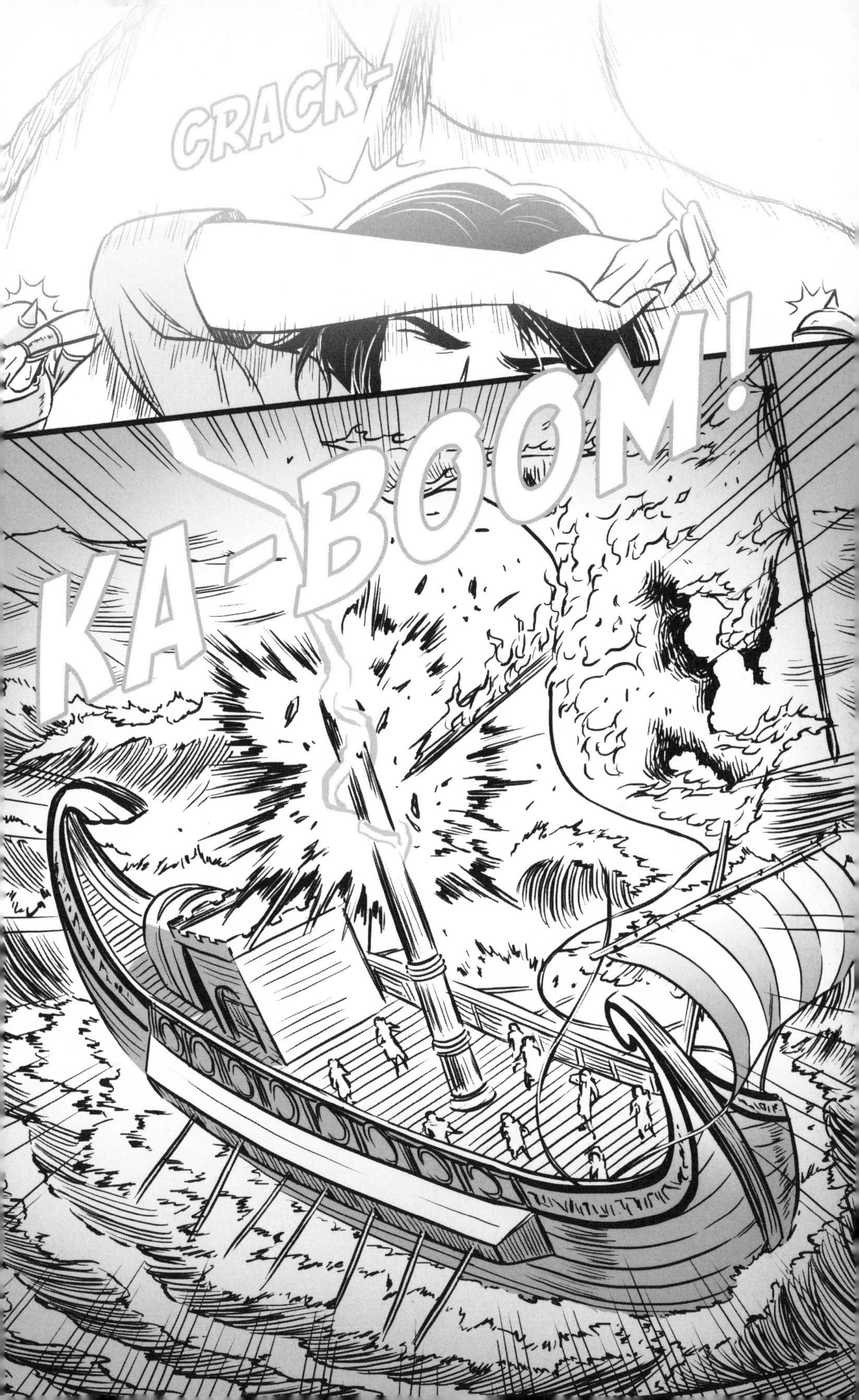
CRACK-
KA-BOOM!

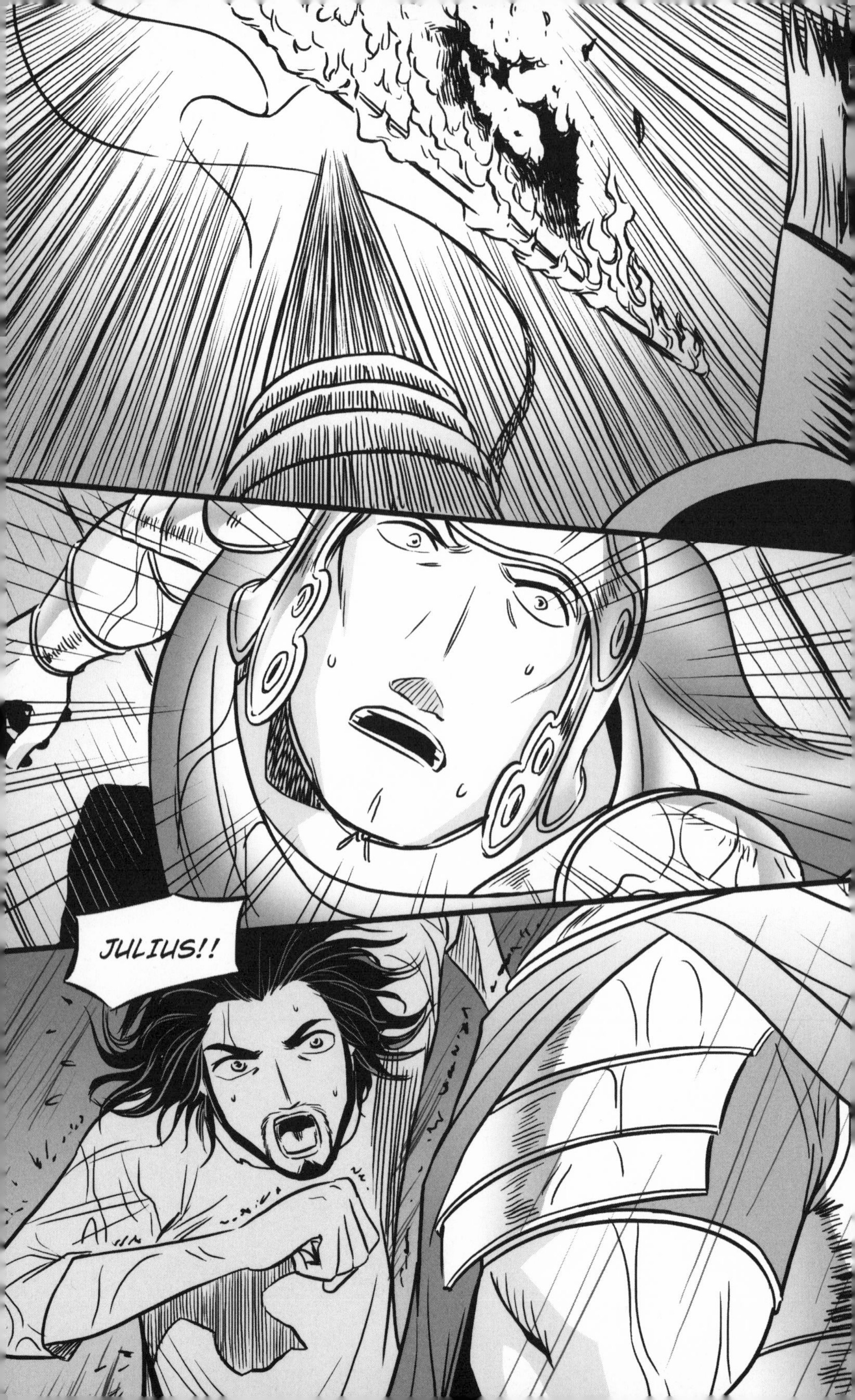
JULIUS!!

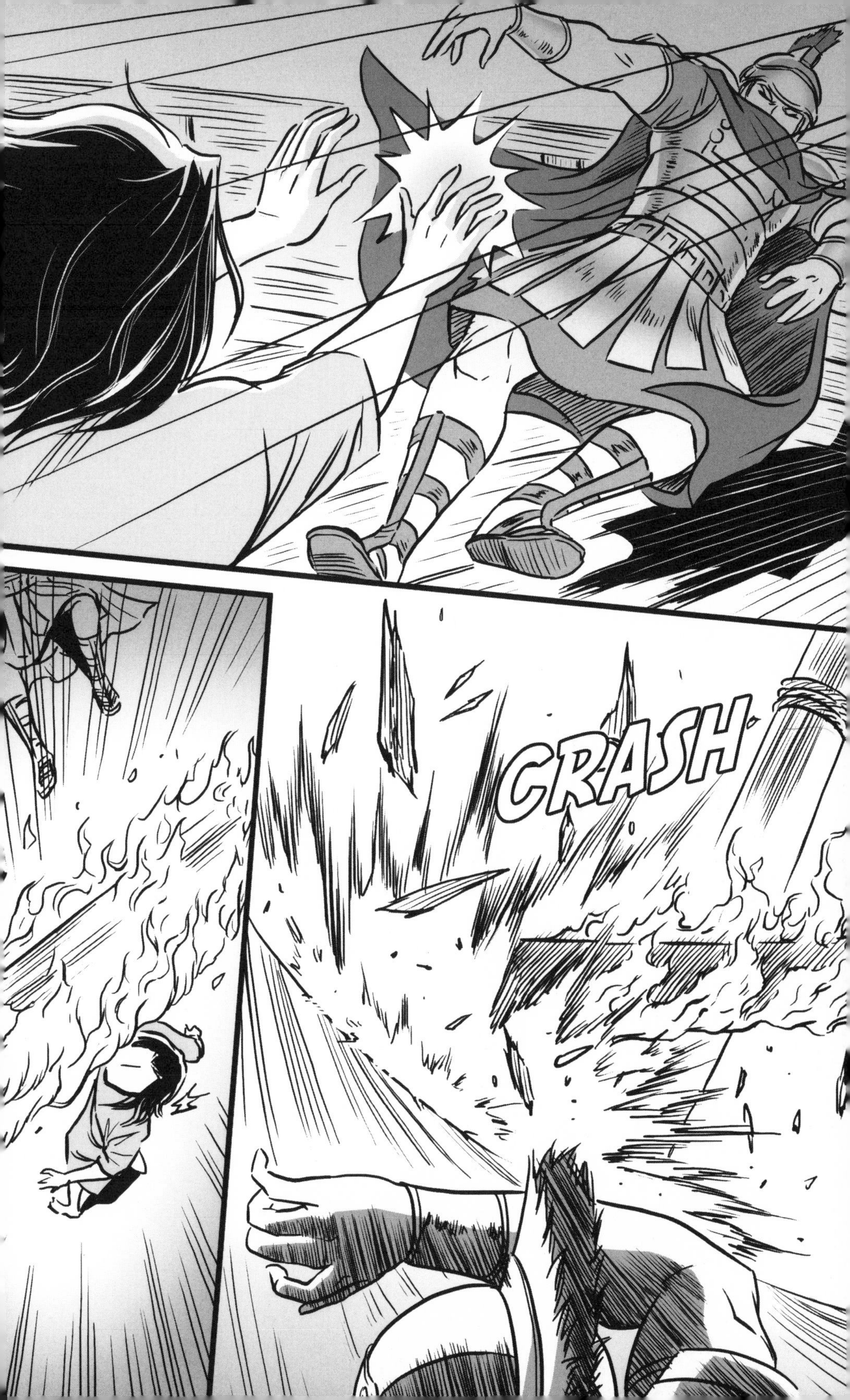
CRASH

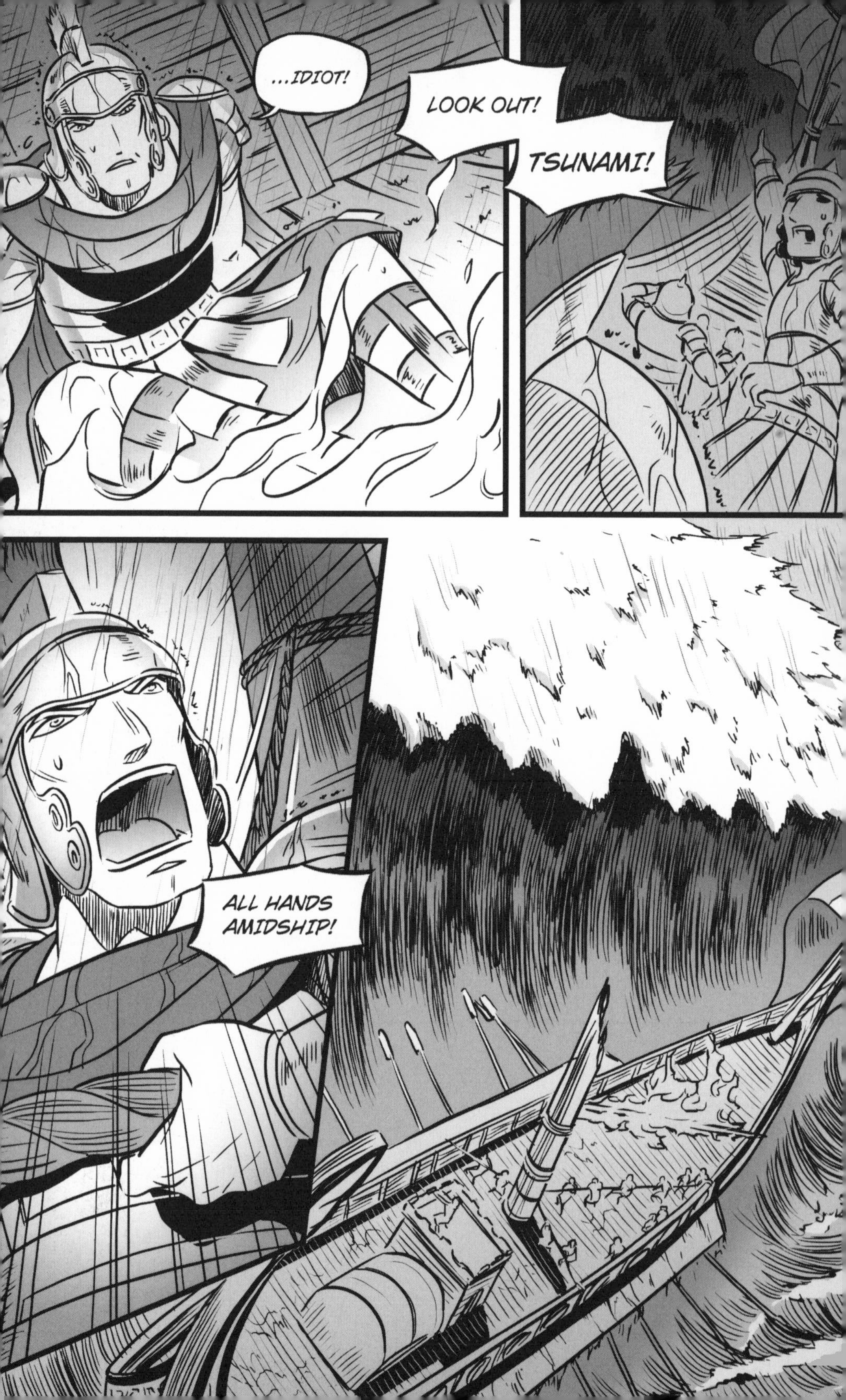
...IDIOT!
LOOK OUT!
TSUNAMI!
ALL HANDS AMIDSHIP!

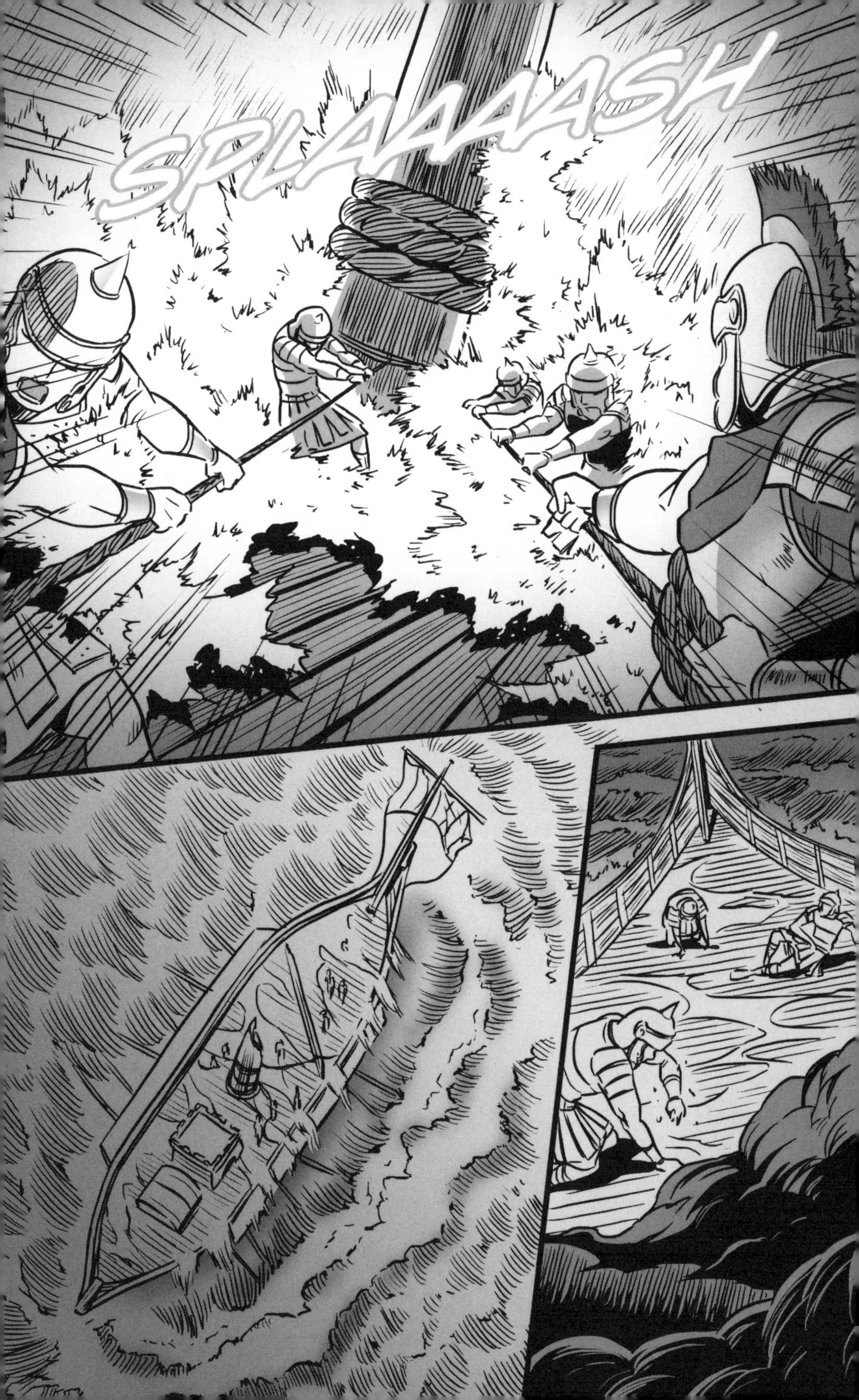
SPLAAAASH

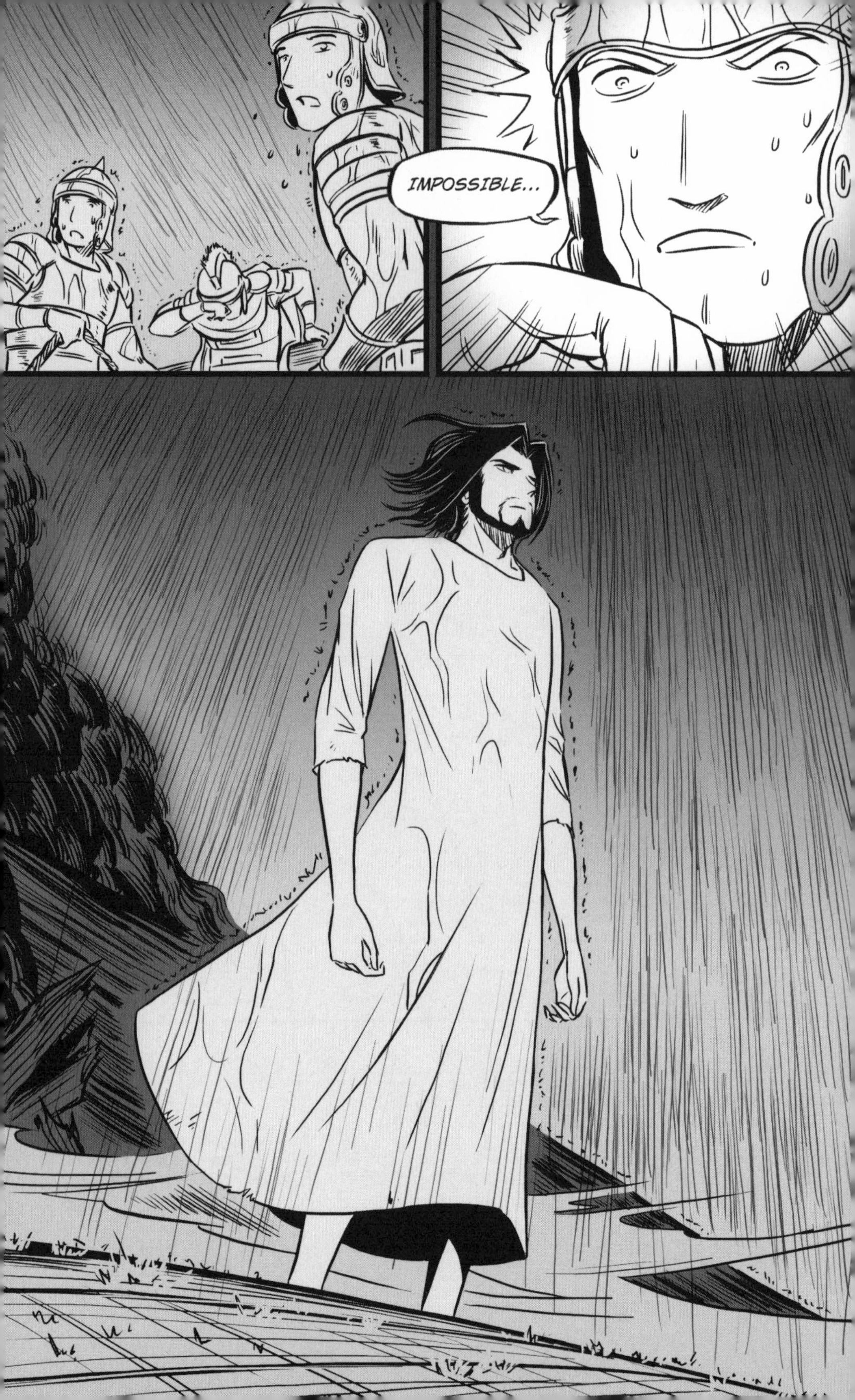
IMPOSSIBLE...

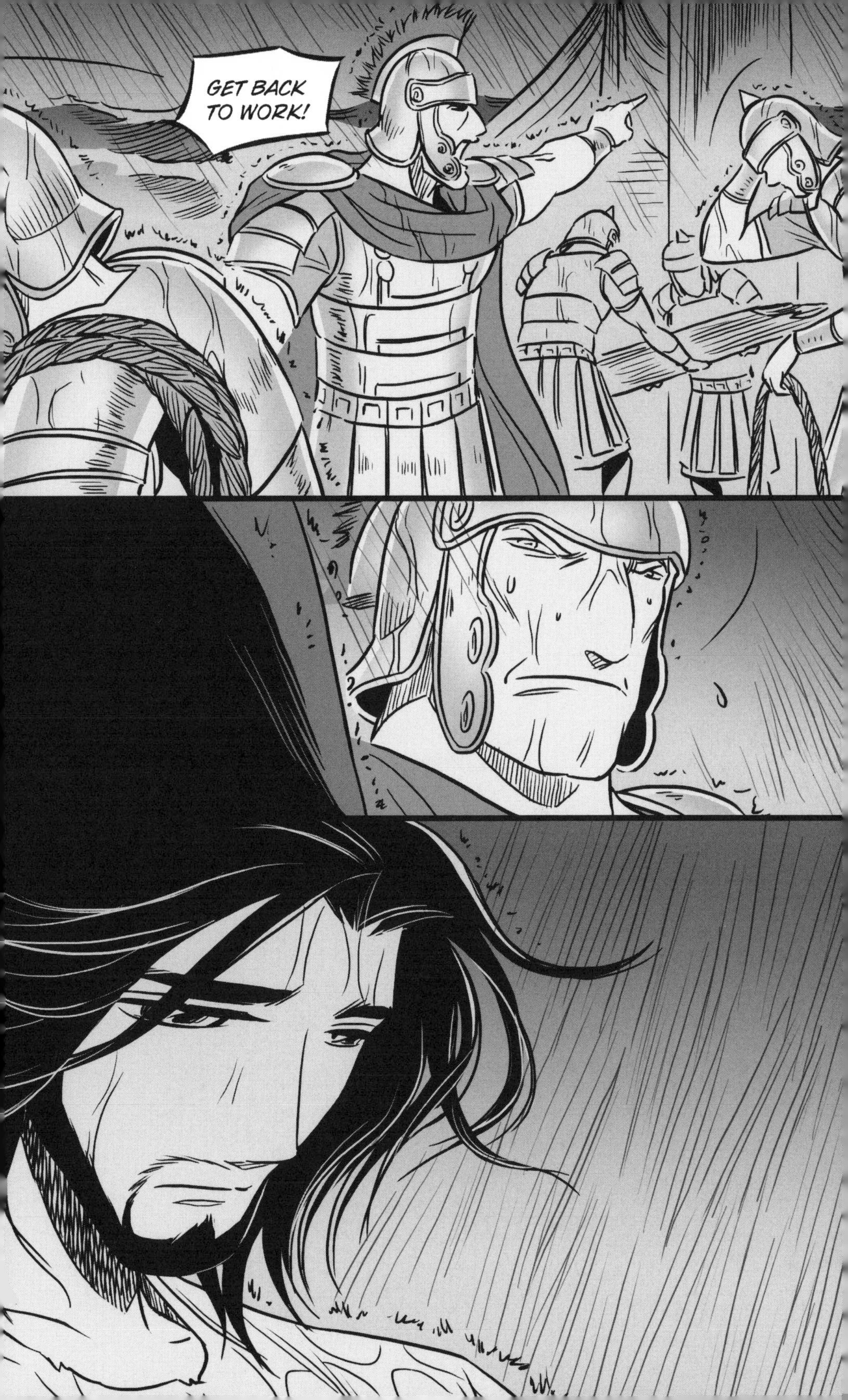
GET BACK TO WORK!

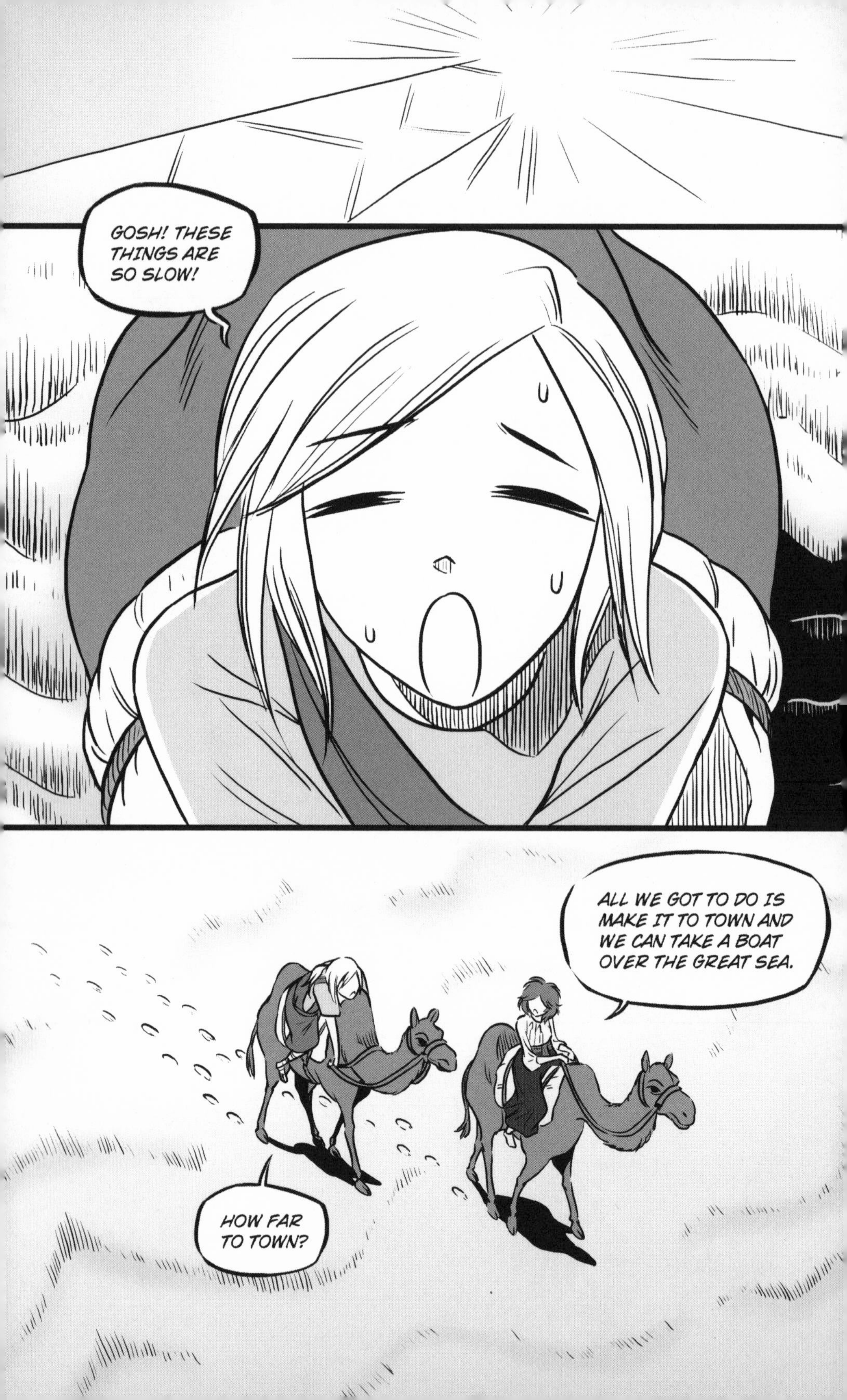
GOSH! THESE THINGS ARE SO SLOW!
ALL WE GOT TO DO IS MAKE IT TO TOWN AND WE CAN TAKE A BOAT OVER THE GREAT SEA.
HOW FAR TO TOWN?

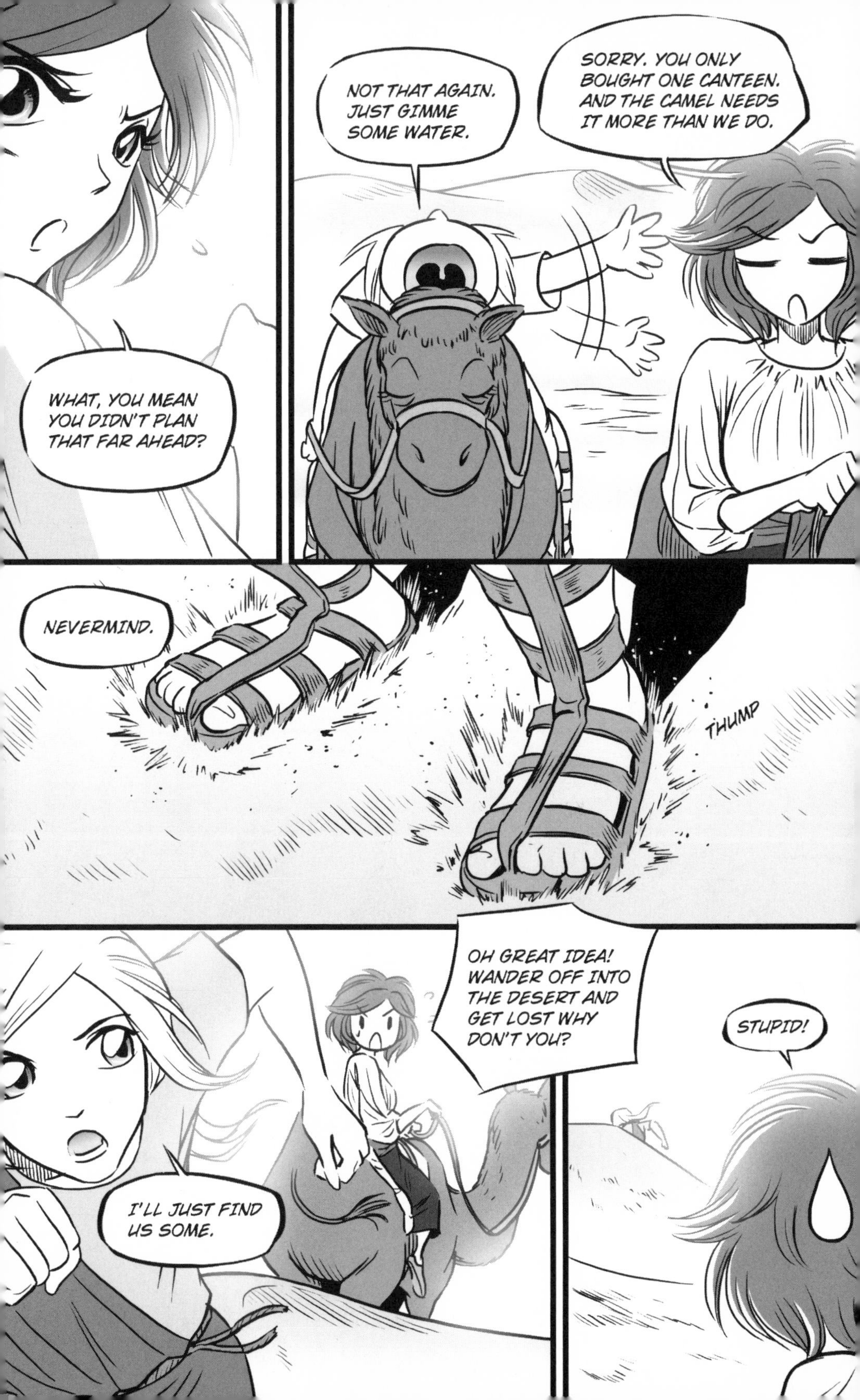
WHAT, YOU MEAN YOU DIDN'T PLAN THAT FAR AHEAD?
NOT THAT AGAIN. JUST GIMME SOME WATER.
SORRY. YOU ONLY BOUGHT ONE CANTEEN. AND THE CAMEL NEEDS IT MORE THAN WE DO.
NEVERMIND.
THUMP
I'LL JUST FIND US SOME.
OH GREAT IDEA! WANDER OFF INTO THE DESERT AND GET LOST WHY DON'T YOU?
STUPID!

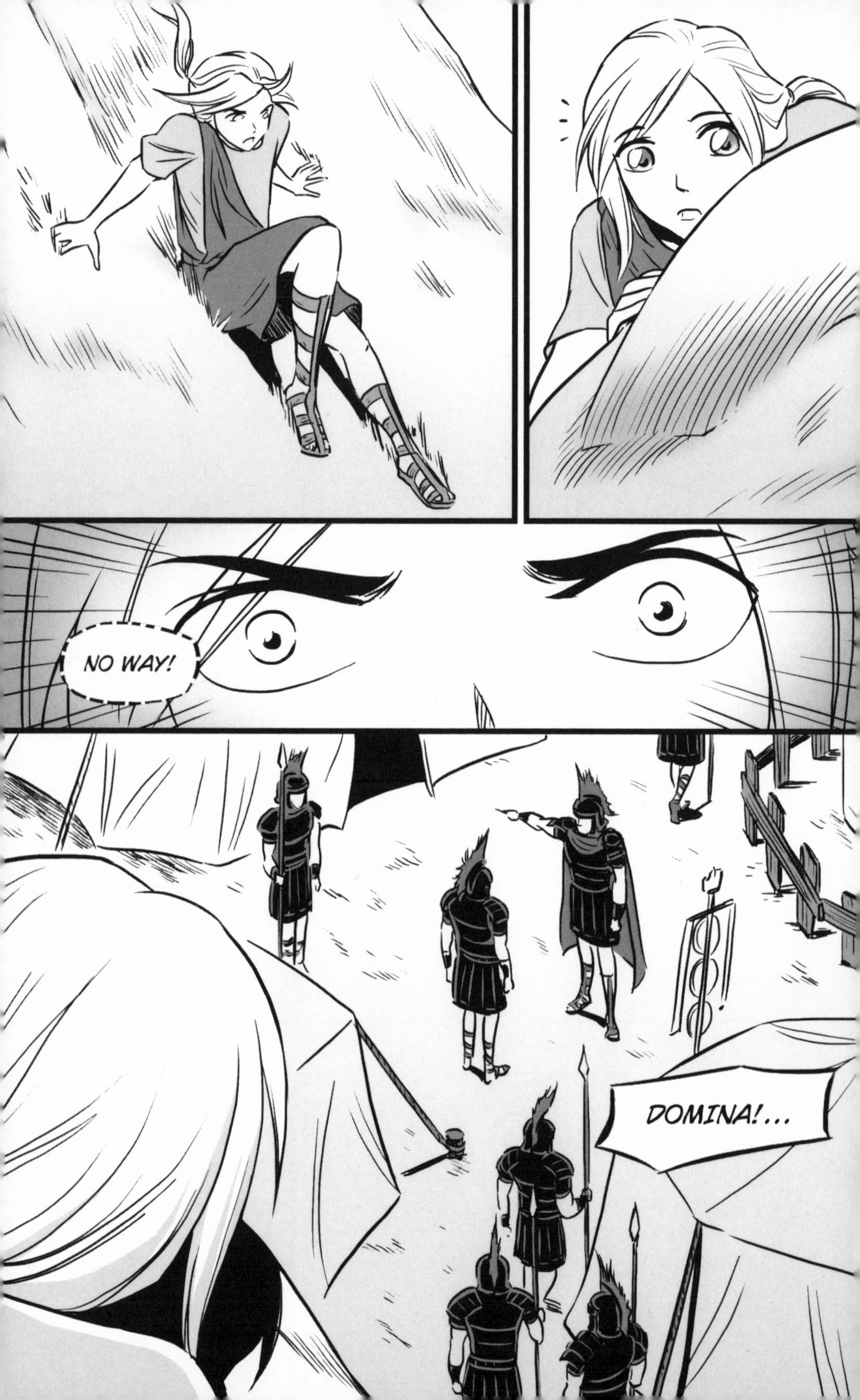
NO WAY!
DOMINA!...

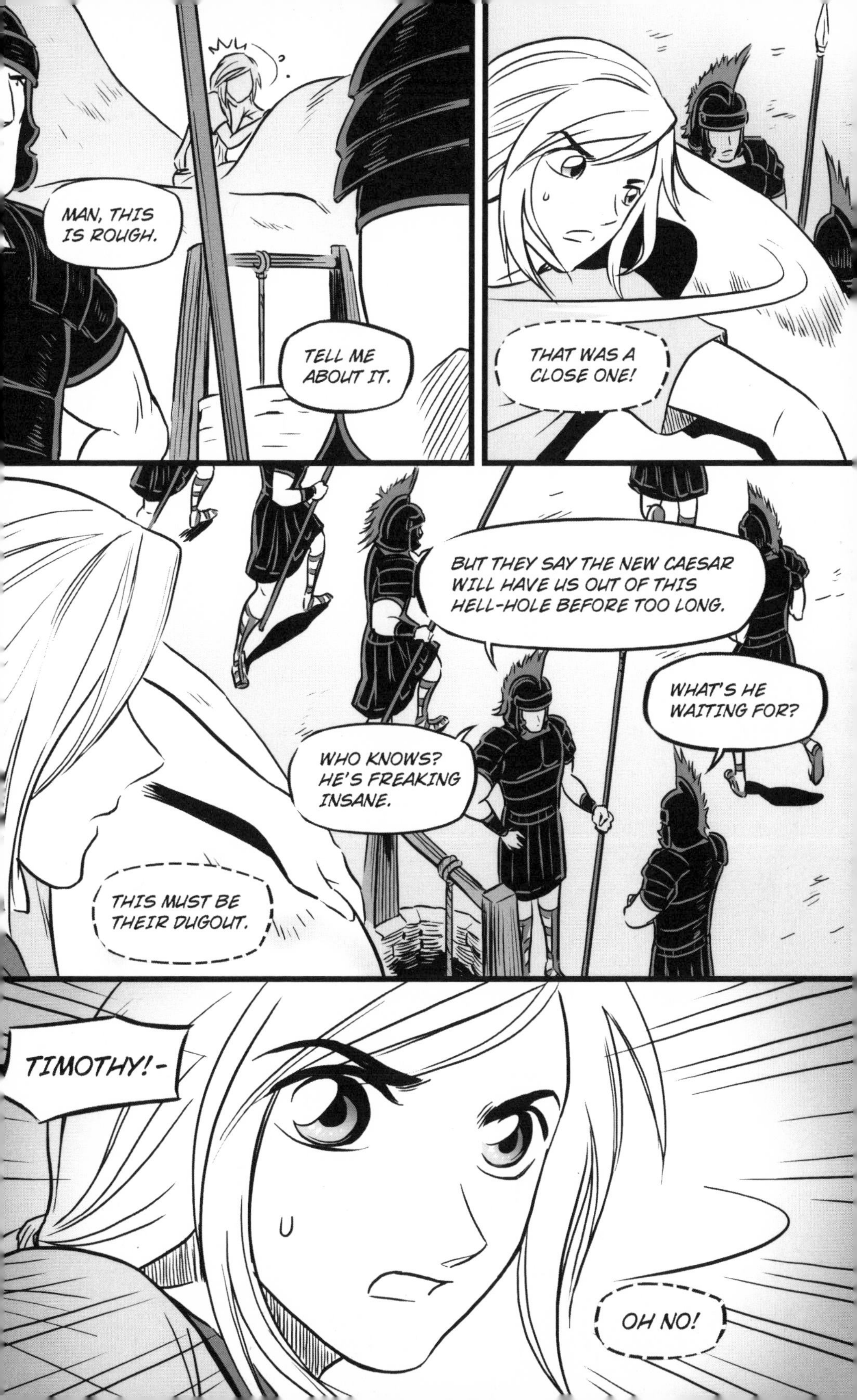
MAN, THIS IS ROUGH.
TELL ME ABOUT IT.
THAT WAS A CLOSE ONE!
BUT THEY SAY THE NEW CAESAR WILL HAVE US OUT OF THIS HELL-HOLE BEFORE TOO LONG.
WHAT'S HE WAITING FOR?
WHO KNOWS? HE'S FREAKING INSANE.
THIS MUST BE THEIR DUGOUT.
TIMOTHY!-
OH NO!

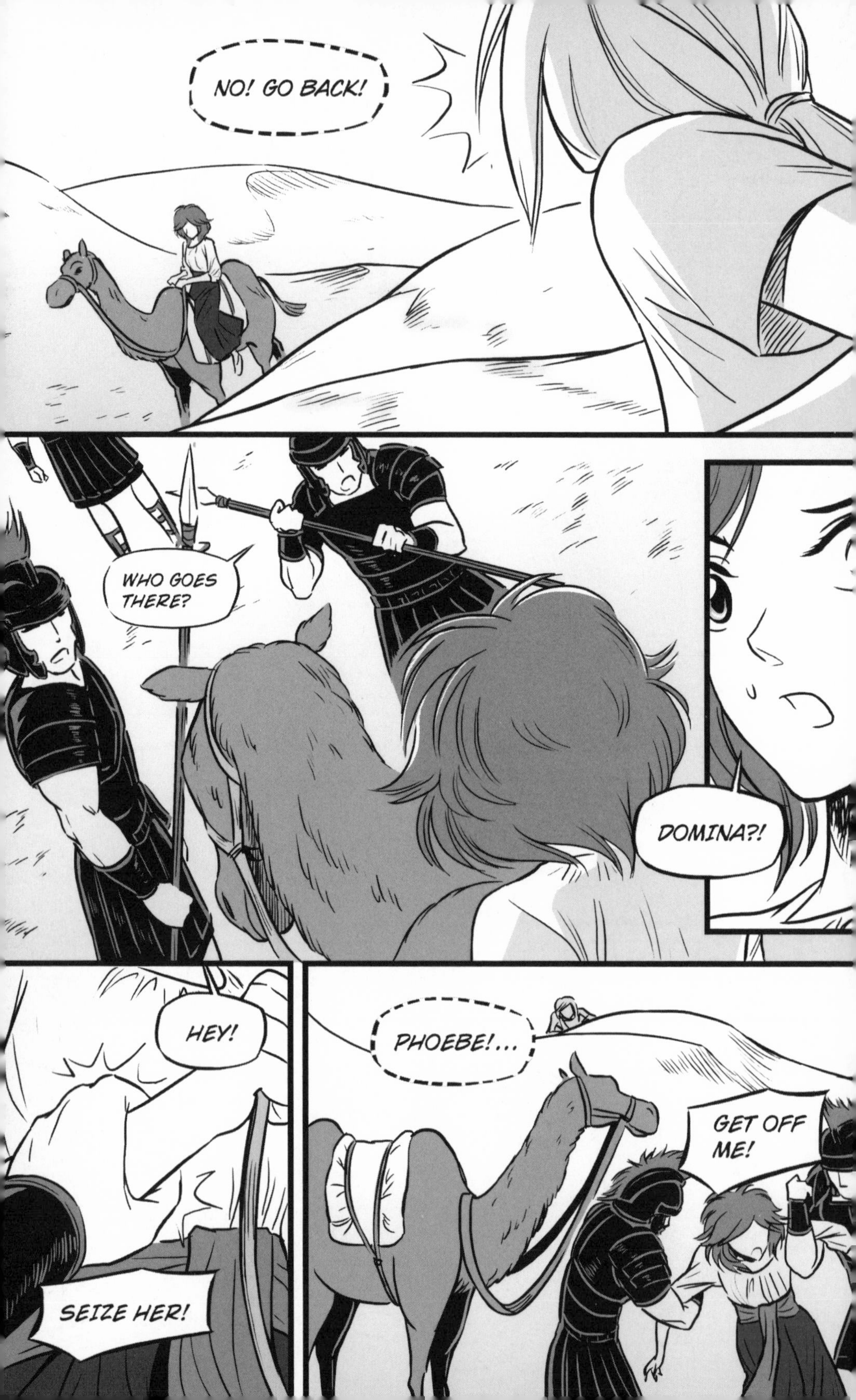
NO! GO BACK!
WHO GOES THERE?
DOMINA?!
HEY!
SEIZE HER!
PHOEBE!...
GET OFF ME!

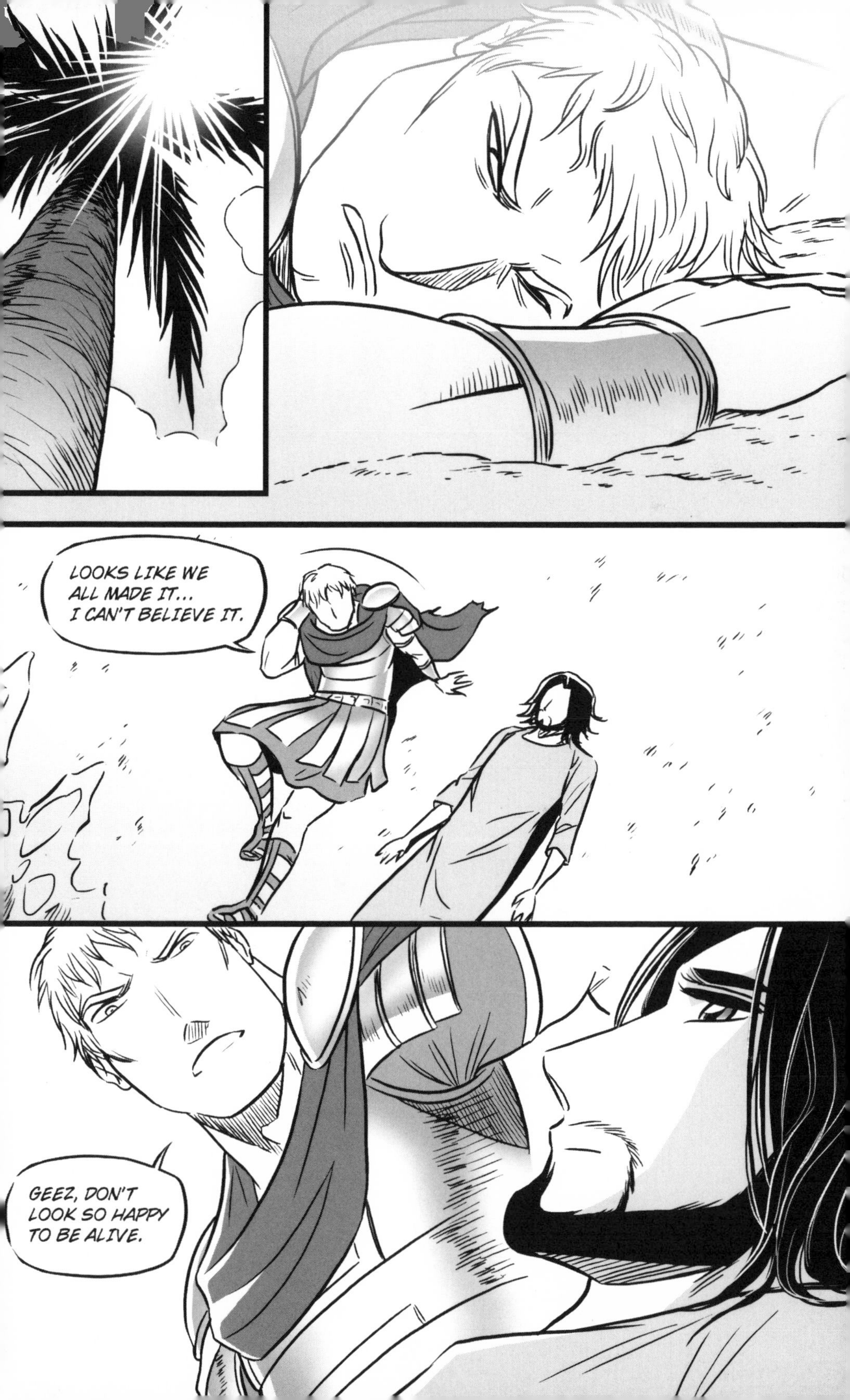
LOOKS LIKE WE ALL MADE IT... I CAN'T BELIEVE IT.
GEEZ, DON'T LOOK SO HAPPY TO BE ALIVE.

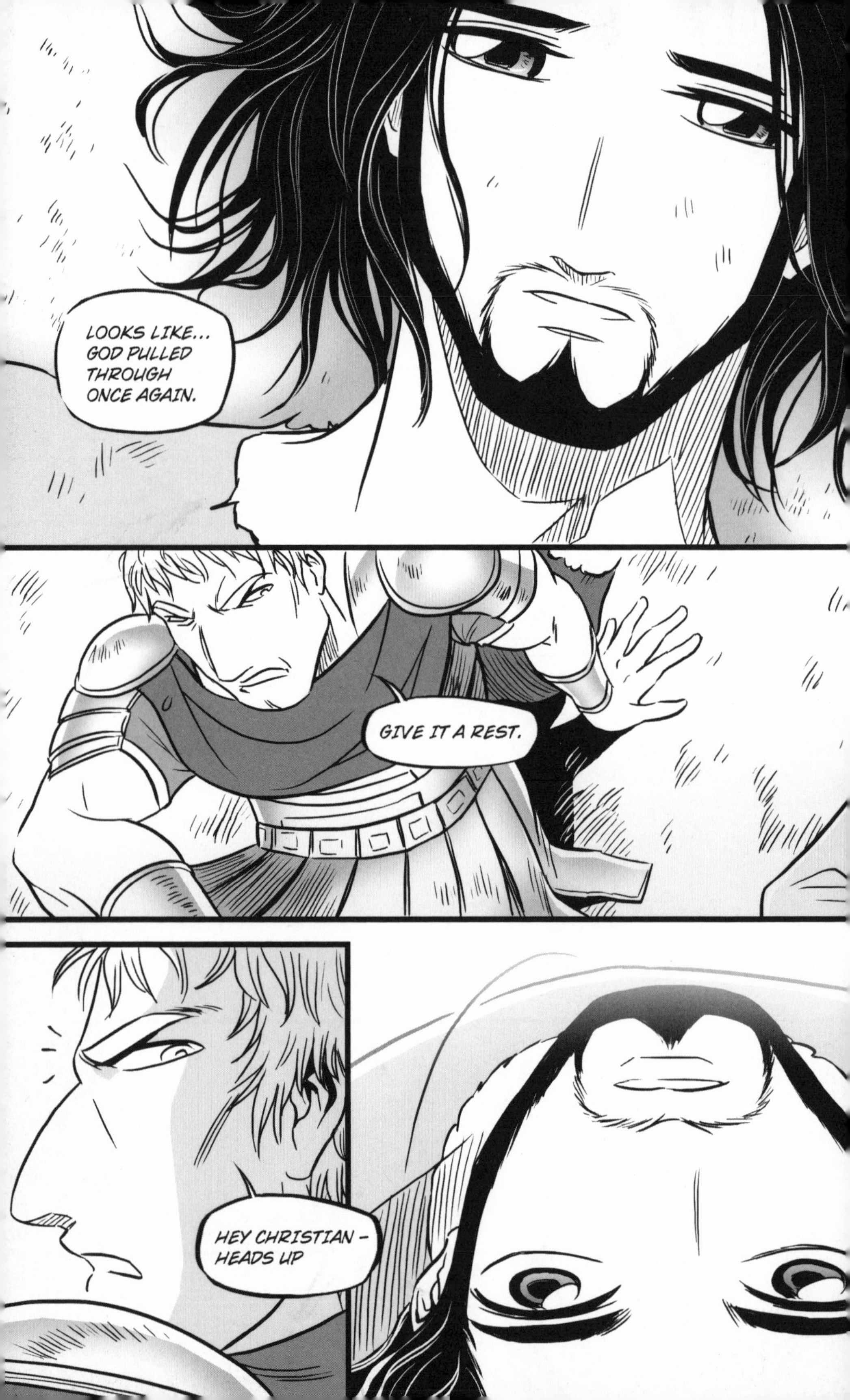
LOOKS LIKE... GOD PULLED THROUGH ONCE AGAIN.
GIVE IT A REST.
HEY CHRISTIAN - HEADS UP

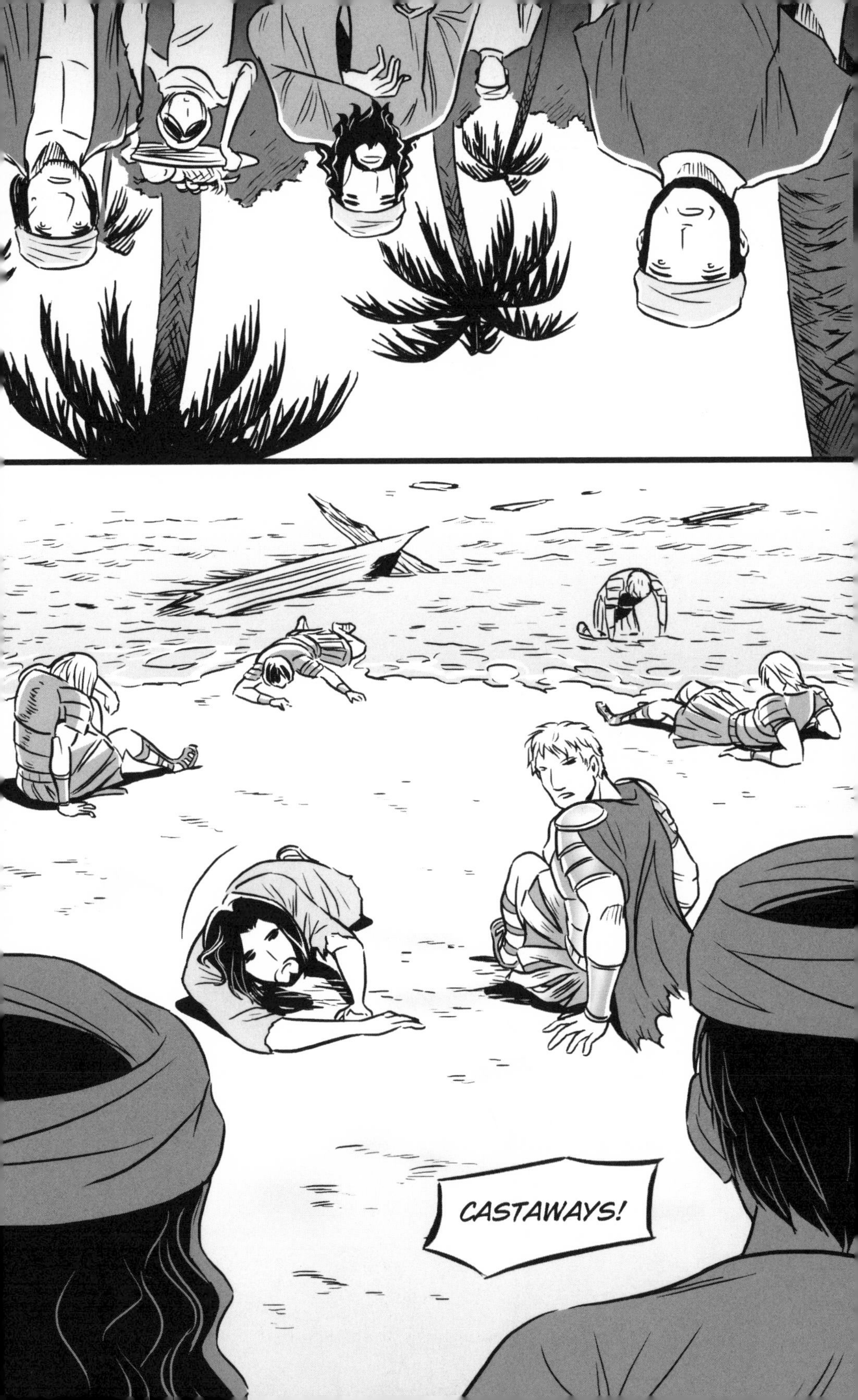
CASTAWAYS!

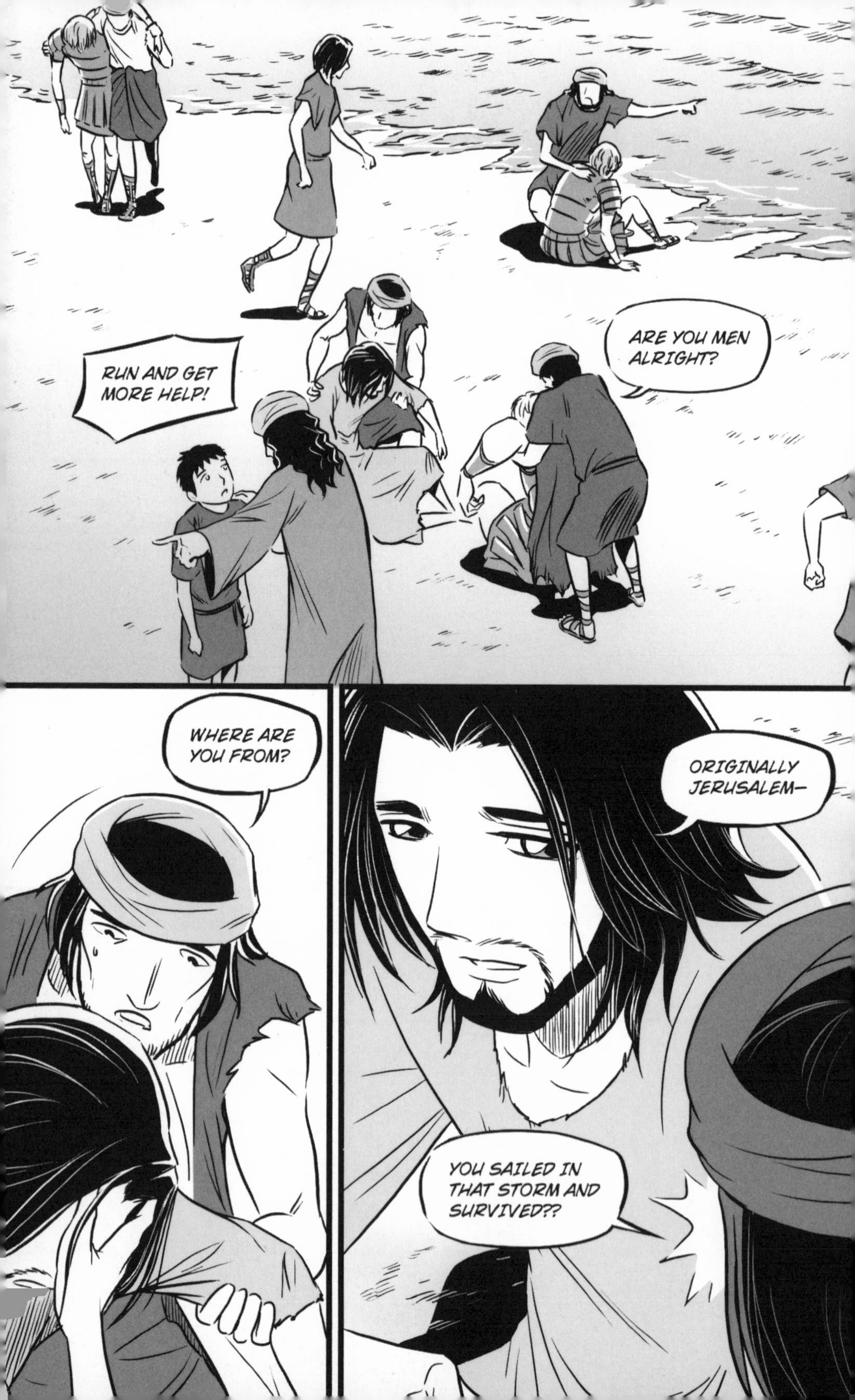
RUN AND GET MORE HELP!
ARE YOU MEN ALRIGHT?
WHERE ARE YOU FROM?
ORIGINALLY JERUSALEM–
YOU SAILED IN THAT STORM AND SURVIVED??

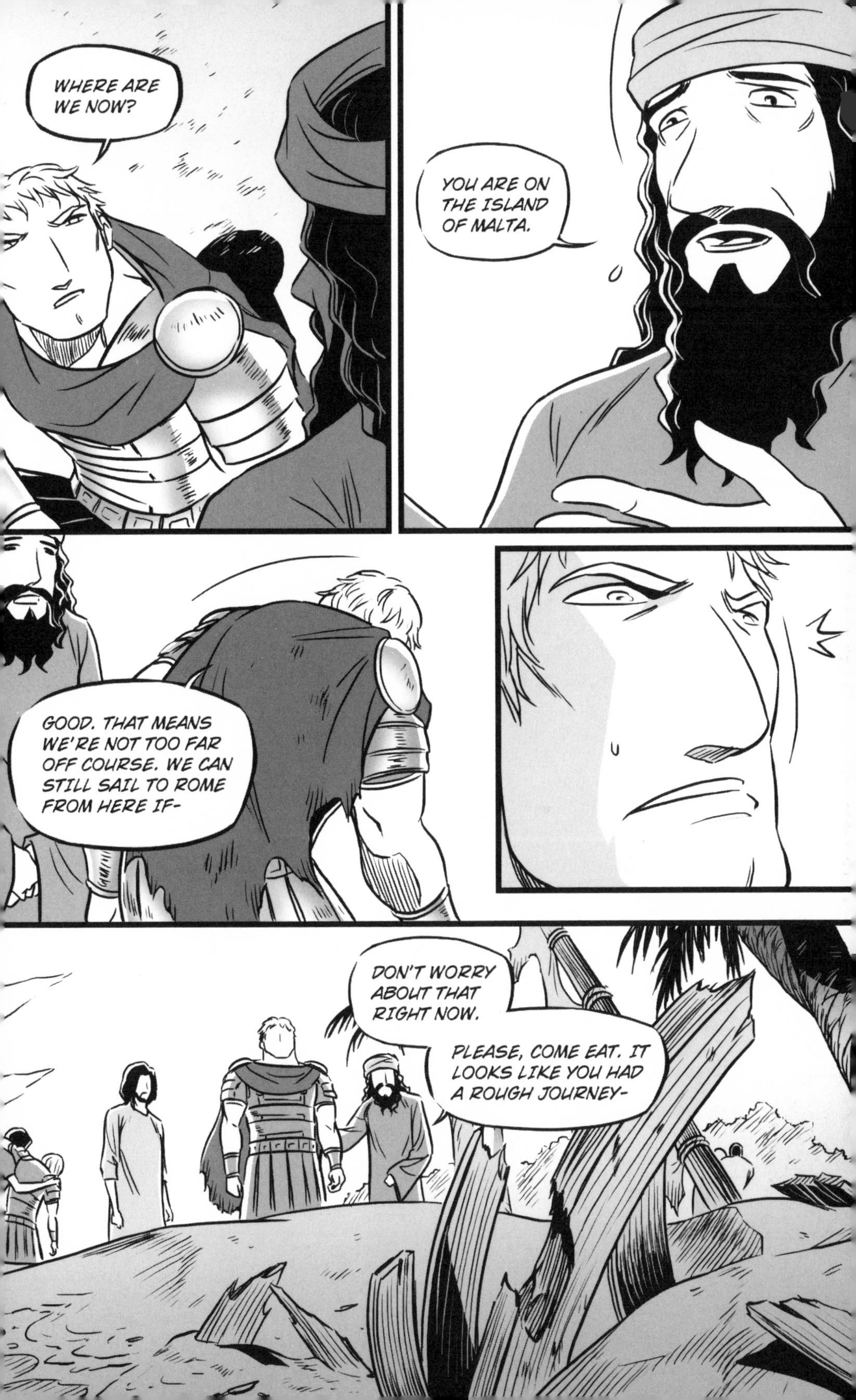
WHERE ARE WE NOW?
YOU ARE ON THE ISLAND OF MALTA.
GOOD. THAT MEANS WE'RE NOT TOO FAR OFF COURSE. WE CAN STILL SAIL TO ROME FROM HERE IF-
DON'T WORRY ABOUT THAT RIGHT NOW.
PLEASE, COME EAT. IT LOOKS LIKE YOU HAD A ROUGH JOURNEY-

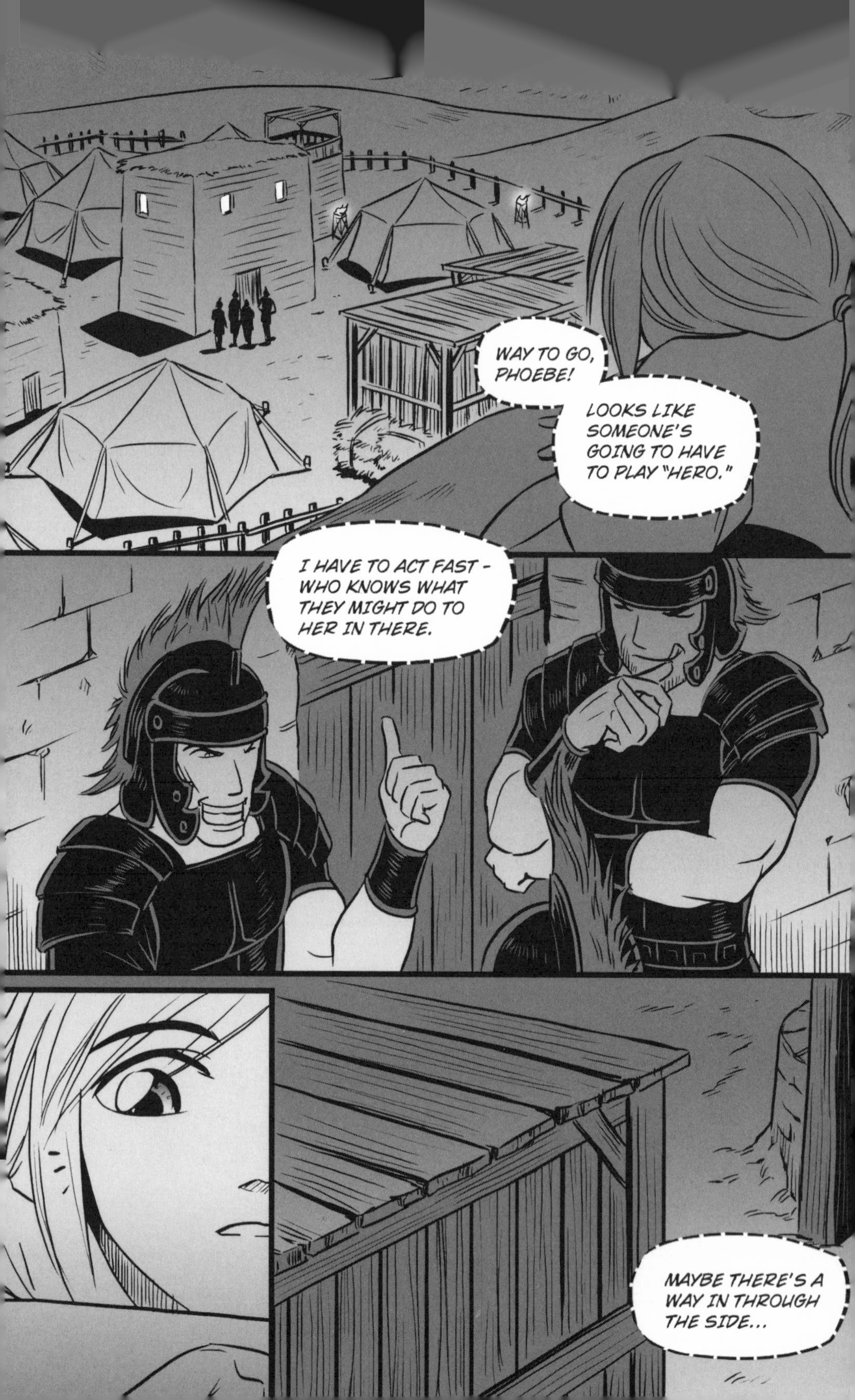
WAY TO GO, PHOEBE!
LOOKS LIKE SOMEONE'S GOING TO HAVE TO PLAY "HERO."
I HAVE TO ACT FAST - WHO KNOWS WHAT THEY MIGHT DO TO HER IN THERE.
MAYBE THERE'S A WAY IN THROUGH THE SIDE...

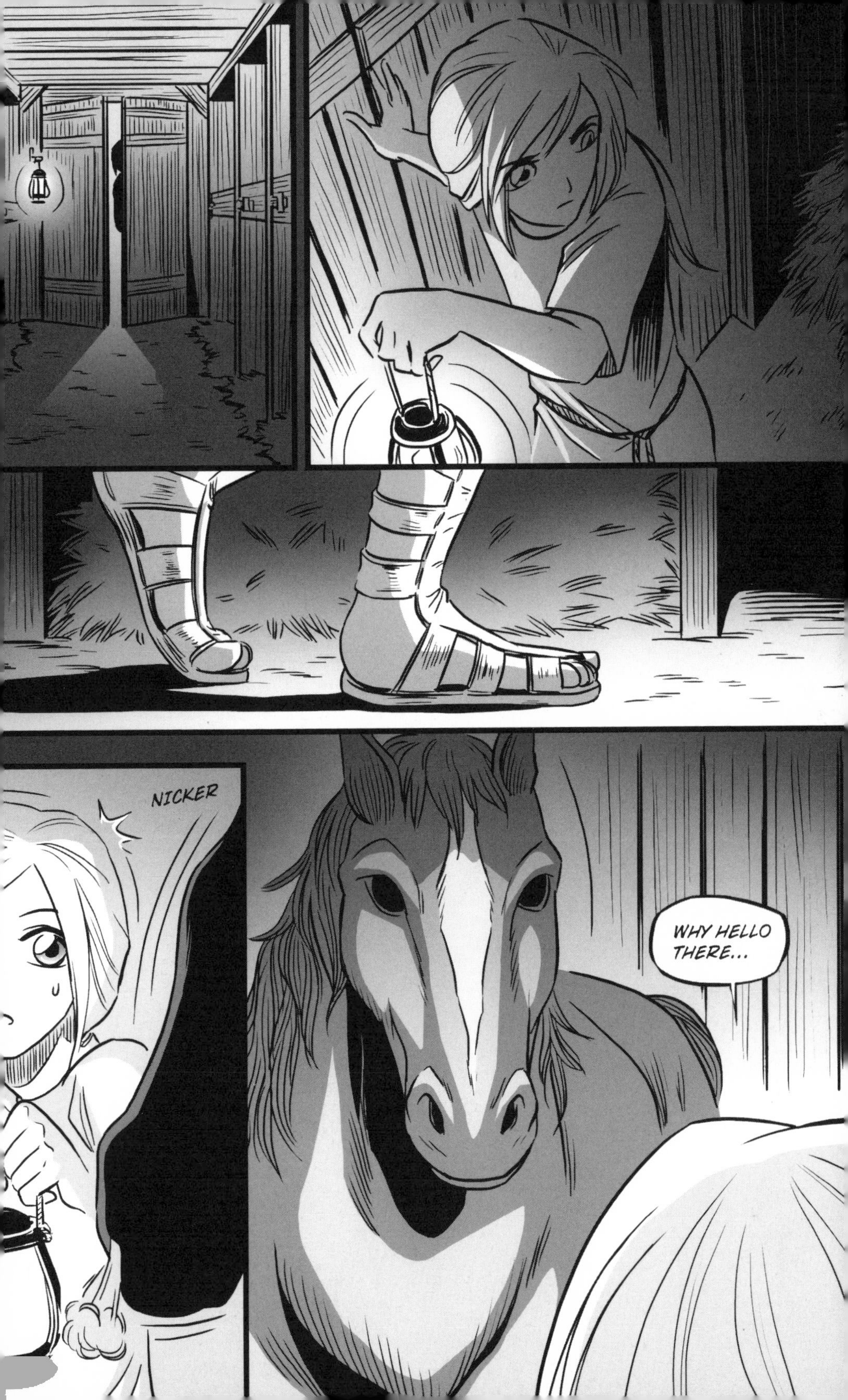
NICKER
WHY HELLO THERE...

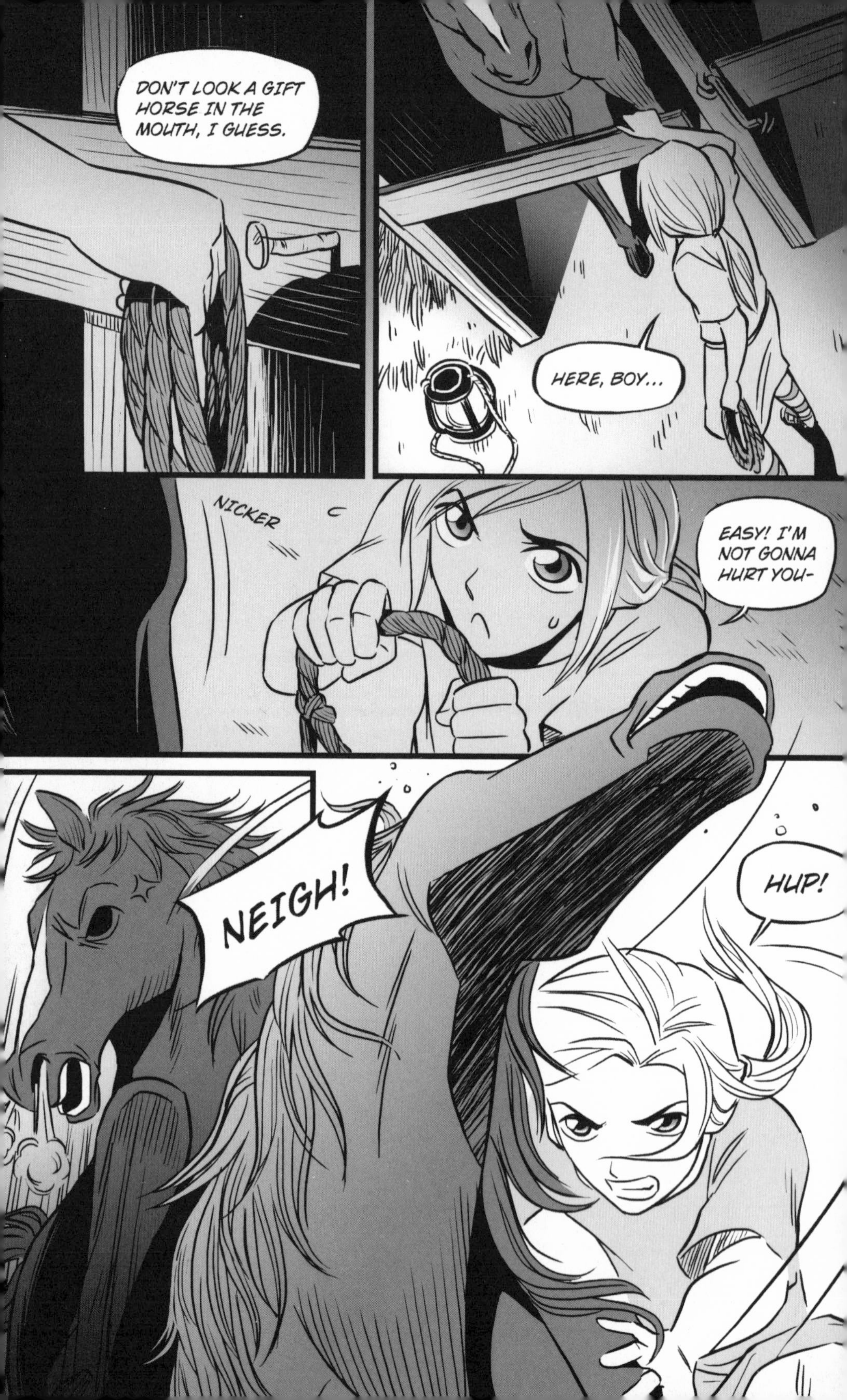
DON'T LOOK A GIFT HORSE IN THE MOUTH, I GUESS.
HERE, BOY...
NICKER
EASY! I'M NOT GONNA HURT YOU-
NEIGH!
HUP!

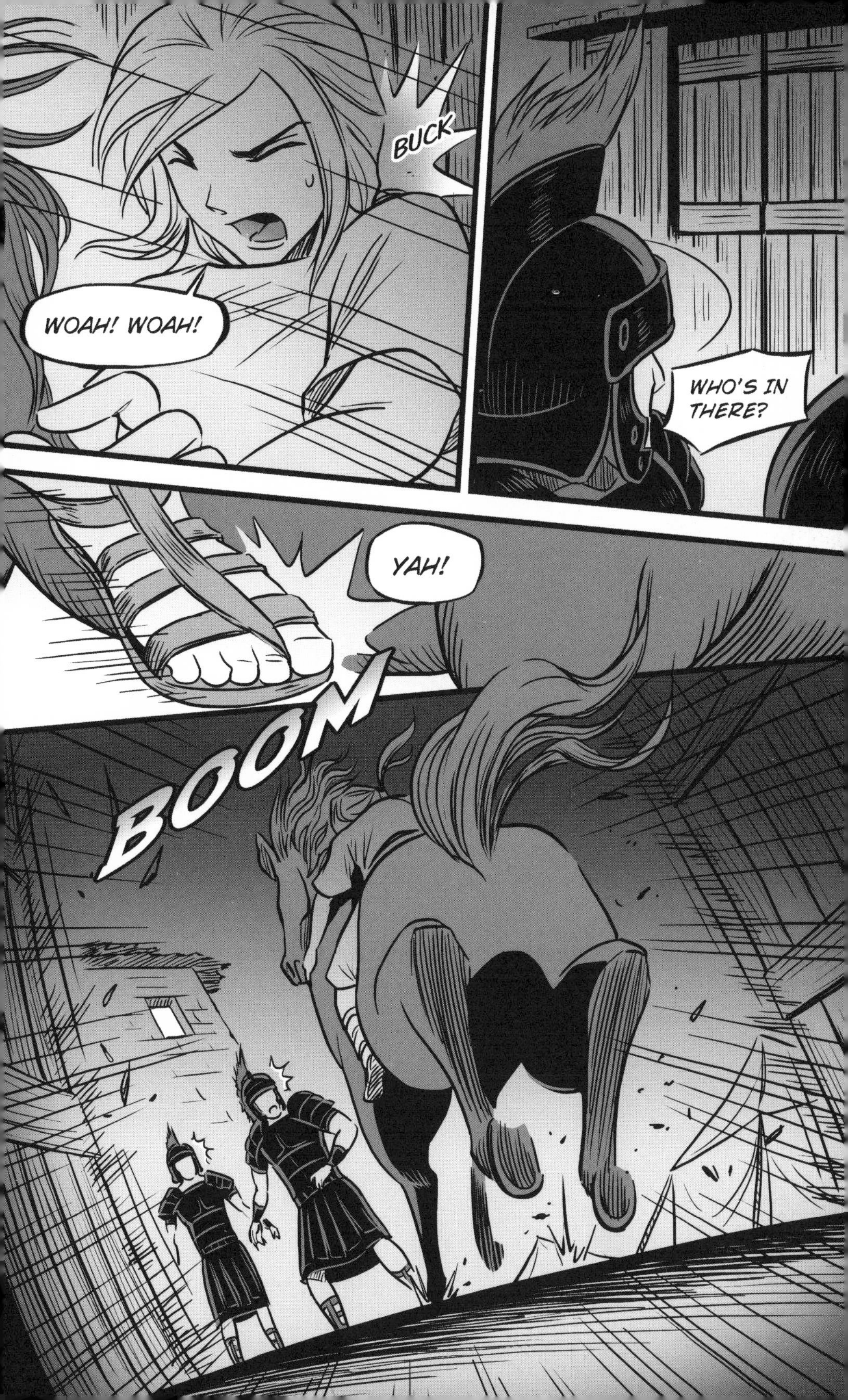
BUCK
WOAH! WOAH!
WHO'S IN THERE?
YAH!
BOOM

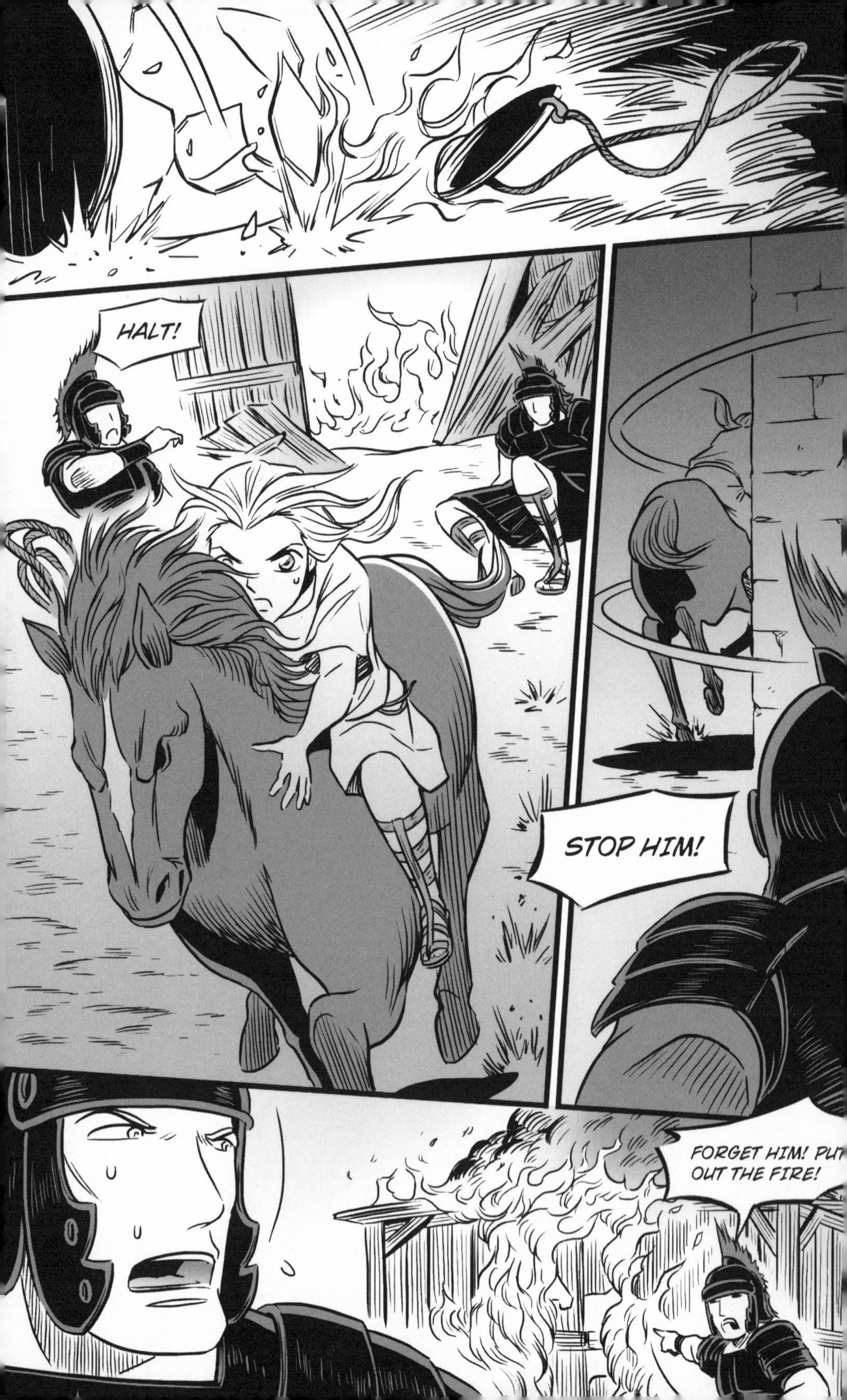
HALT!
STOP HIM!
FORGET HIM! PUT OUT THE FIRE!

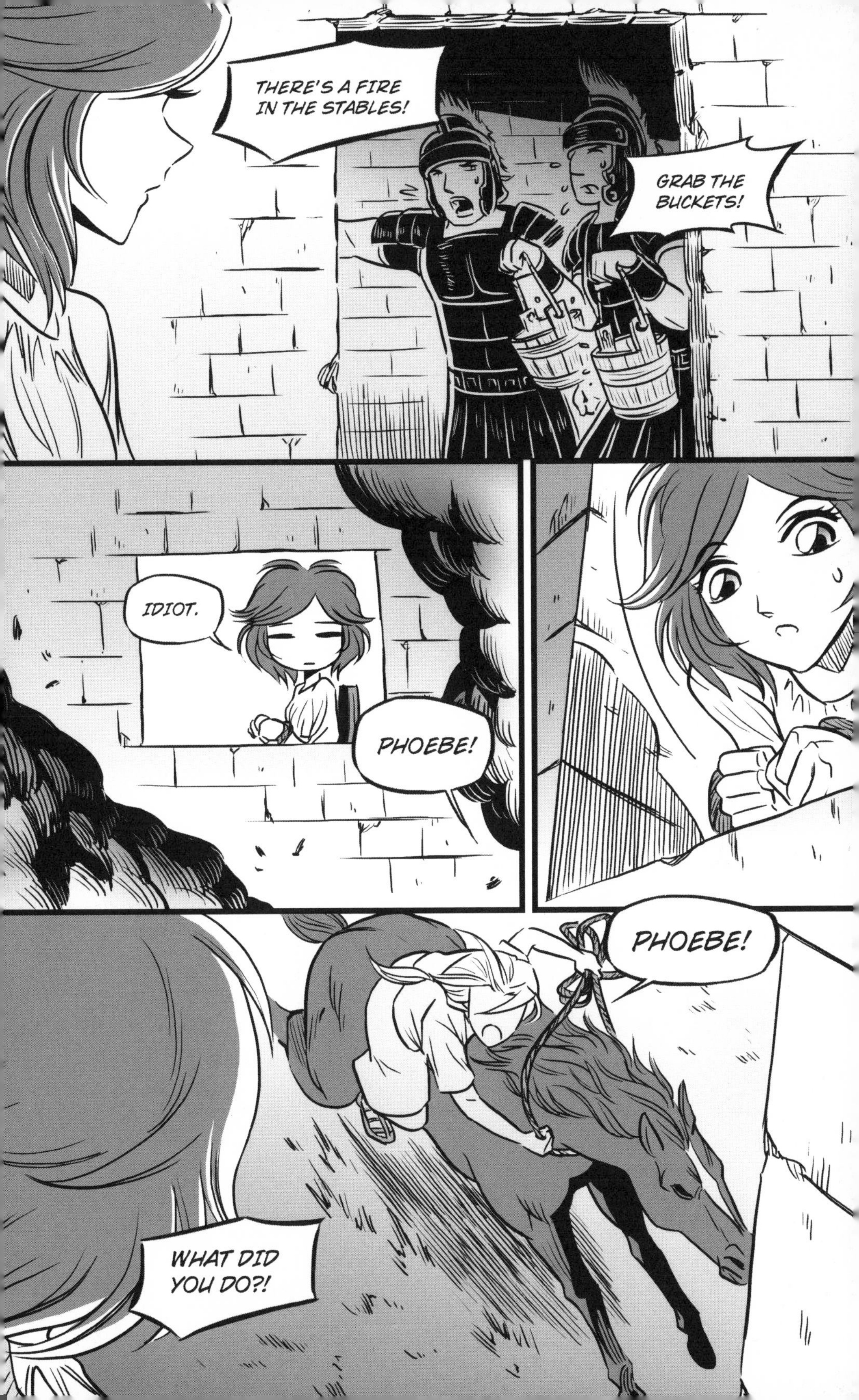
THERE'S A FIRE IN THE STABLES!
GRAB THE BUCKETS!
IDIOT.
PHOEBE!
PHOEBE!
WHAT DID YOU DO?!

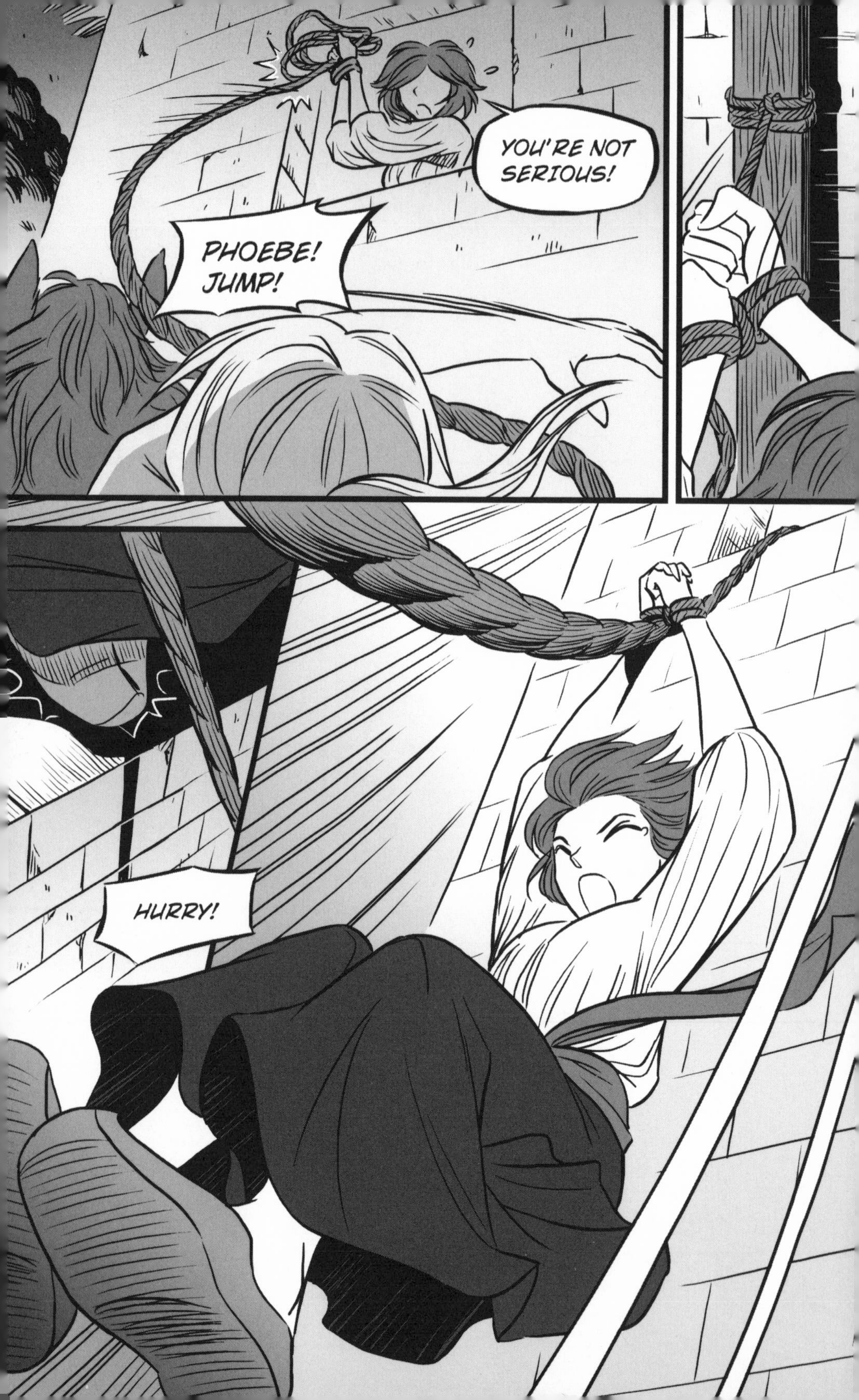
YOU'RE NOT SERIOUS!
PHOEBE! JUMP!
HURRY!

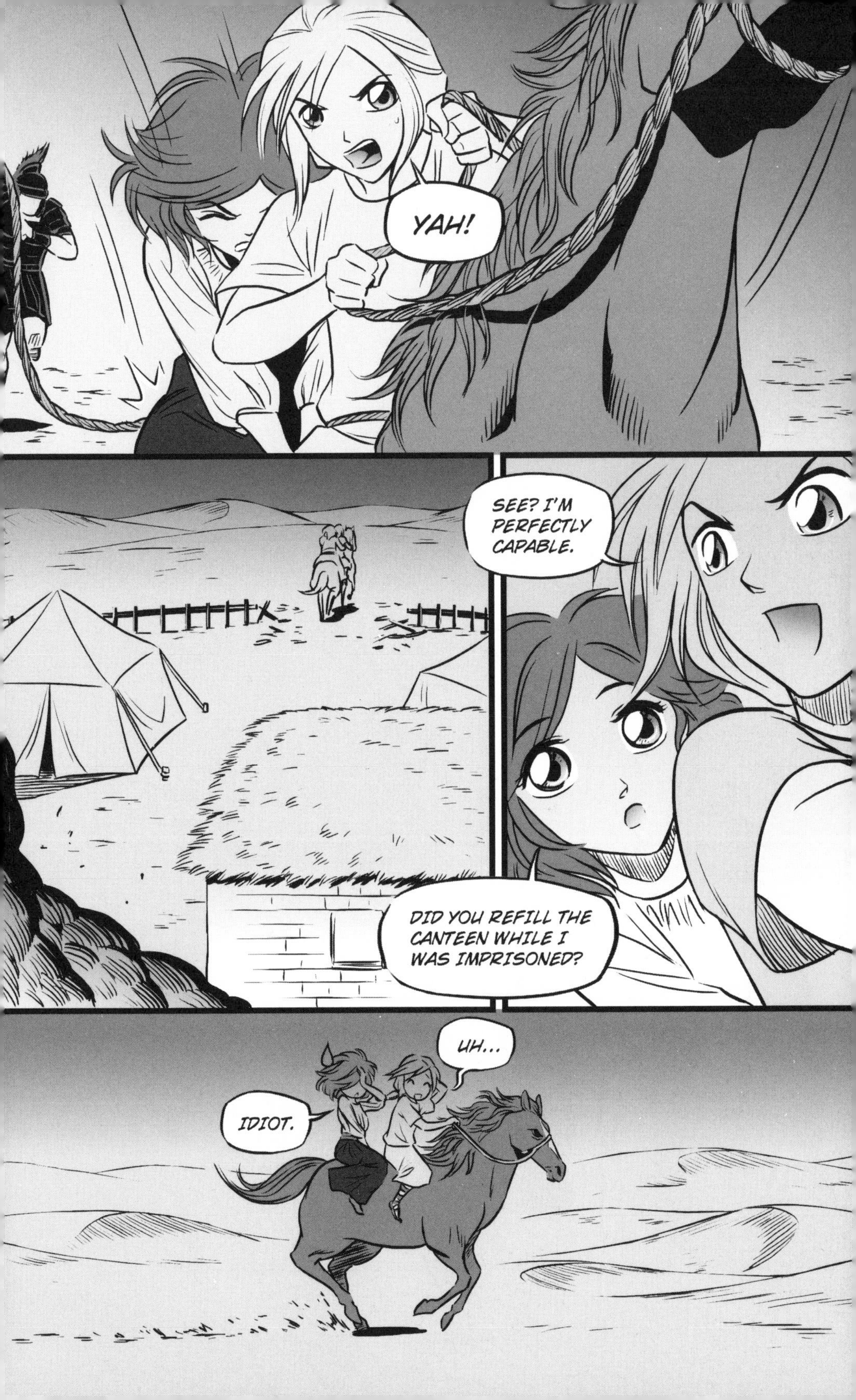
YAH!
SEE? I'M PERFECTLY CAPABLE.
DID YOU REFILL THE CANTEEN WHILE I WAS IMPRISONED?
UH...
IDIOT.

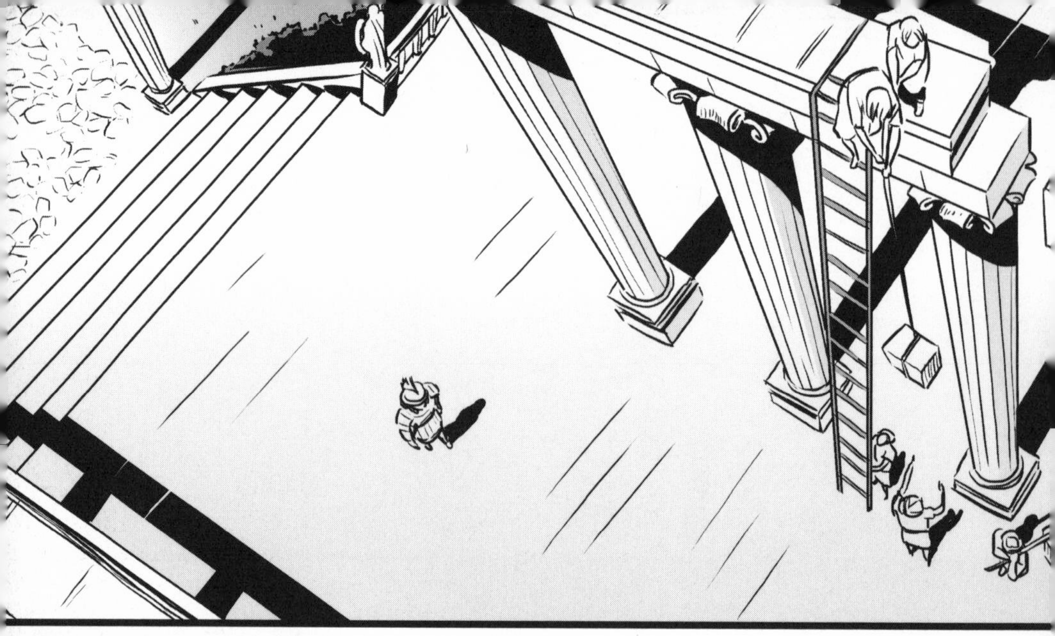

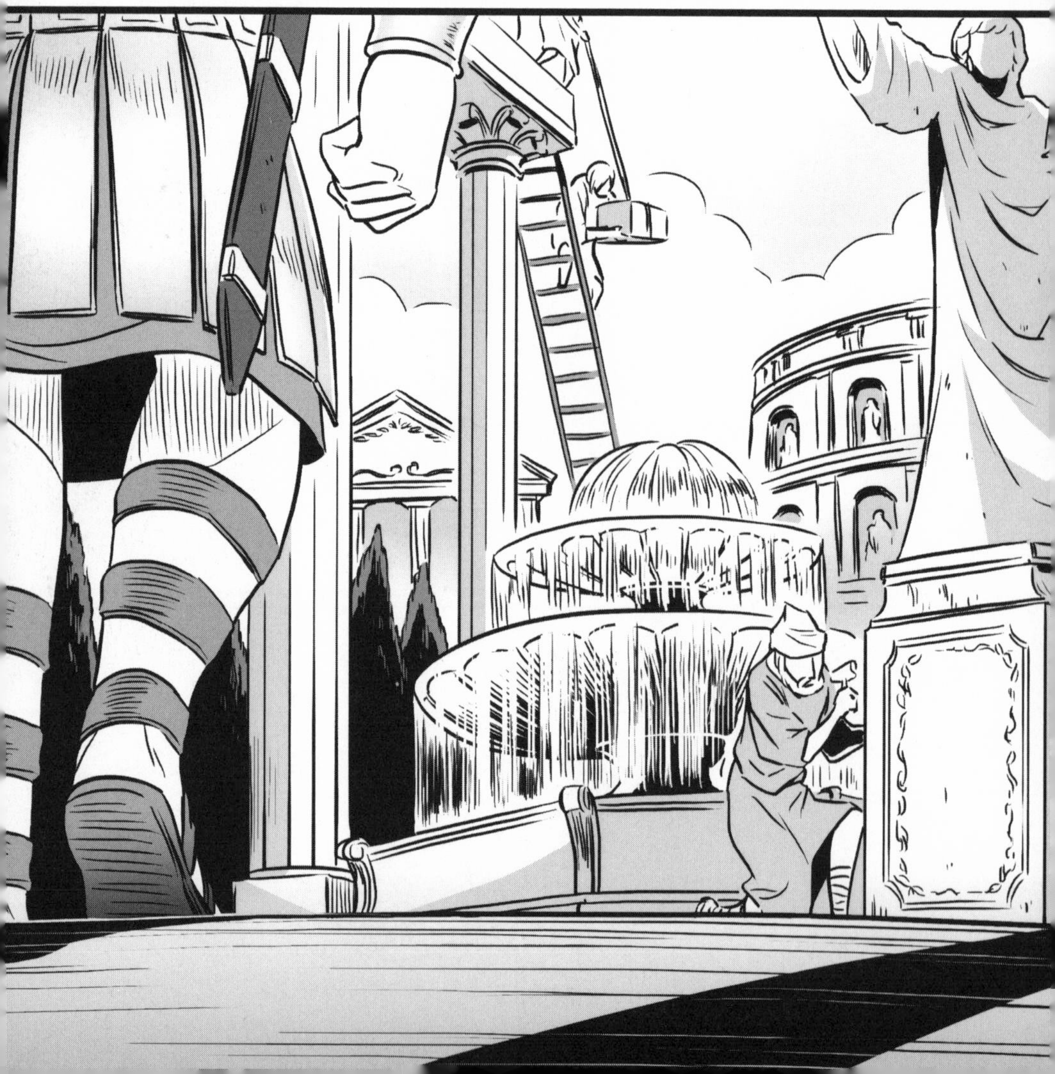

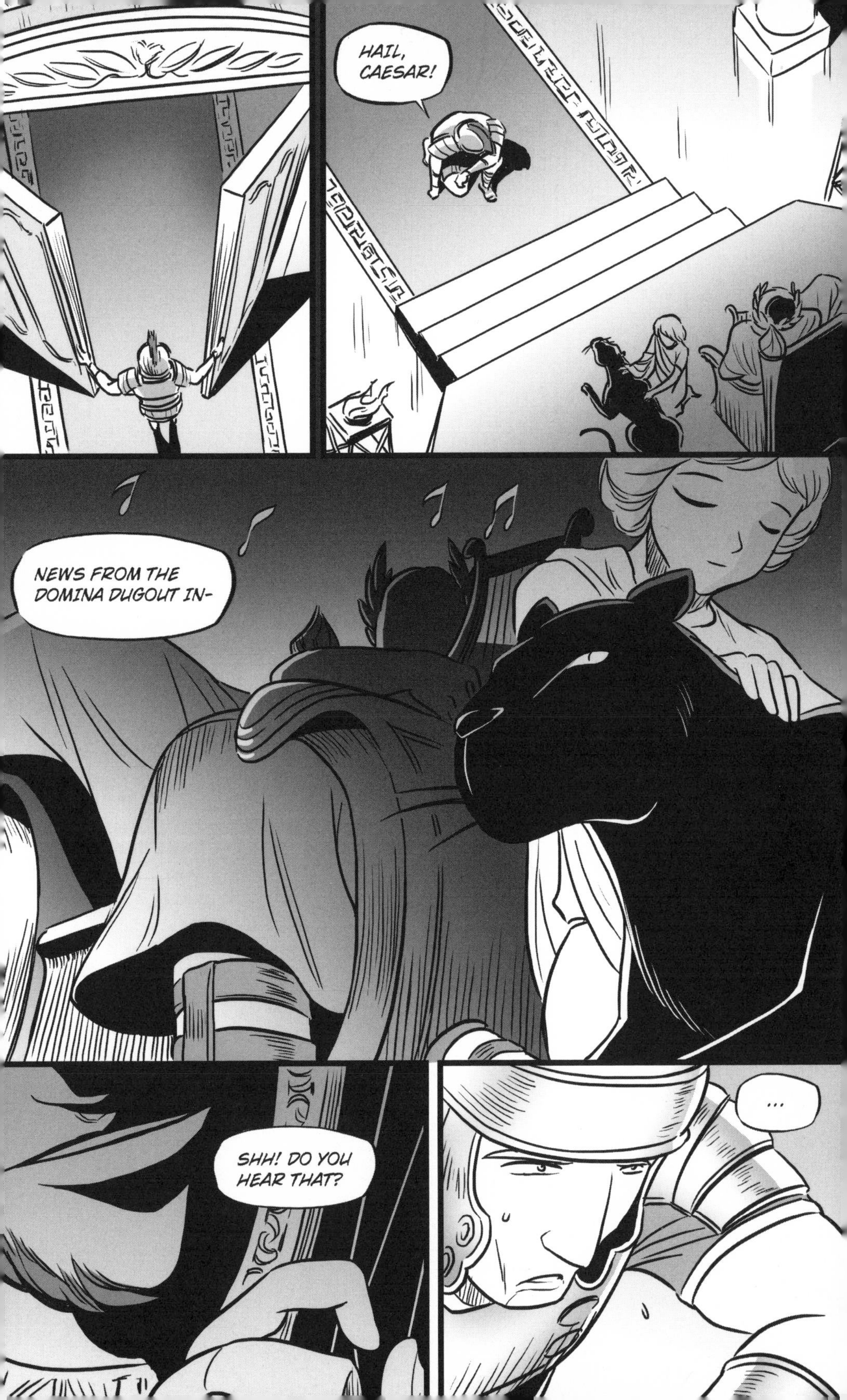
HAIL, CAESAR!
NEWS FROM THE DOMINA DUGOUT IN-
SHH! DO YOU HEAR THAT?
...

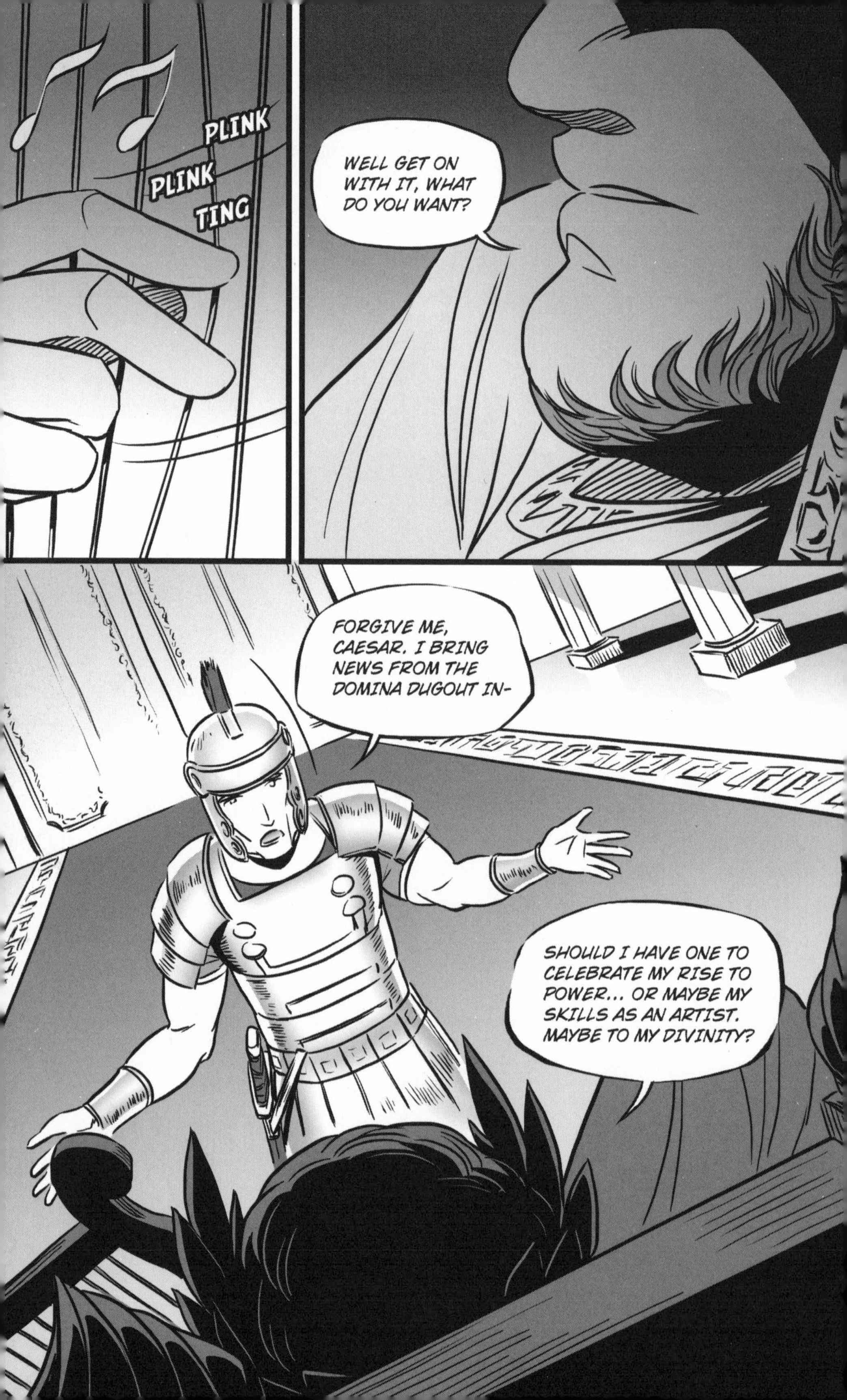
PLINK
PLINK
TING
WELL GET ON WITH IT, WHAT DO YOU WANT?
FORGIVE ME, CAESAR. I BRING NEWS FROM THE DOMINA DUGOUT IN-
SHOULD I HAVE ONE TO CELEBRATE MY RISE TO POWER... OR MAYBE MY SKILLS AS AN ARTIST. MAYBE TO MY DIVINITY?

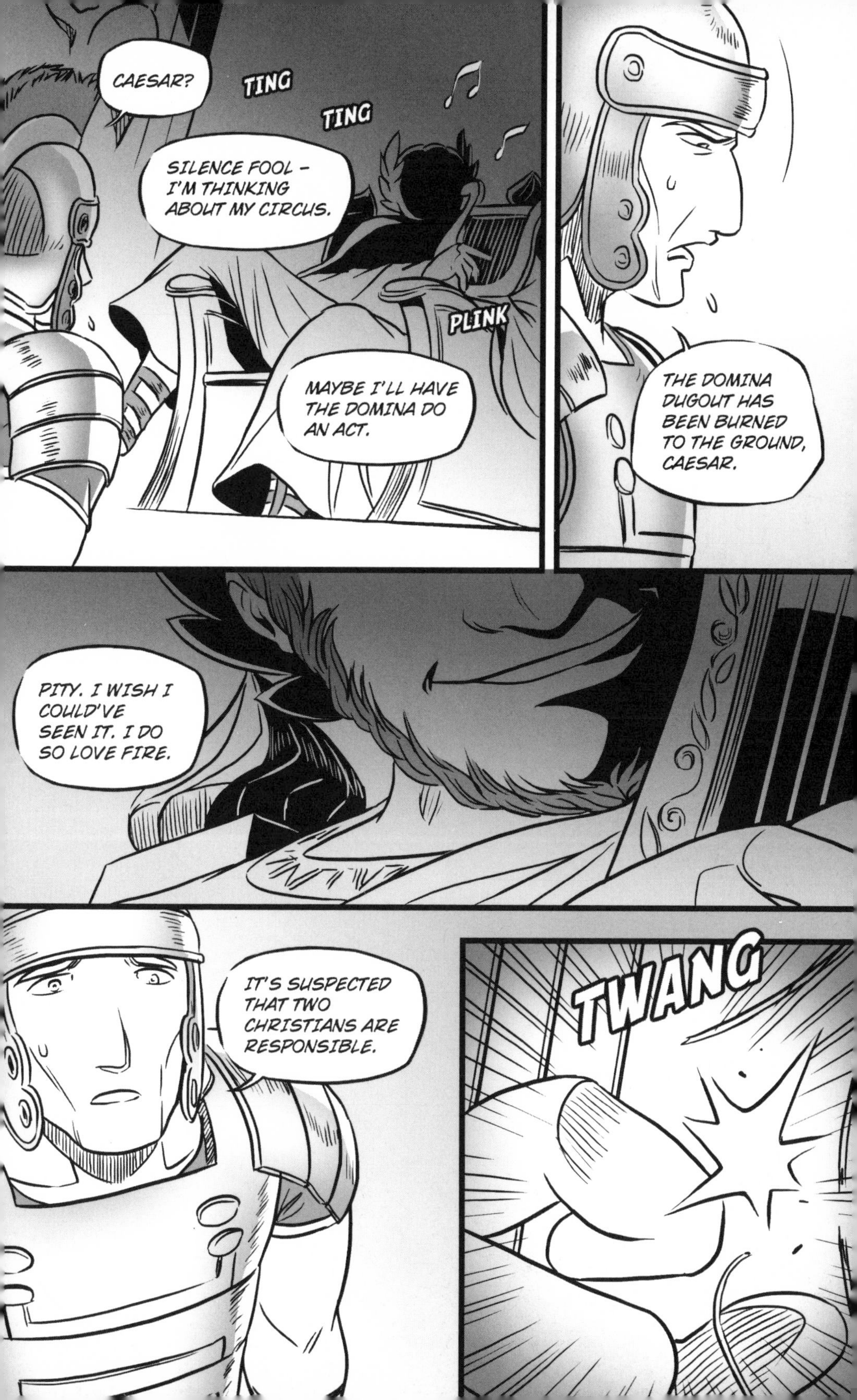
CAESAR?
TING
TING
SILENCE FOOL - I'M THINKING ABOUT MY CIRCUS.
PLINK
MAYBE I'LL HAVE THE DOMINA DO AN ACT.
THE DOMINA DUGOUT HAS BEEN BURNED TO THE GROUND, CAESAR.
PITY. I WISH I COULD'VE SEEN IT. I DO SO LOVE FIRE.
IT'S SUSPECTED THAT TWO CHRISTIANS ARE RESPONSIBLE.
TWANG

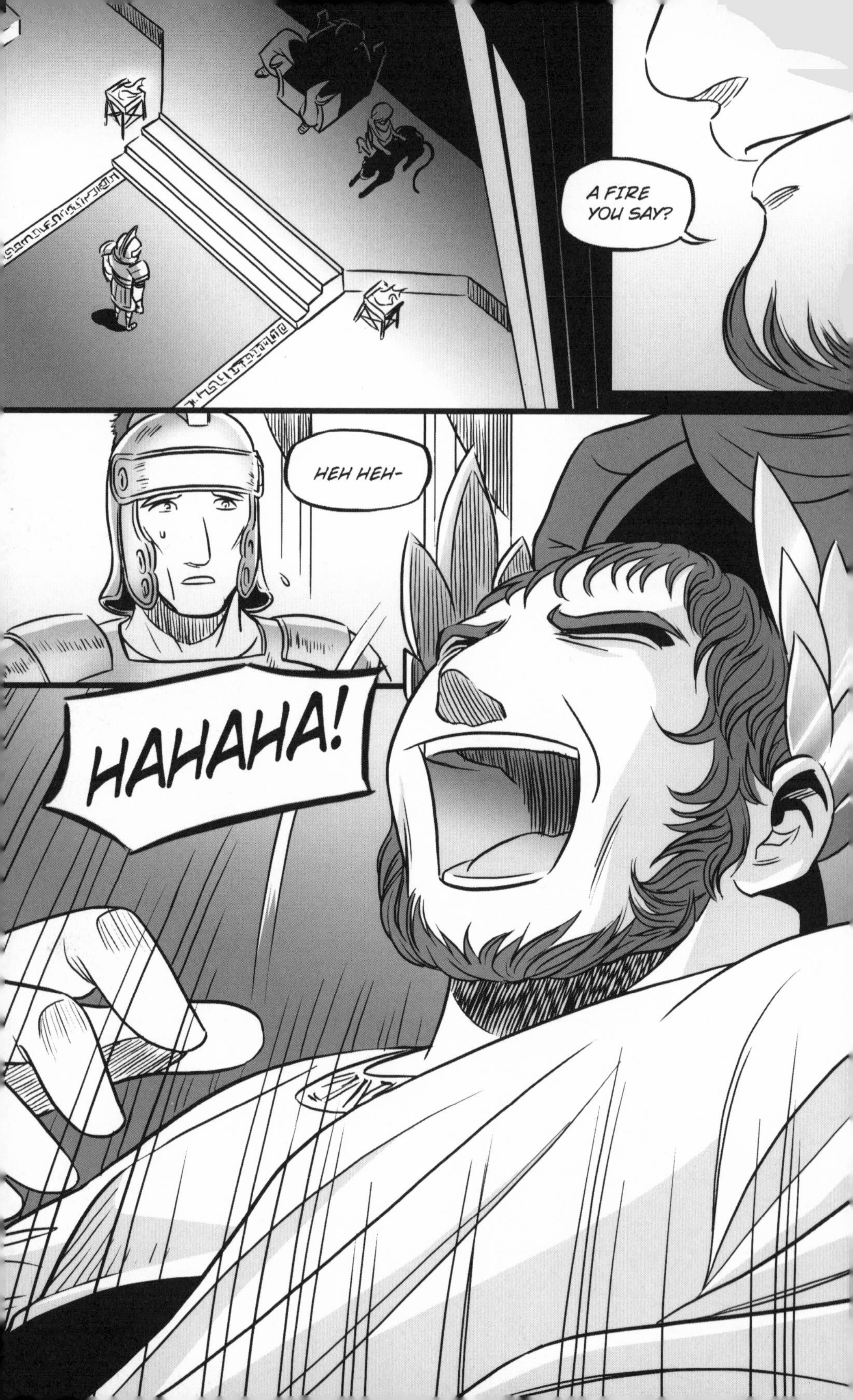
A FIRE YOU SAY?
HEH HEH-
HAHAHA!

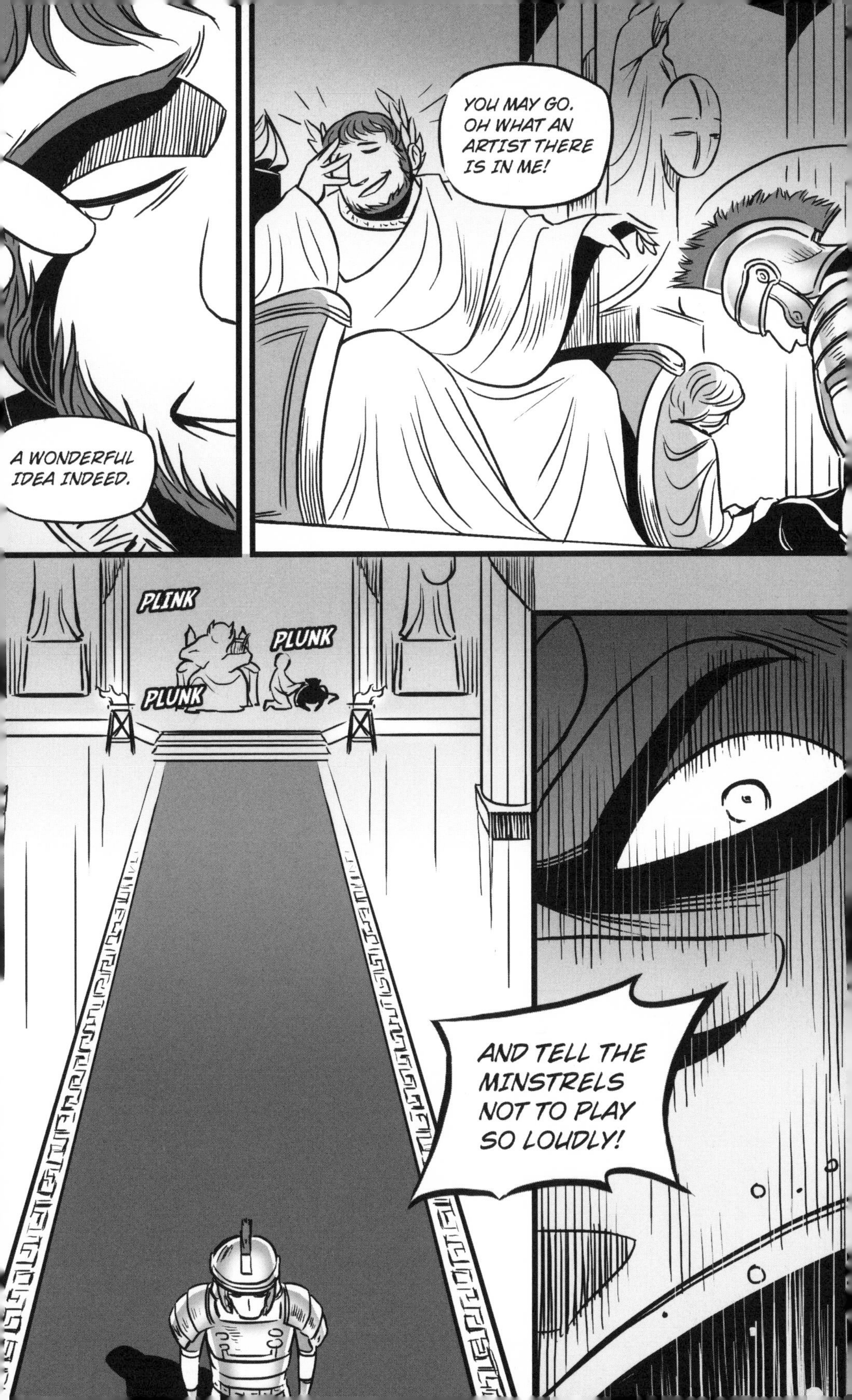
A WONDERFUL IDEA INDEED.
YOU MAY GO. OH WHAT AN ARTIST THERE IS IN ME!
PLINK
PLUNK
PLUNK
AND TELL THE MINSTRELS NOT TO PLAY SO LOUDLY!

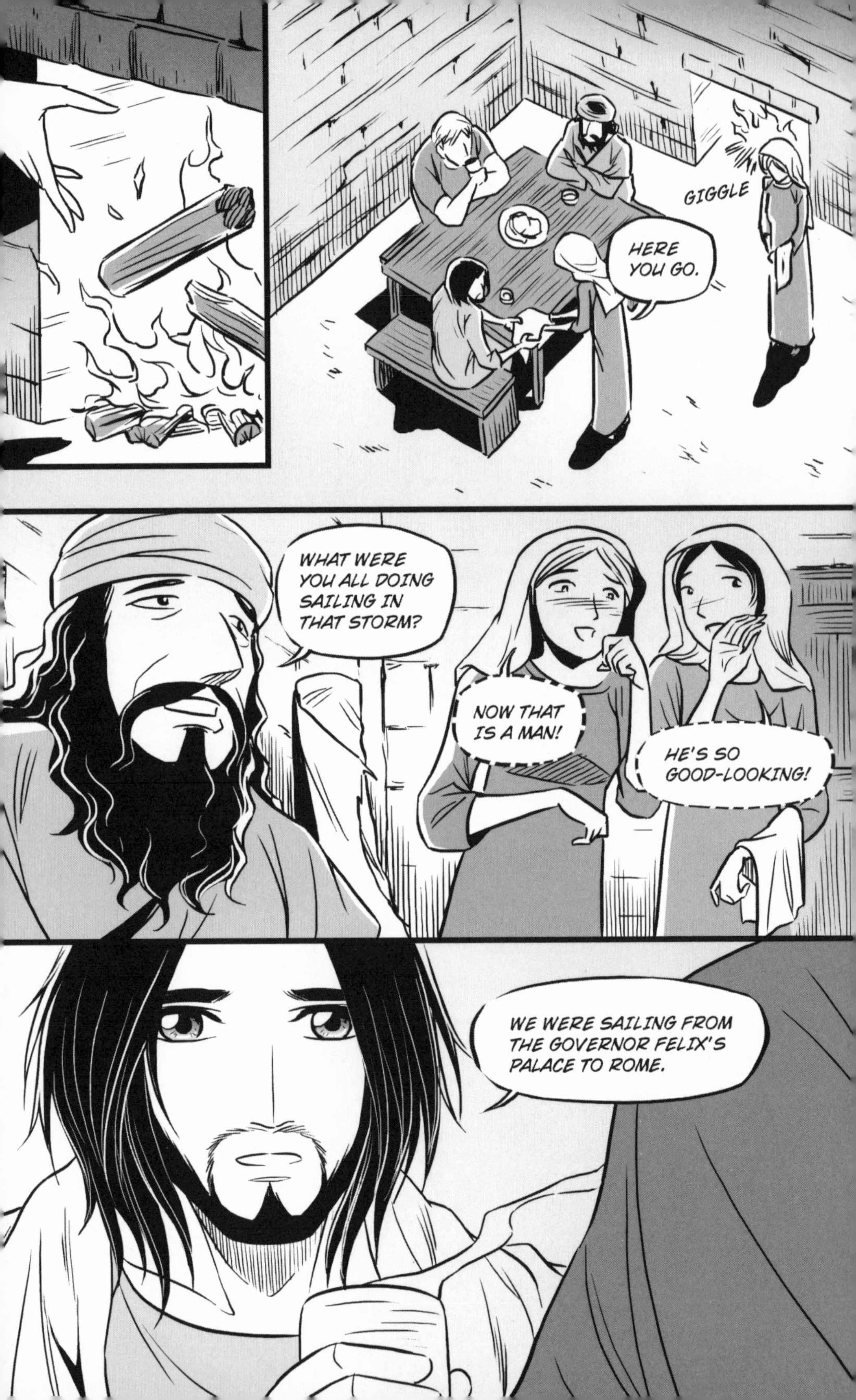
GIGGLE
HERE YOU GO.
WHAT WERE YOU ALL DOING SAILING IN THAT STORM?
NOW THAT IS A MAN!
HE'S SO GOOD-LOOKING!
WE WERE SAILING FROM THE GOVERNOR FELIX'S PALACE TO ROME.

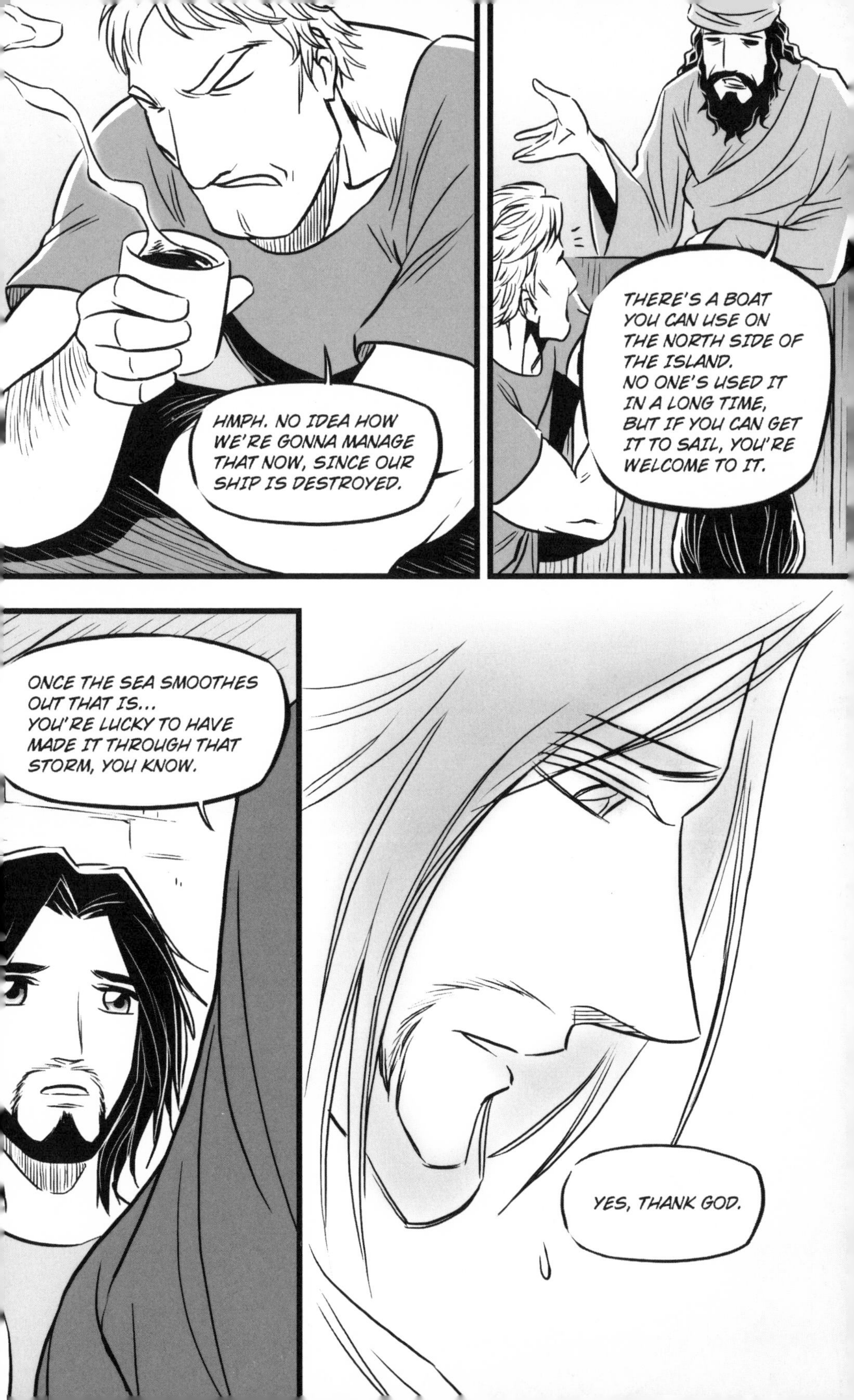
HMPH. NO IDEA HOW WE'RE GONNA MANAGE THAT NOW, SINCE OUR SHIP IS DESTROYED.
THERE'S A BOAT YOU CAN USE ON THE NORTH SIDE OF THE ISLAND. NO ONE'S USED IT IN A LONG TIME, BUT IF YOU CAN GET IT TO SAIL, YOU'RE WELCOME TO IT.
ONCE THE SEA SMOOTHES OUT THAT IS... YOU'RE LUCKY TO HAVE MADE IT THROUGH THAT STORM, YOU KNOW.
YES, THANK GOD.

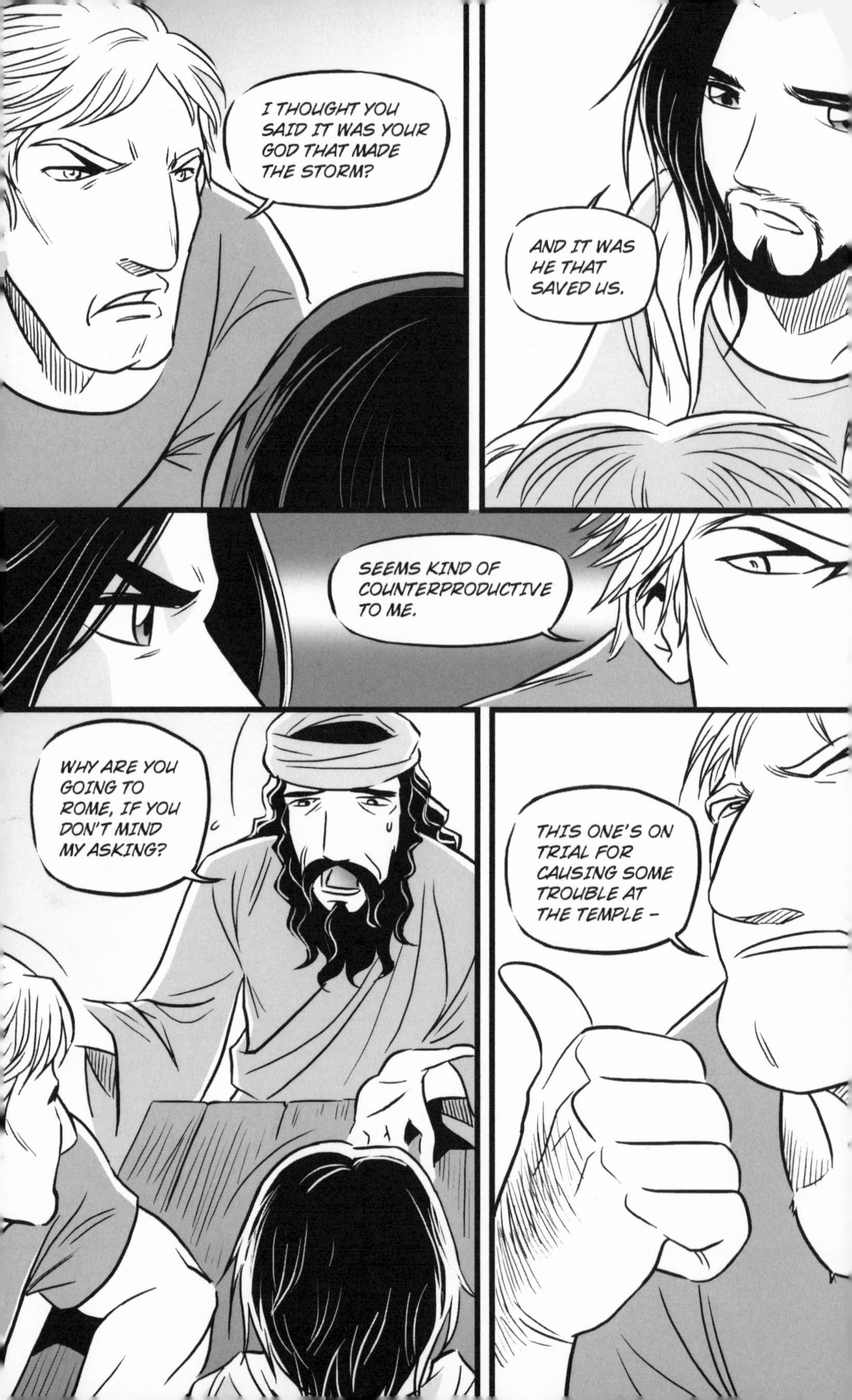
I THOUGHT YOU SAID IT WAS YOUR GOD THAT MADE THE STORM?
AND IT WAS HE THAT SAVED US.
SEEMS KIND OF COUNTERPRODUCTIVE TO ME.
WHY ARE YOU GOING TO ROME, IF YOU DON'T MIND MY ASKING?
THIS ONE'S ON TRIAL FOR CAUSING SOME TROUBLE AT THE TEMPLE -

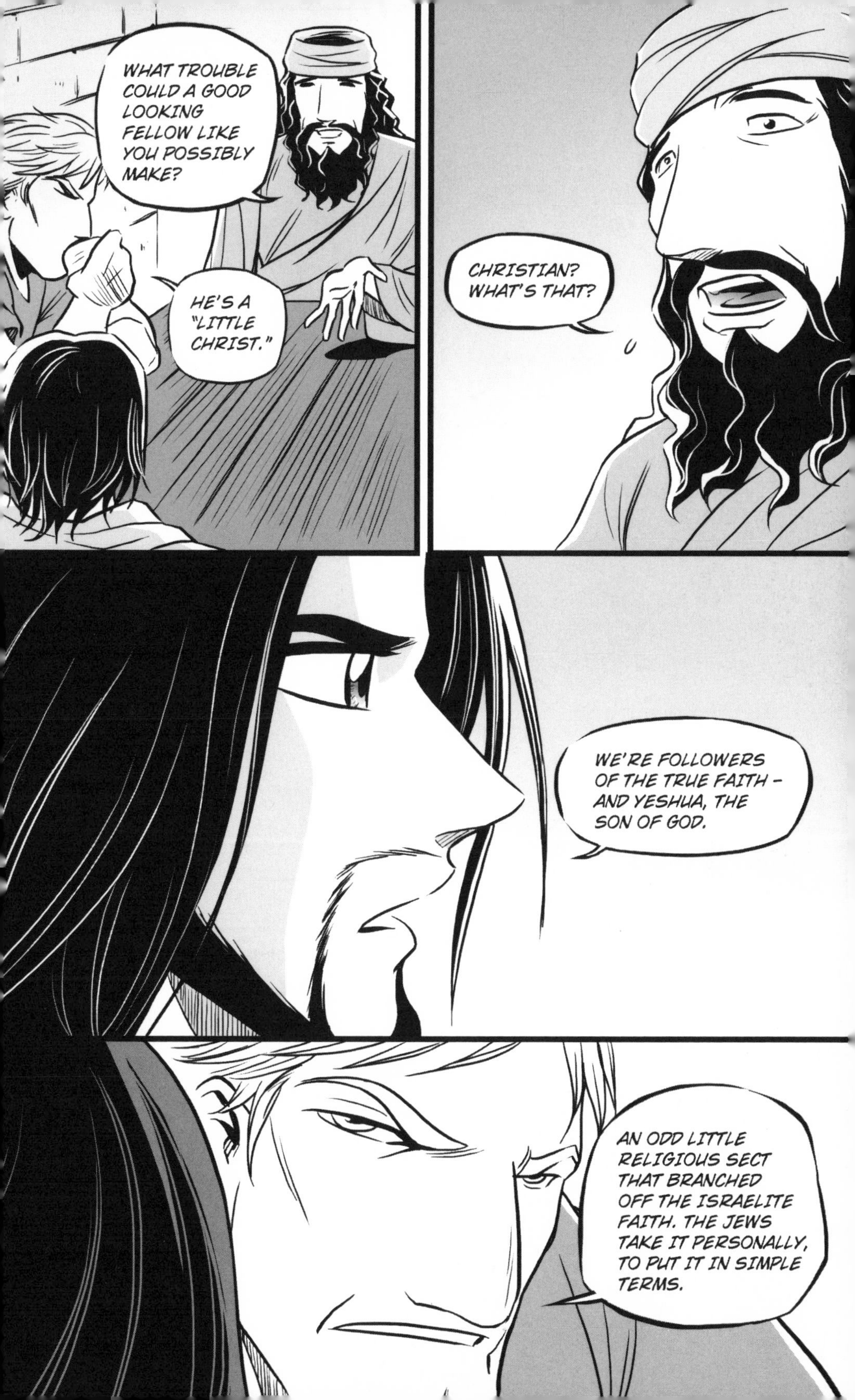
WHAT TROUBLE COULD A GOOD LOOKING FELLOW LIKE YOU POSSIBLY MAKE?
HE'S A "LITTLE CHRIST."
CHRISTIAN? WHAT'S THAT?
WE'RE FOLLOWERS OF THE TRUE FAITH - AND YESHUA, THE SON OF GOD.
AN ODD LITTLE RELIGIOUS SECT THAT BRANCHED OFF THE ISRAELITE FAITH. THE JEWS TAKE IT PERSONALLY, TO PUT IT IN SIMPLE TERMS.

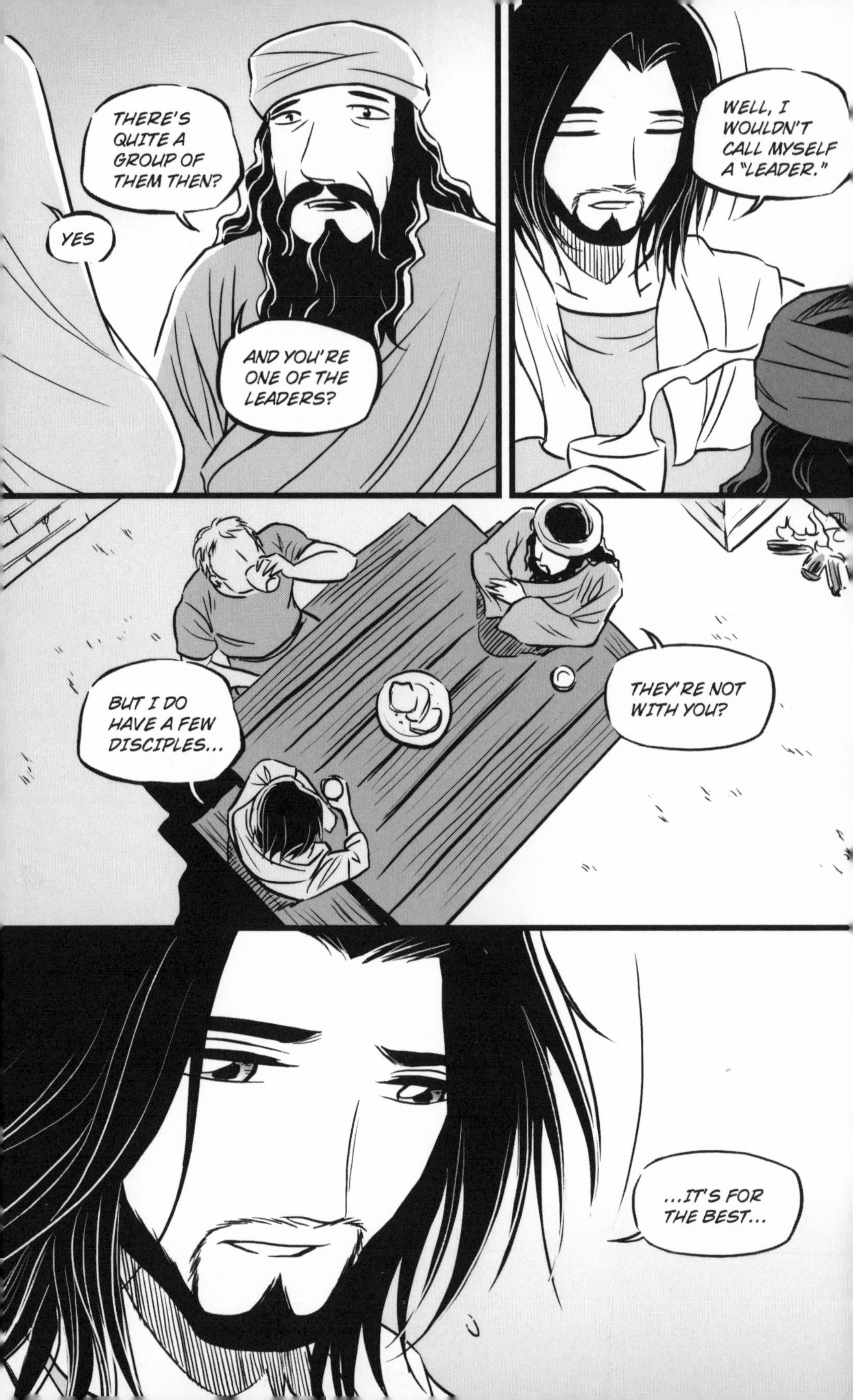
THERE'S QUITE A GROUP OF THEM THEN?
YES
AND YOU'RE ONE OF THE LEADERS?
WELL, I WOULDN'T CALL MYSELF A "LEADER."
BUT I DO HAVE A FEW DISCIPLES...
THEY'RE NOT WITH YOU?
...IT'S FOR THE BEST...

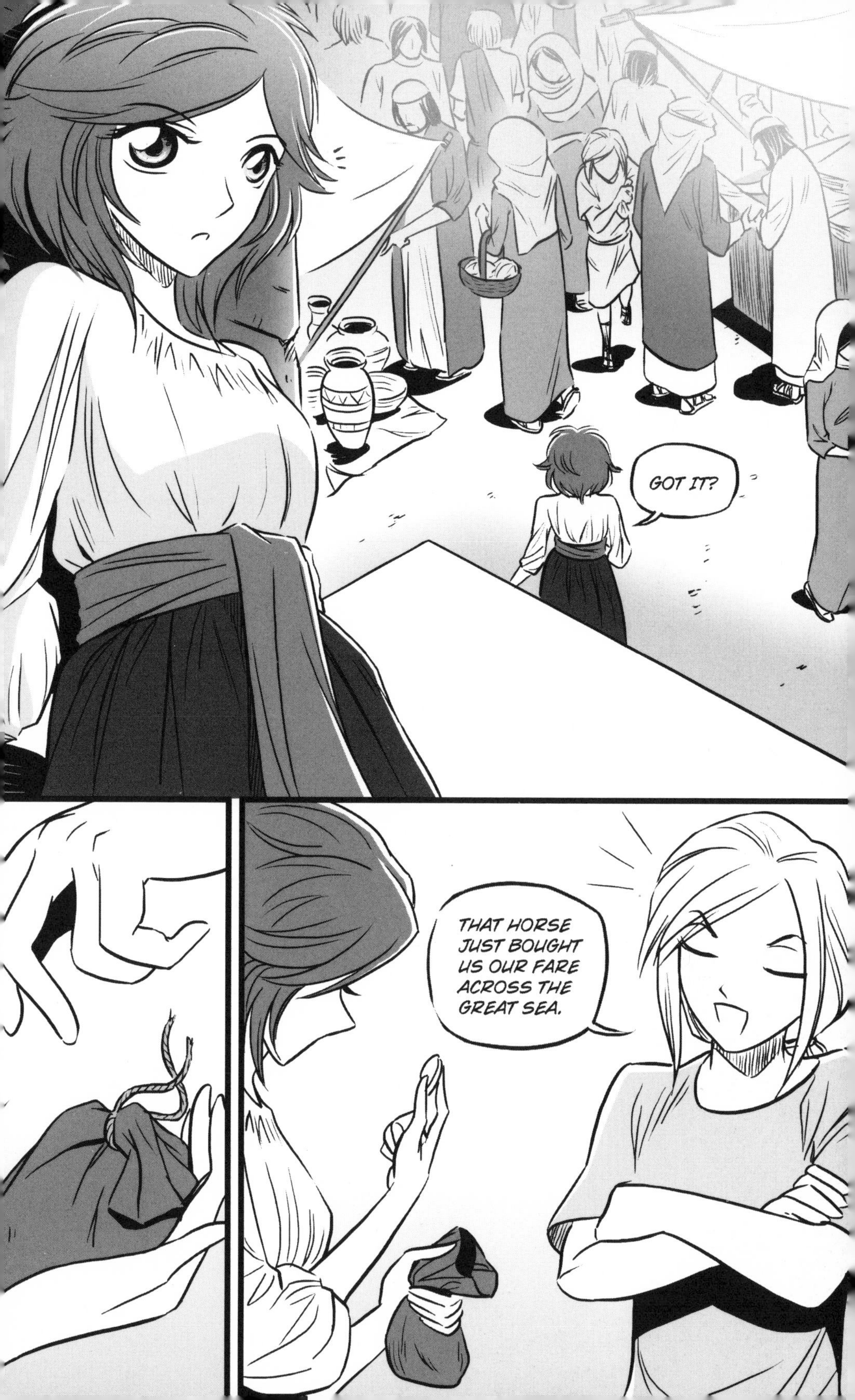
GOT IT?
THAT HORSE JUST BOUGHT US OUR FARE ACROSS THE GREAT SEA.

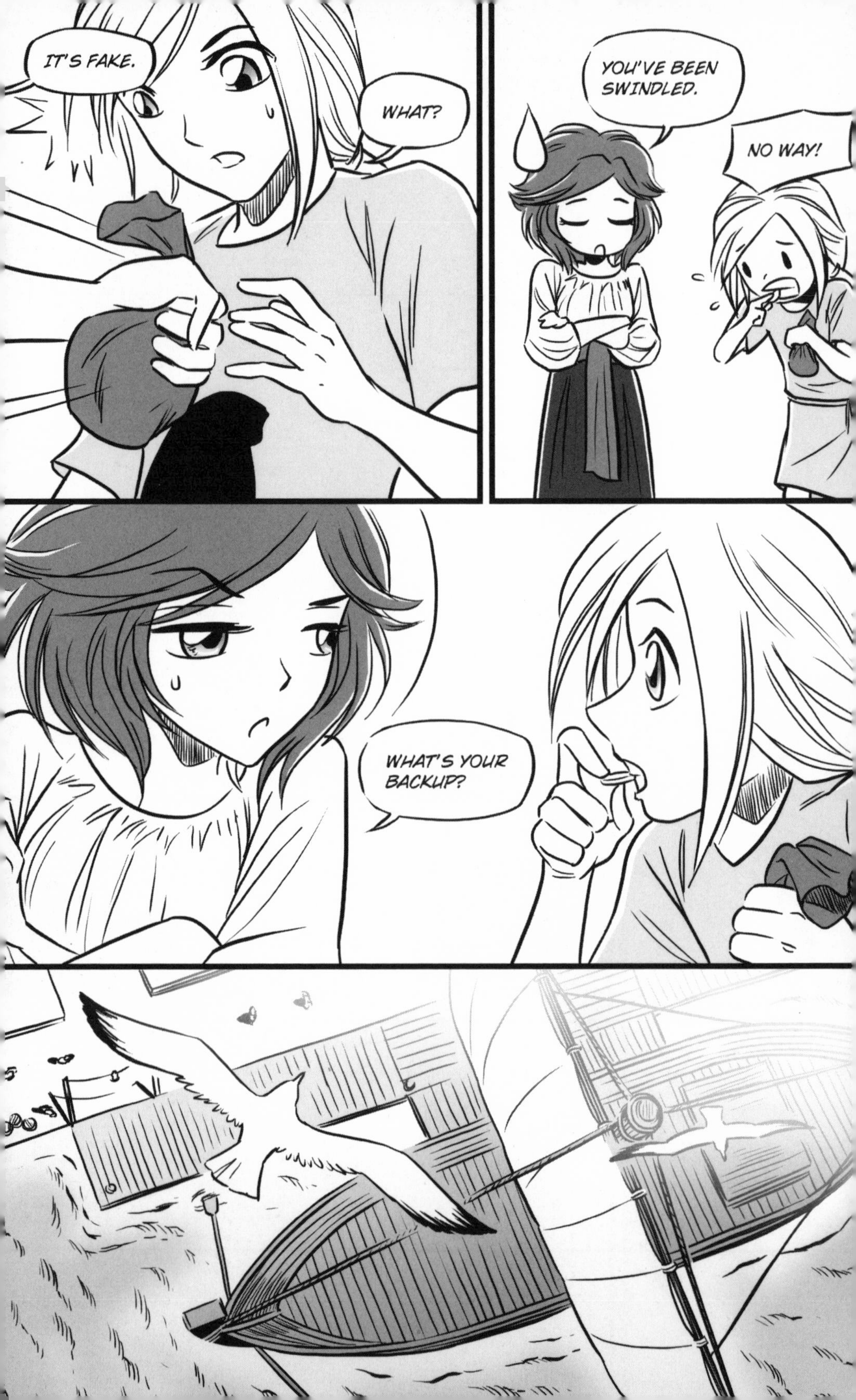
IT'S FAKE.
WHAT?
YOU'VE BEEN SWINDLED.
NO WAY!
WHAT'S YOUR BACKUP?

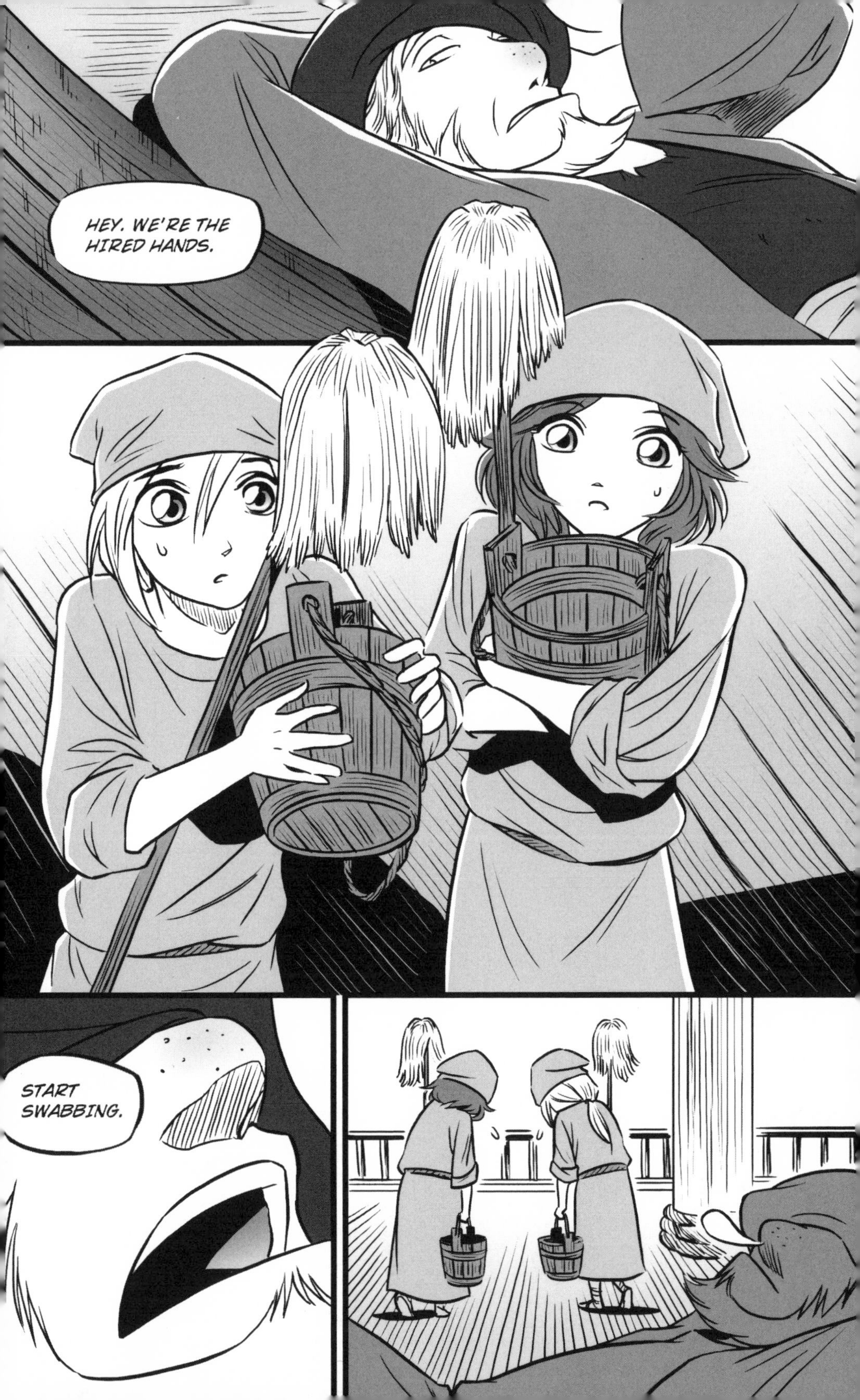
HEY. WE'RE THE HIRED HANDS.
START SWABBING.

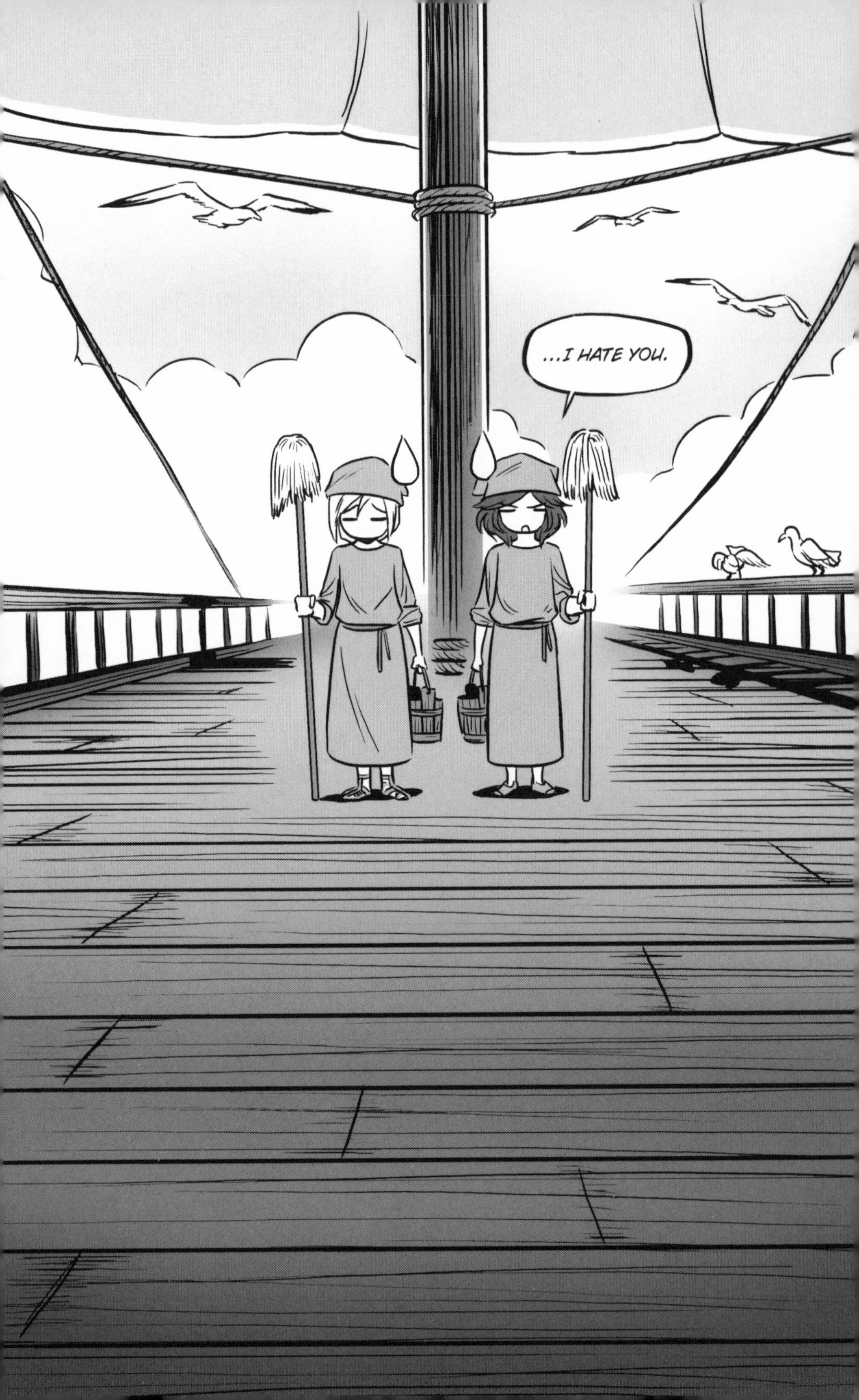
...I HATE YOU.

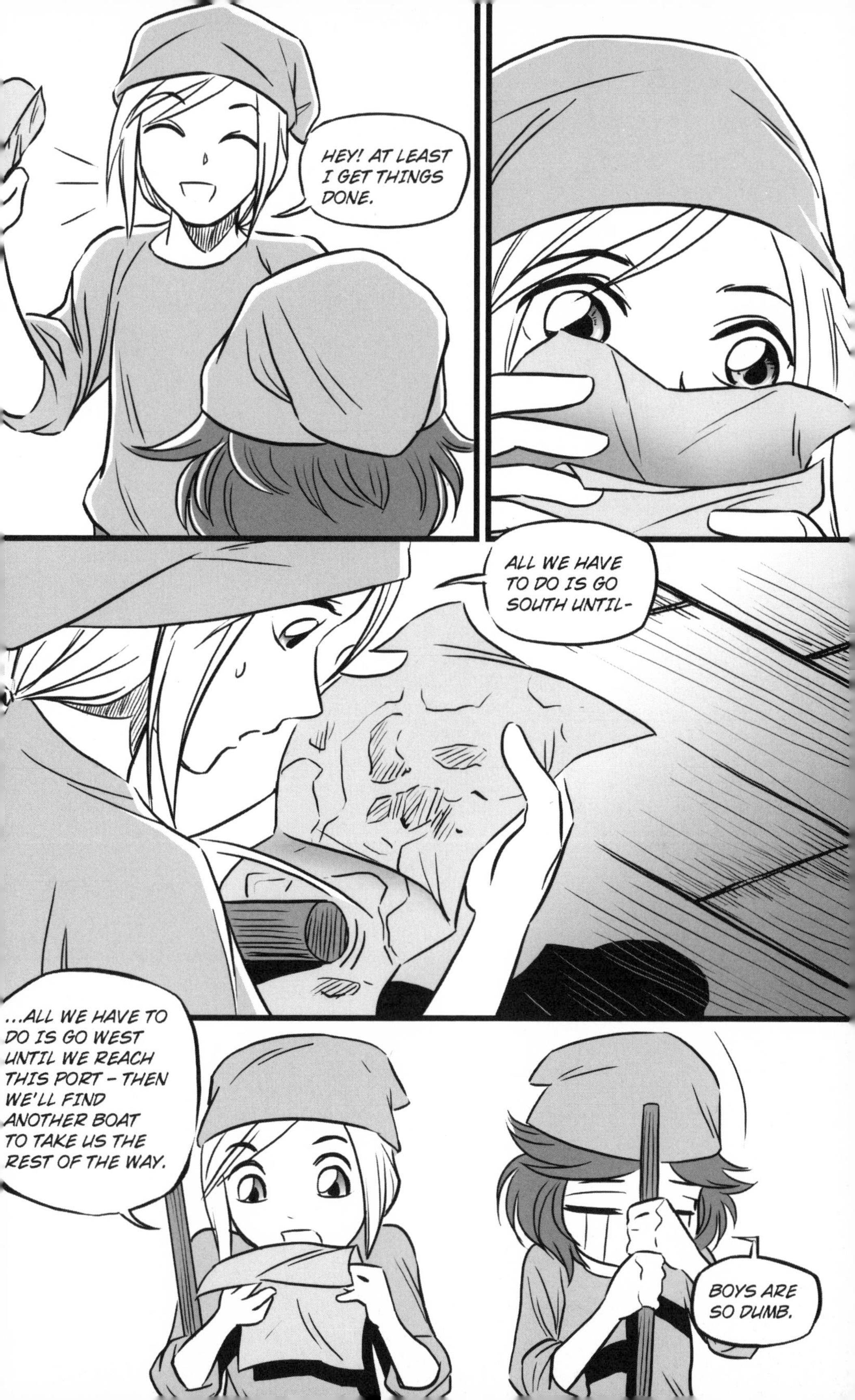
HEY! AT LEAST I GET THINGS DONE.
ALL WE HAVE TO DO IS GO SOUTH UNTIL-
...ALL WE HAVE TO DO IS GO WEST UNTIL WE REACH THIS PORT - THEN WE'LL FIND ANOTHER BOAT TO TAKE US THE REST OF THE WAY.
BOYS ARE SO DUMB.

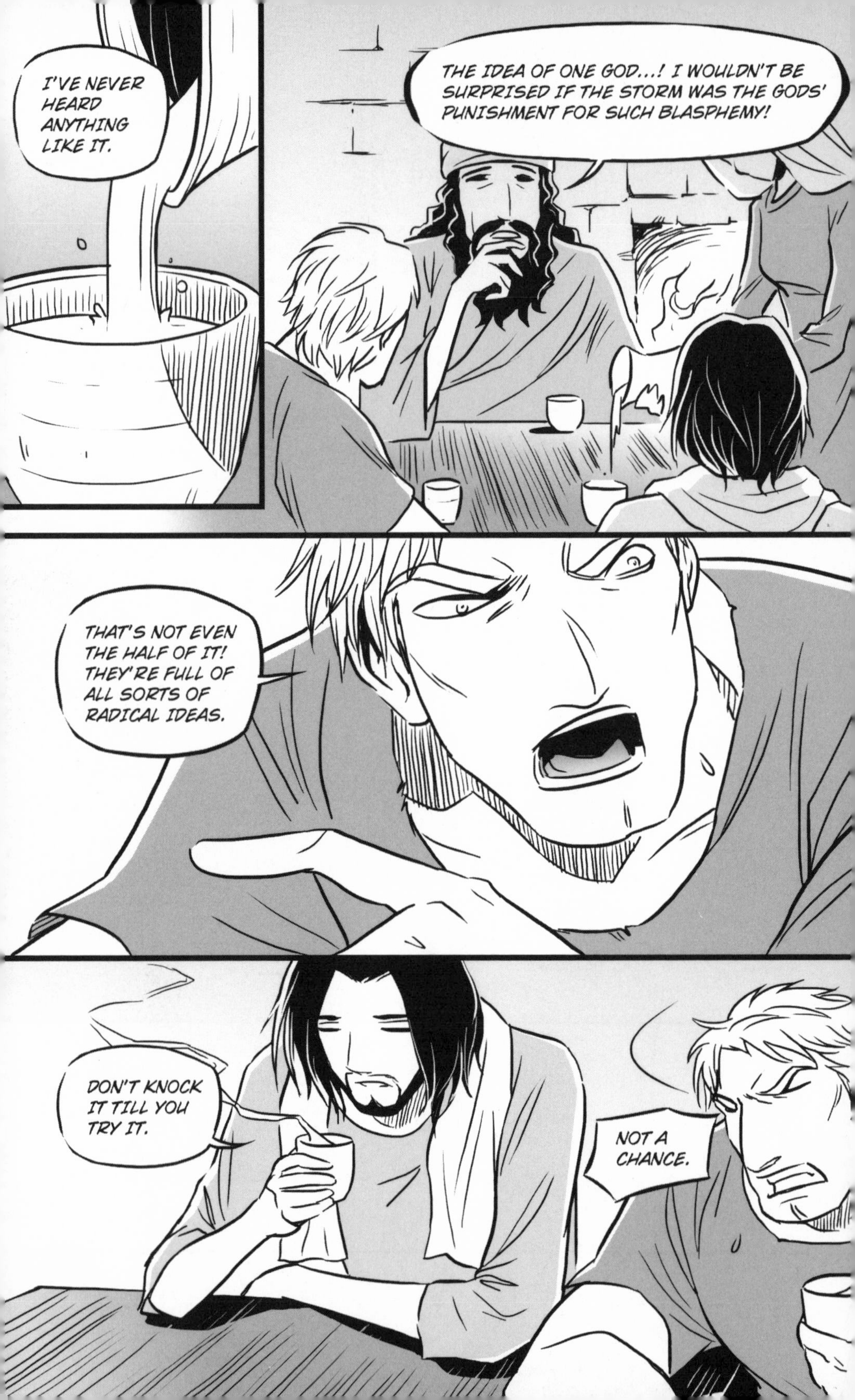
I'VE NEVER HEARD ANYTHING LIKE IT.
THE IDEA OF ONE GOD...! I WOULDN'T BE SURPRISED IF THE STORM WAS THE GODS' PUNISHMENT FOR SUCH BLASPHEMY!
THAT'S NOT EVEN THE HALF OF IT! THEY'RE FULL OF ALL SORTS OF RADICAL IDEAS.
DON'T KNOCK IT TILL YOU TRY IT.
NOT A CHANCE.

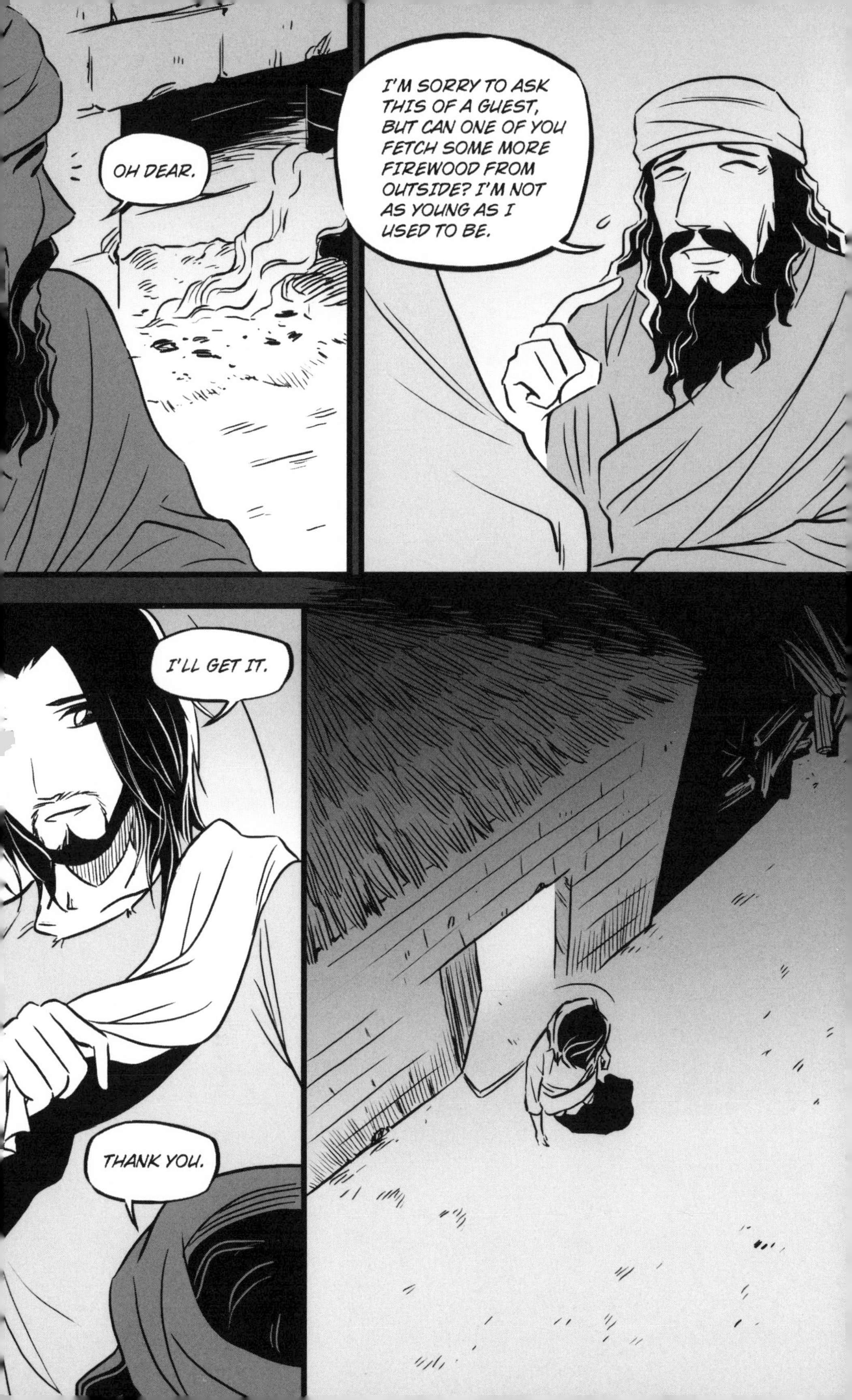
OH DEAR.
I'M SORRY TO ASK THIS OF A GUEST, BUT CAN ONE OF YOU FETCH SOME MORE FIREWOOD FROM OUTSIDE? I'M NOT AS YOUNG AS I USED TO BE.
I'LL GET IT.
THANK YOU.

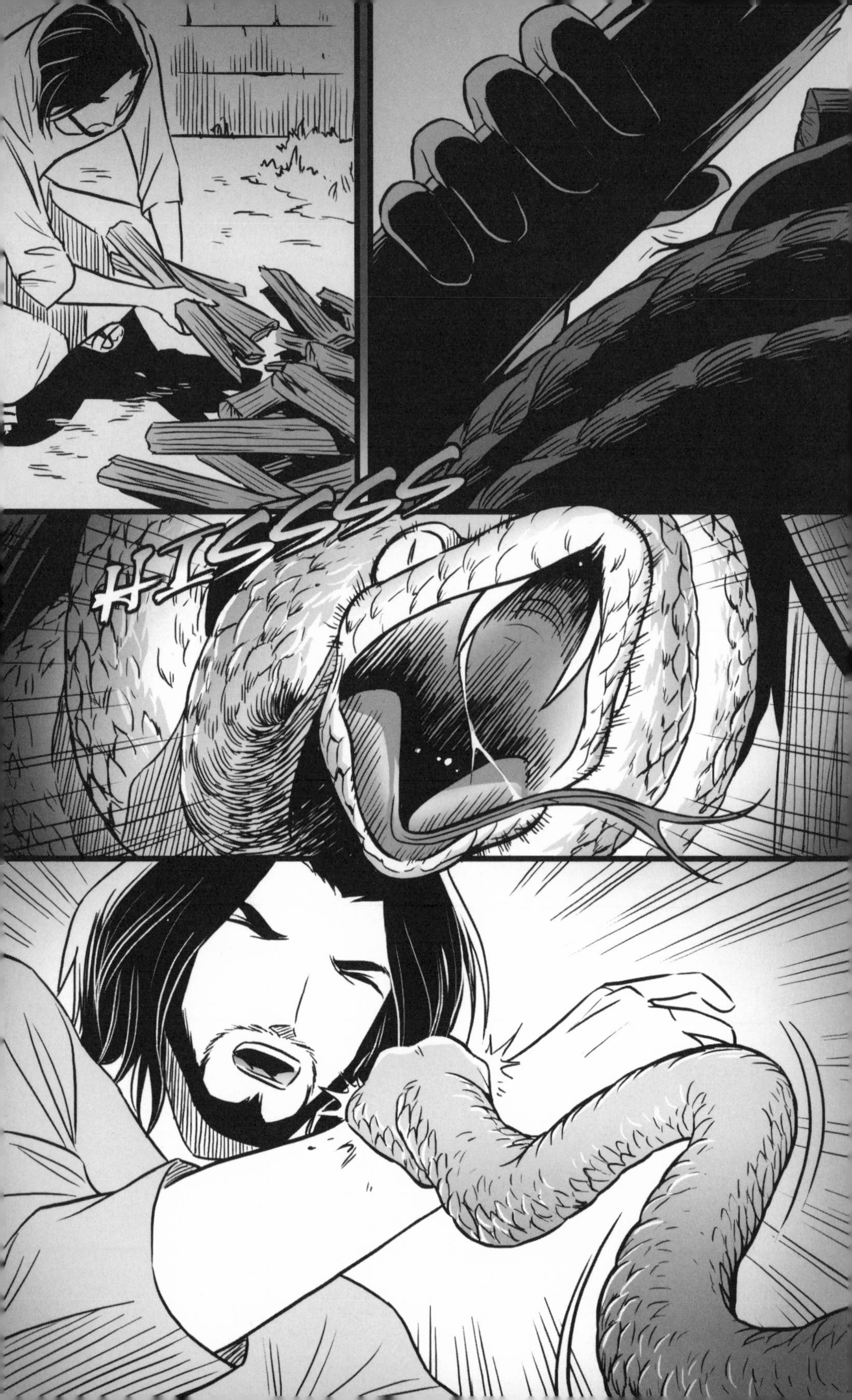
HISSSS

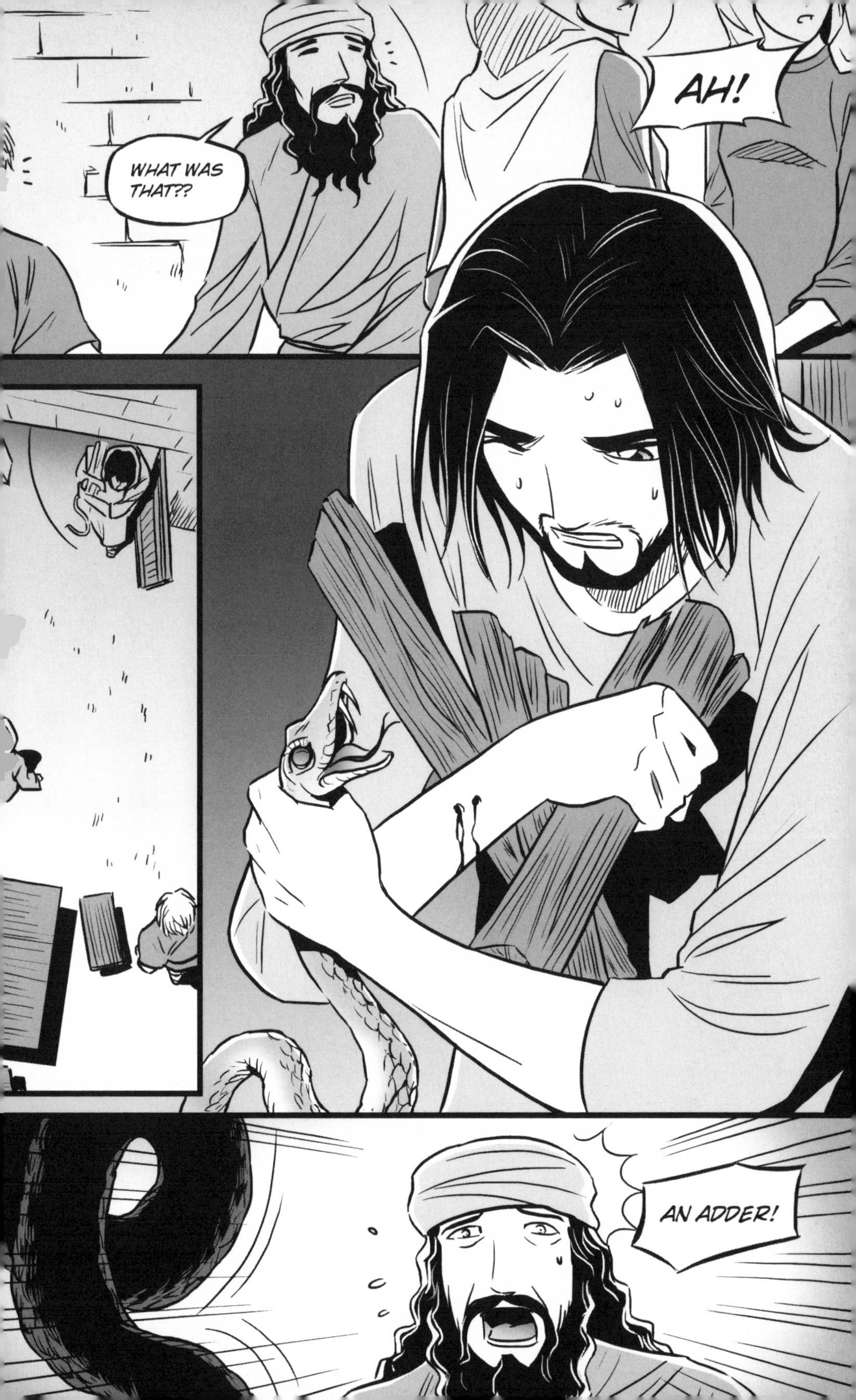
WHAT WAS THAT??
AH!
AN ADDER!

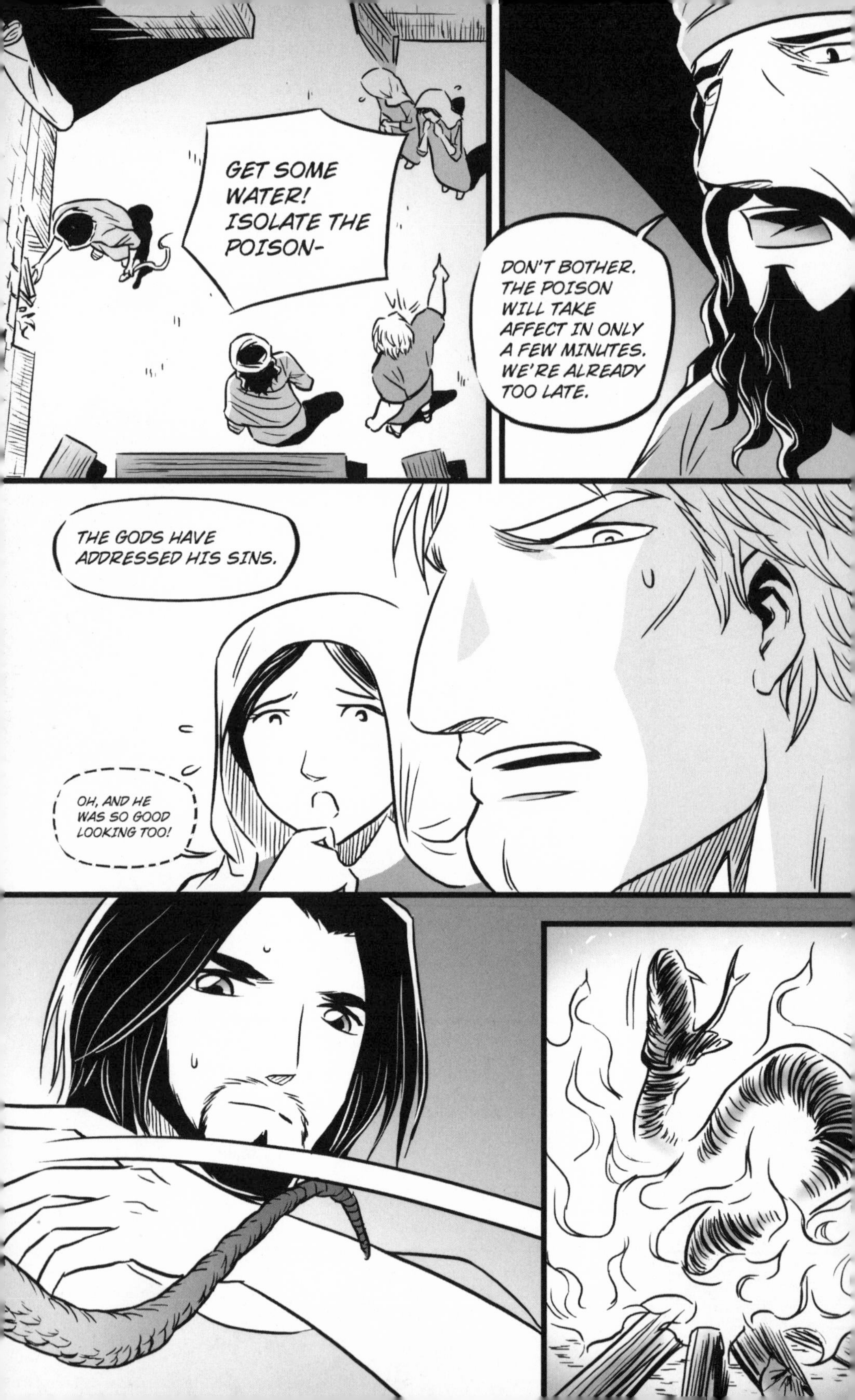
GET SOME WATER! ISOLATE THE POISON-
DON'T BOTHER. THE POISON WILL TAKE AFFECT IN ONLY A FEW MINUTES. WE'RE ALREADY TOO LATE.
THE GODS HAVE ADDRESSED HIS SINS.
OH, AND HE WAS SO GOOD LOOKING TOO!

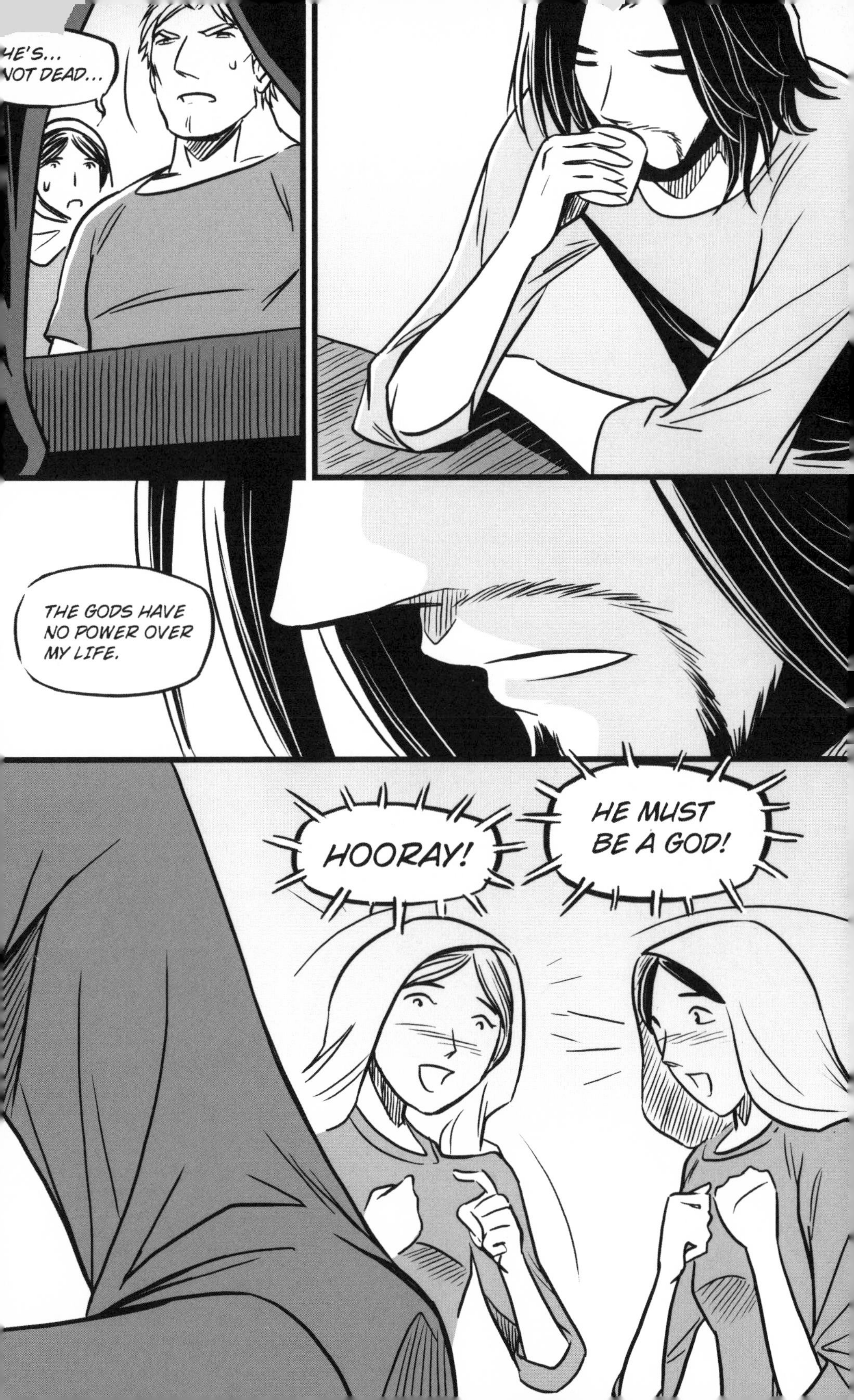
HE'S...
NOT DEAD...
THE GODS HAVE NO POWER OVER MY LIFE.
HOORAY!
HE MUST BE A GOD!

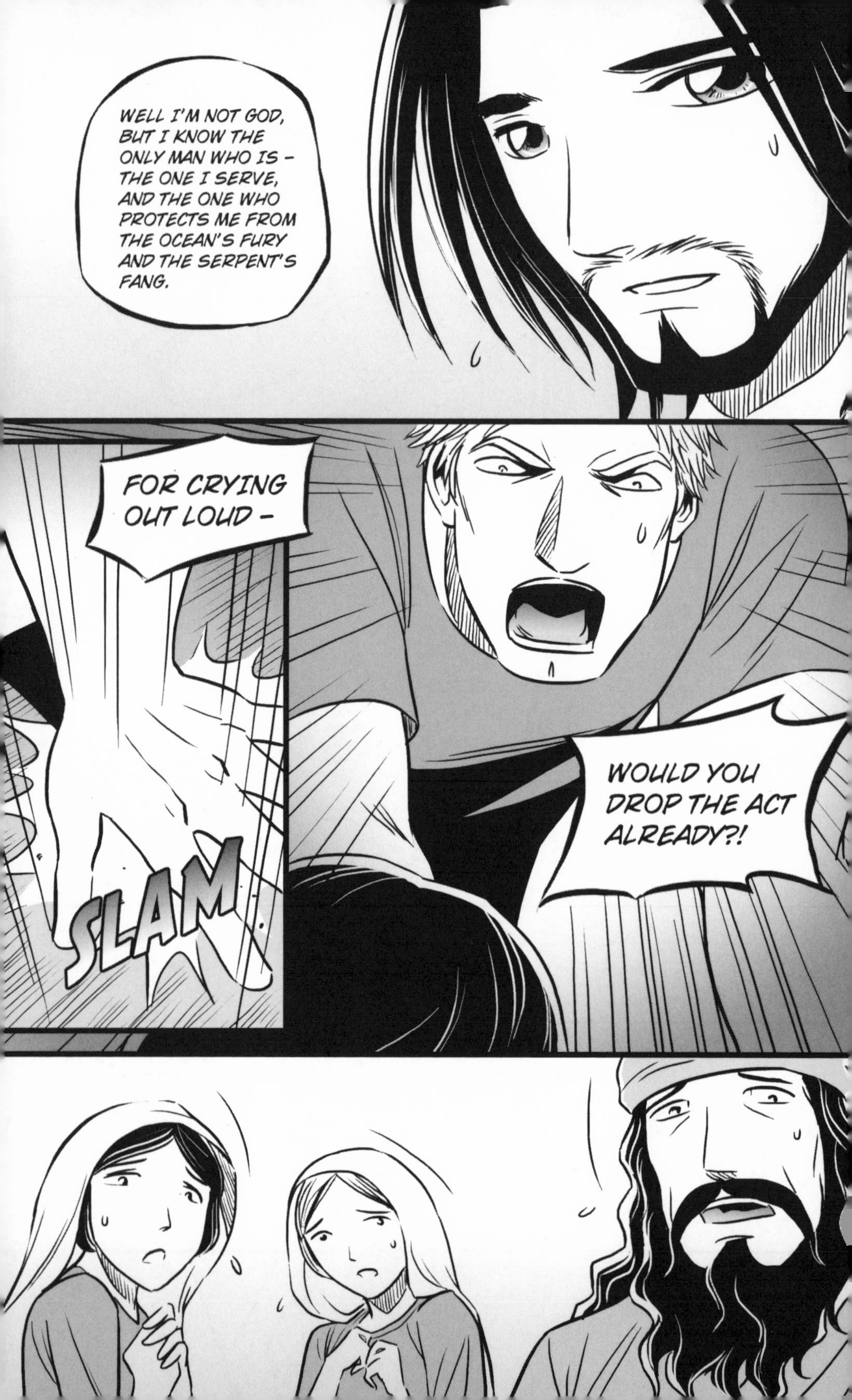
WELL I'M NOT GOD, BUT I KNOW THE ONLY MAN WHO IS - THE ONE I SERVE, AND THE ONE WHO PROTECTS ME FROM THE OCEAN'S FURY AND THE SERPENT'S FANG.
FOR CRYING OUT LOUD -
SLAM
WOULD YOU DROP THE ACT ALREADY?!

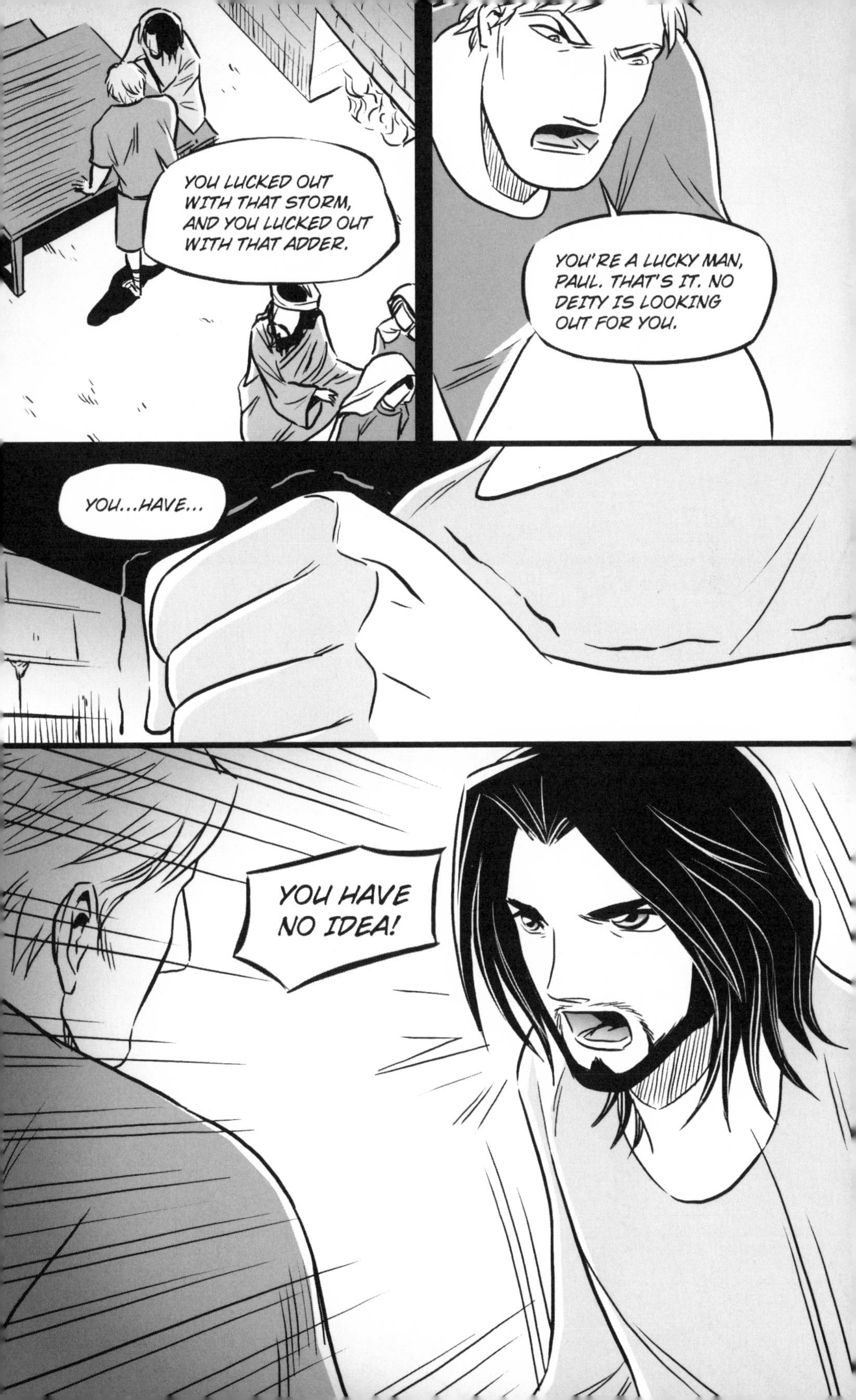
YOU LUCKED OUT WITH THAT STORM, AND YOU LUCKED OUT WITH THAT ADDER.
YOU'RE A LUCKY MAN, PAUL. THAT'S IT. NO DEITY IS LOOKING OUT FOR YOU.
YOU...HAVE...
YOU HAVE NO IDEA!

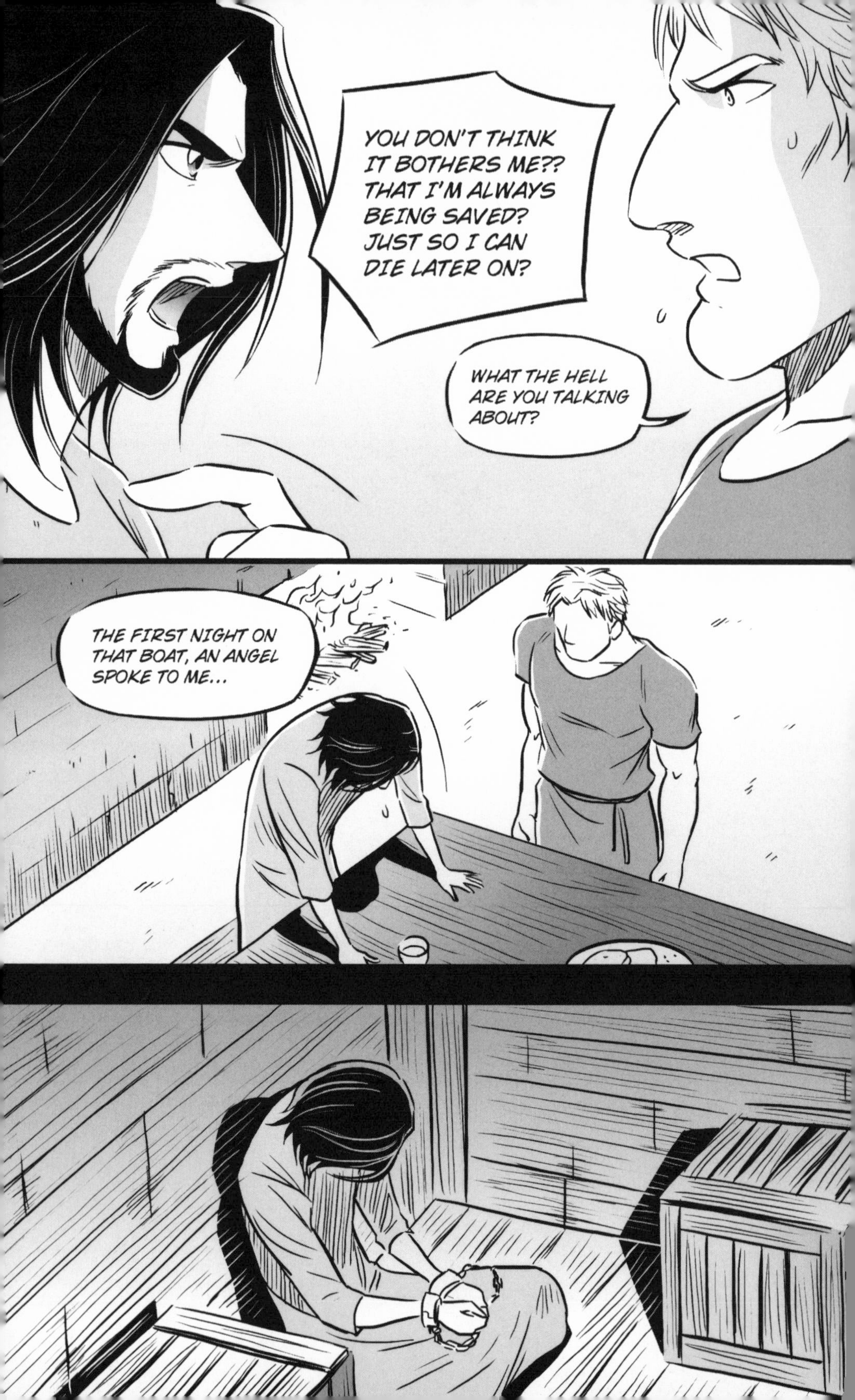
YOU DON'T THINK IT BOTHERS ME?? THAT I'M ALWAYS BEING SAVED? JUST SO I CAN DIE LATER ON?
WHAT THE HELL ARE YOU TALKING ABOUT?
THE FIRST NIGHT ON THAT BOAT, AN ANGEL SPOKE TO ME...

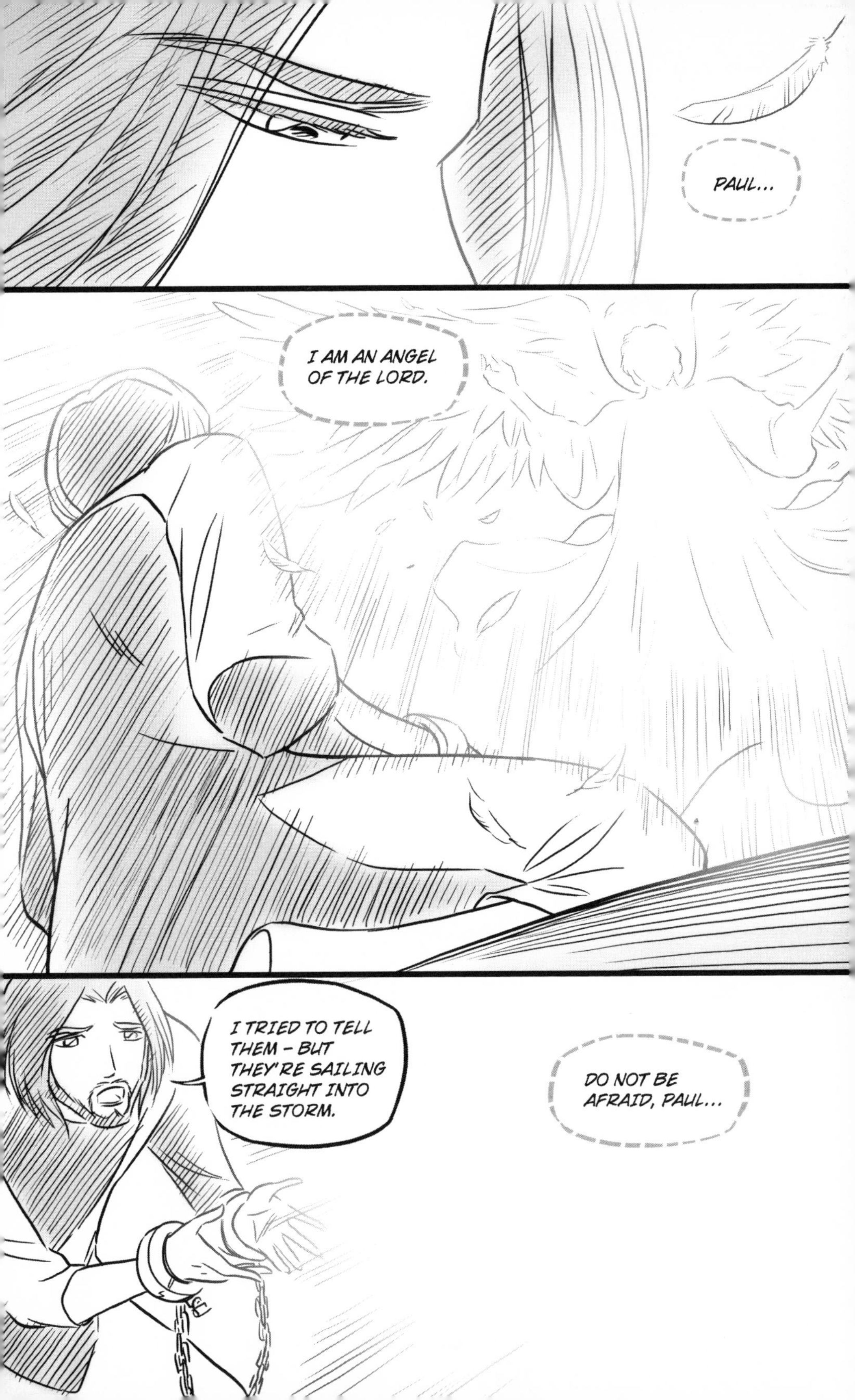
PAUL...
I AM AN ANGEL OF THE LORD.
I TRIED TO TELL THEM - BUT THEY'RE SAILING STRAIGHT INTO THE STORM.
DO NOT BE AFRAID, PAUL...

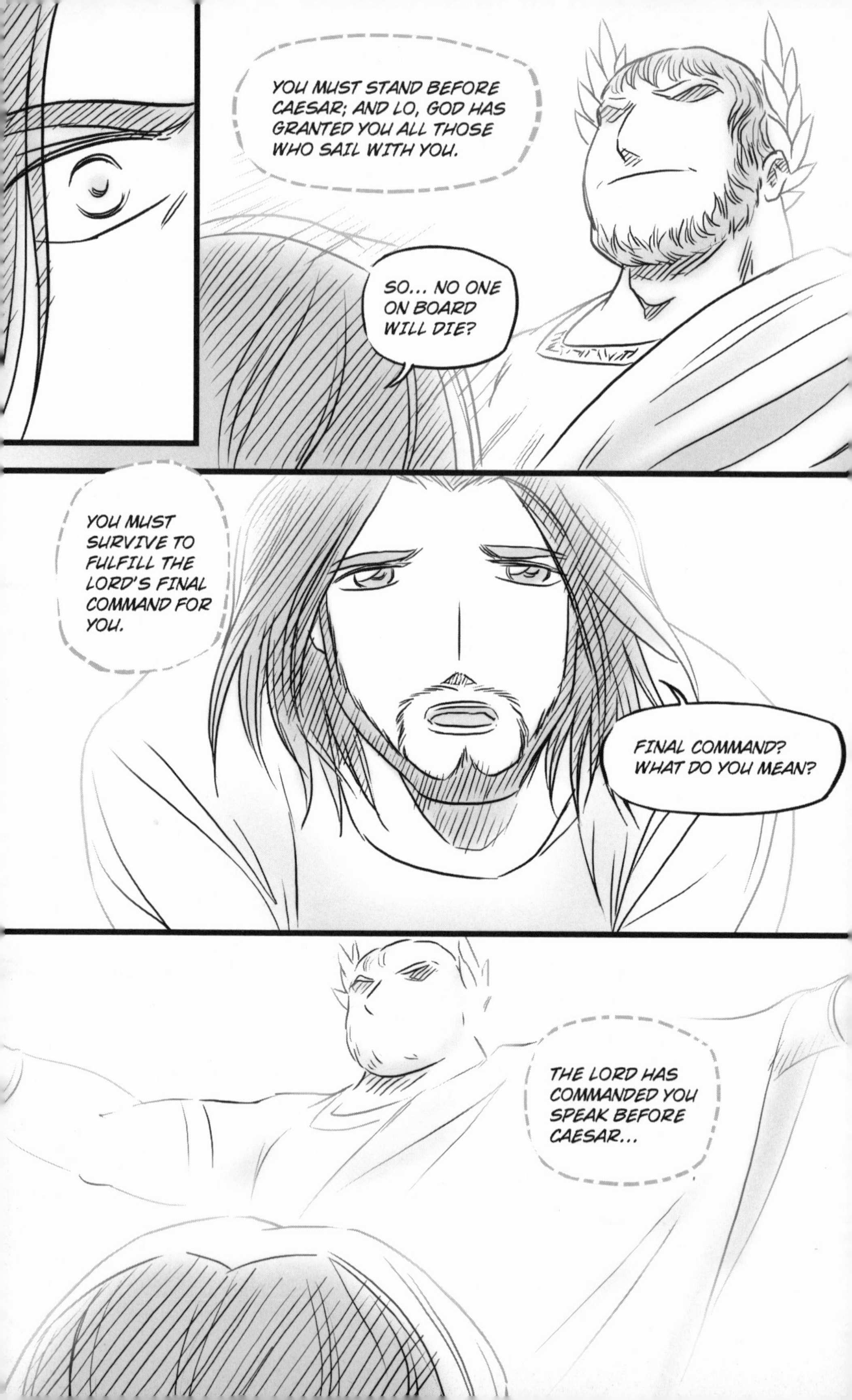
YOU MUST STAND BEFORE CAESAR; AND LO, GOD HAS GRANTED YOU ALL THOSE WHO SAIL WITH YOU.
SO... NO ONE ON BOARD WILL DIE?
YOU MUST SURVIVE TO FULFILL THE LORD'S FINAL COMMAND FOR YOU.
FINAL COMMAND? WHAT DO YOU MEAN?
THE LORD HAS COMMANDED YOU SPEAK BEFORE CAESAR...

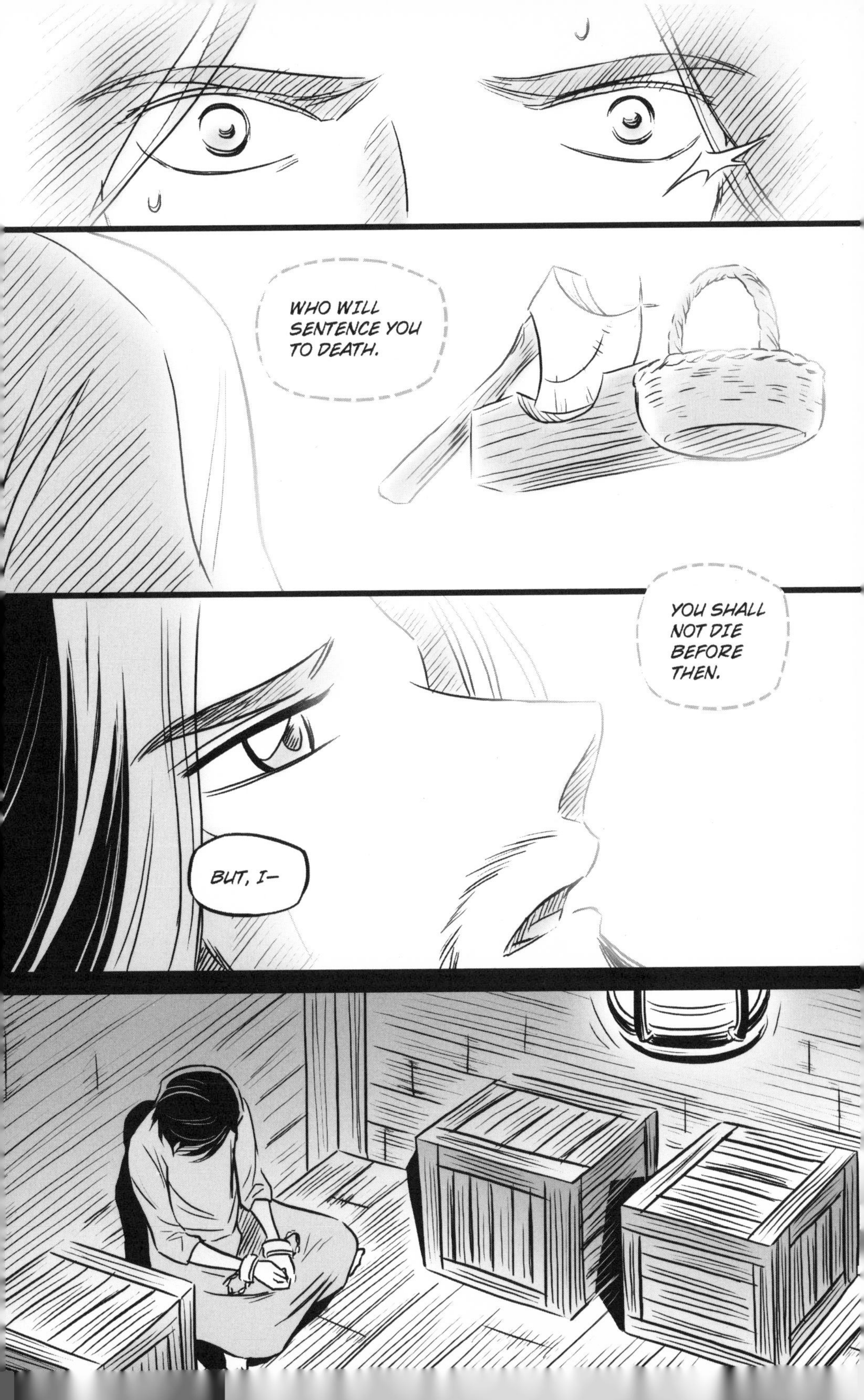
WHO WILL SENTENCE YOU TO DEATH.
YOU SHALL NOT DIE BEFORE THEN.
BUT, I—

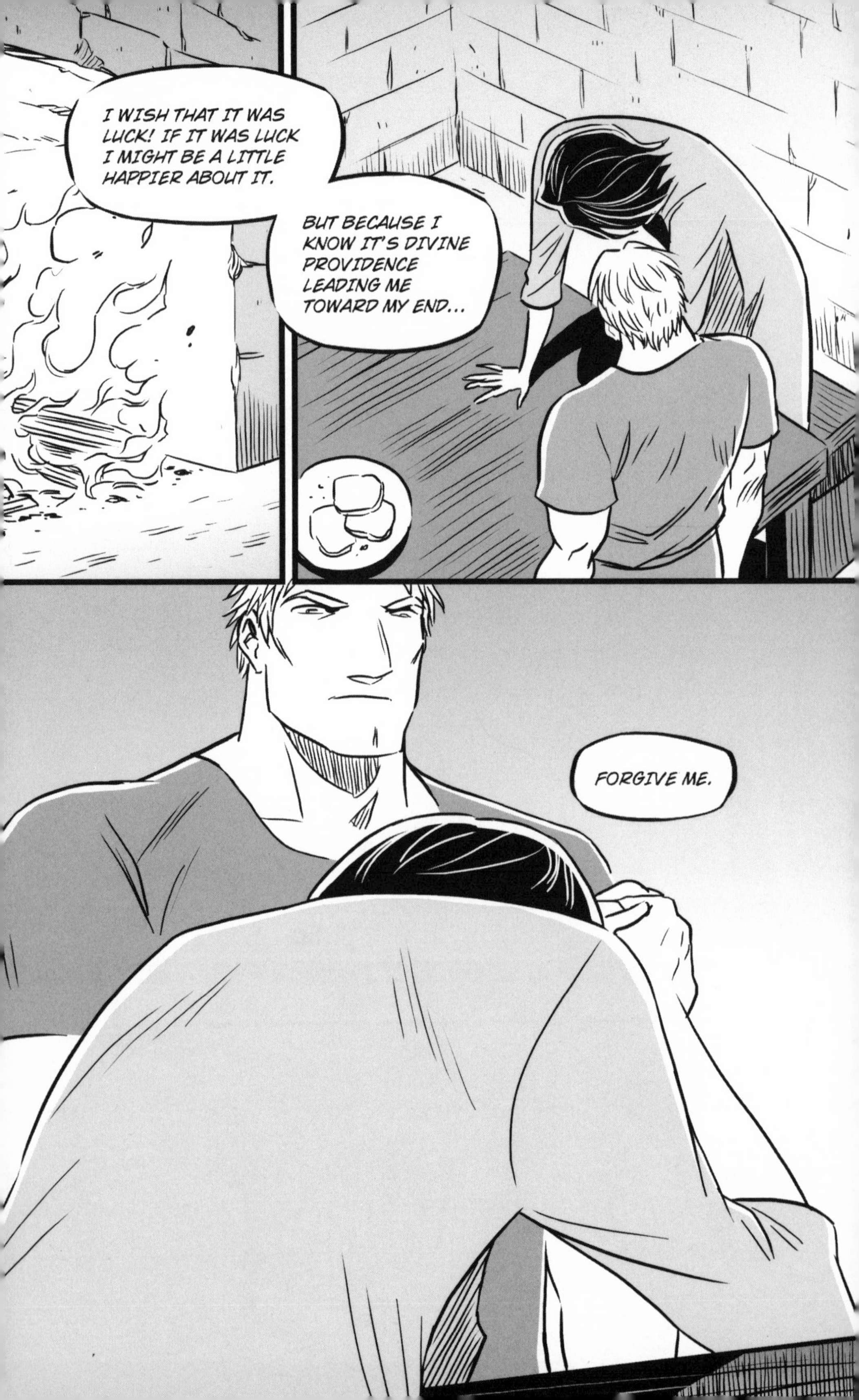
I WISH THAT IT WAS LUCK! IF IT WAS LUCK I MIGHT BE A LITTLE HAPPIER ABOUT IT.
BUT BECAUSE I KNOW IT'S DIVINE PROVIDENCE LEADING ME TOWARD MY END...
FORGIVE ME.

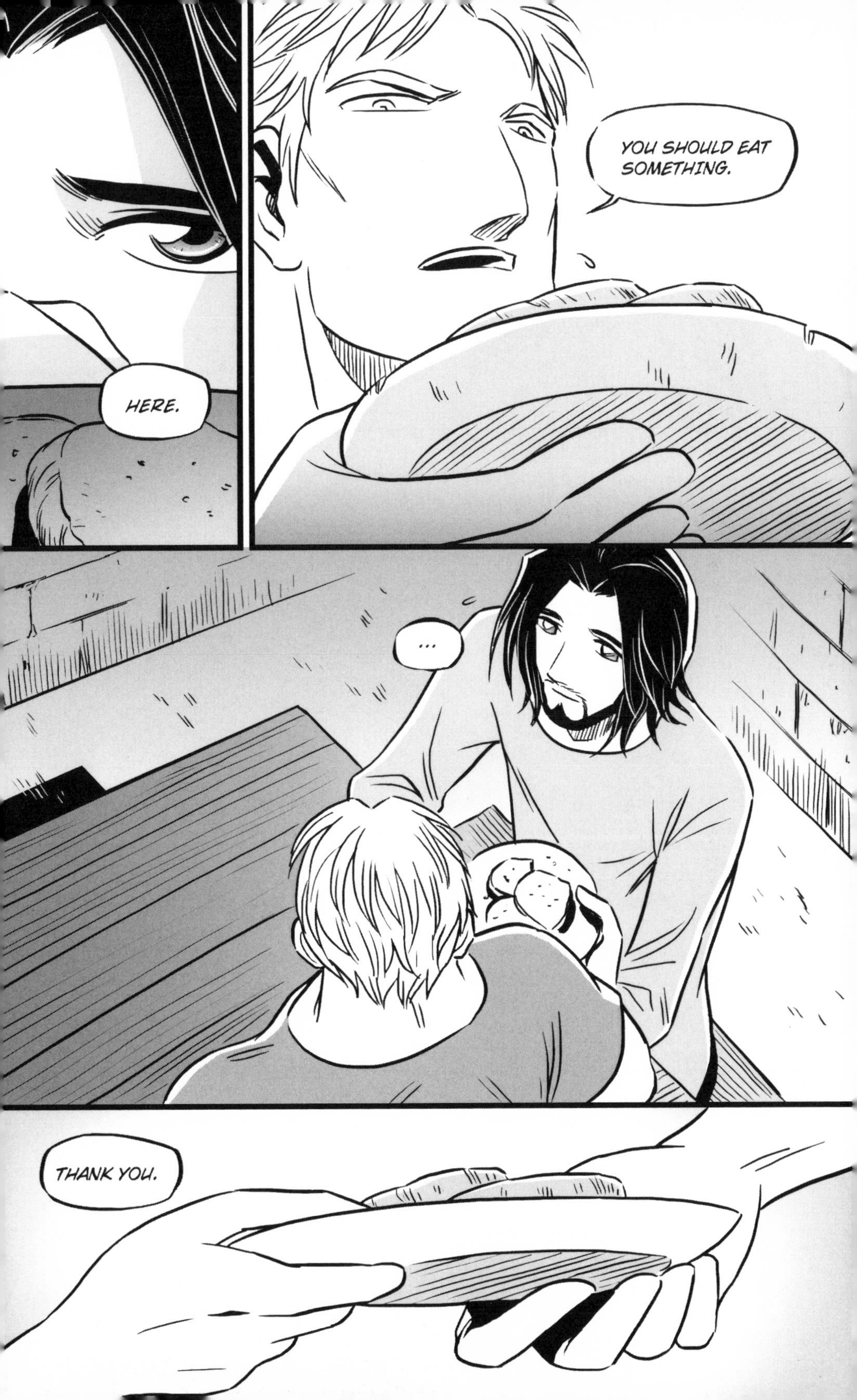
YOU SHOULD EAT SOMETHING.
HERE.
...
THANK YOU.

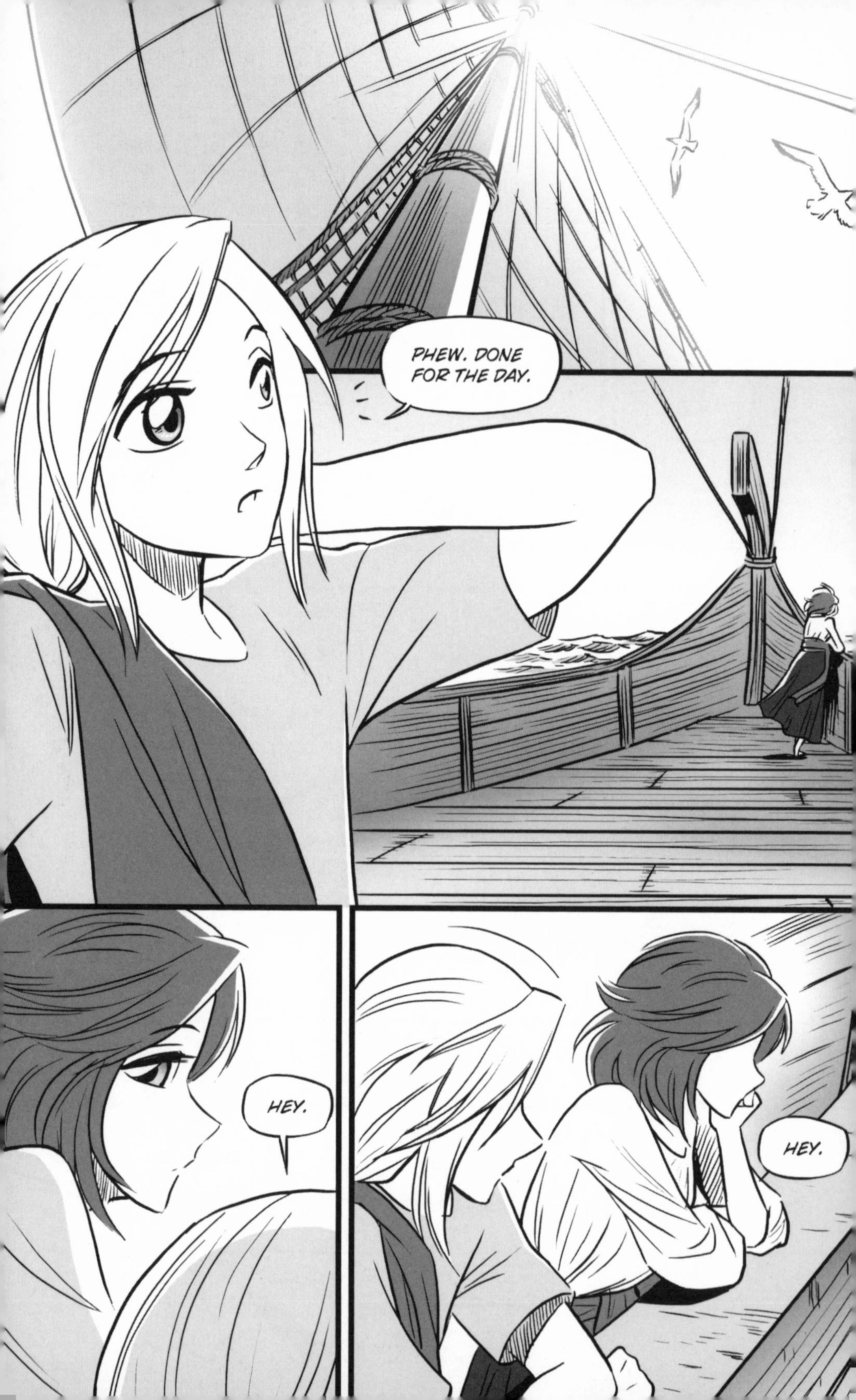
PHEW. DONE FOR THE DAY.
HEY.
HEY.

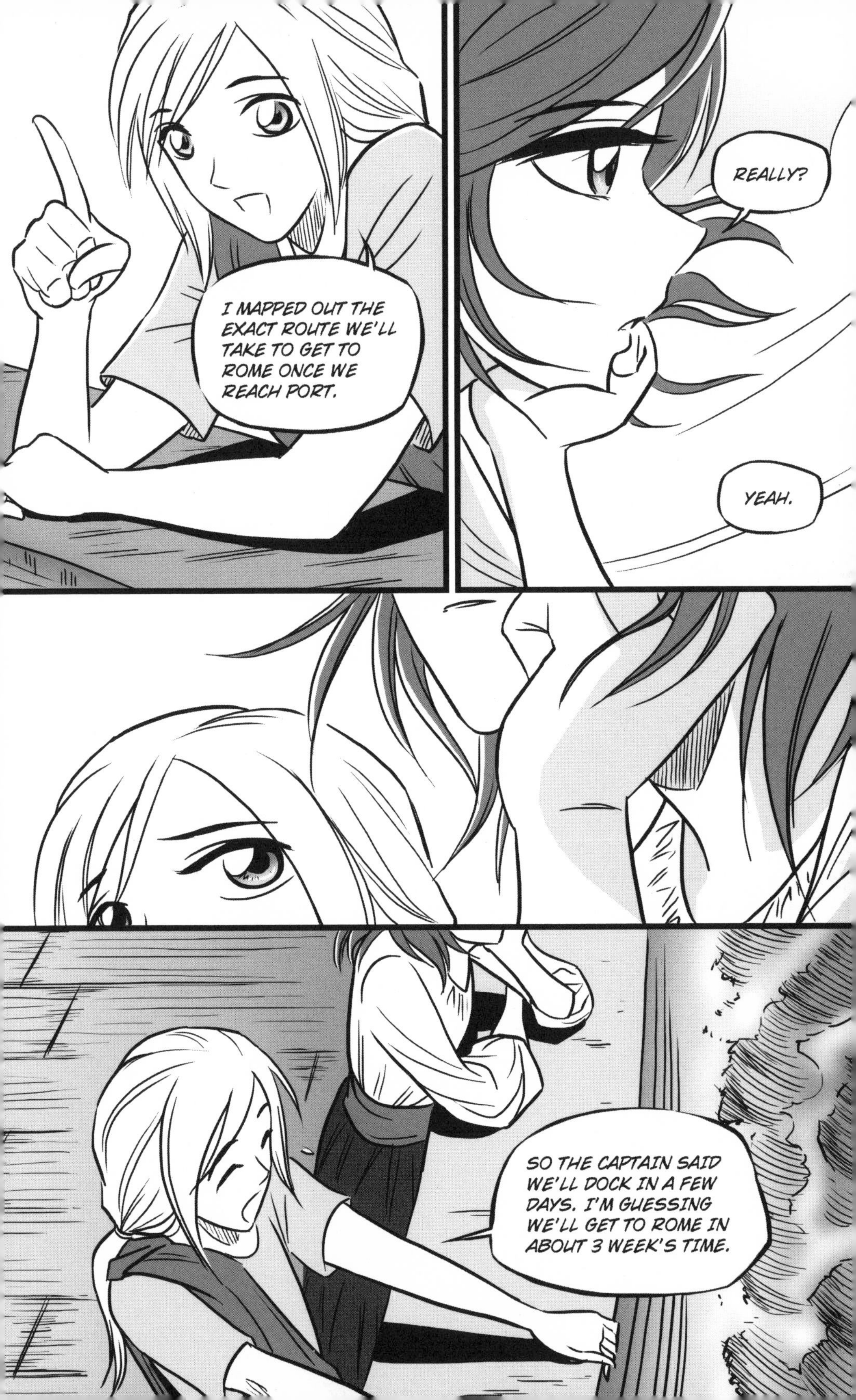
I MAPPED OUT THE EXACT ROUTE WE'LL TAKE TO GET TO ROME ONCE WE REACH PORT.
REALLY?
YEAH.
SO THE CAPTAIN SAID WE'LL DOCK IN A FEW DAYS. I'M GUESSING WE'LL GET TO ROME IN ABOUT 3 WEEK'S TIME.

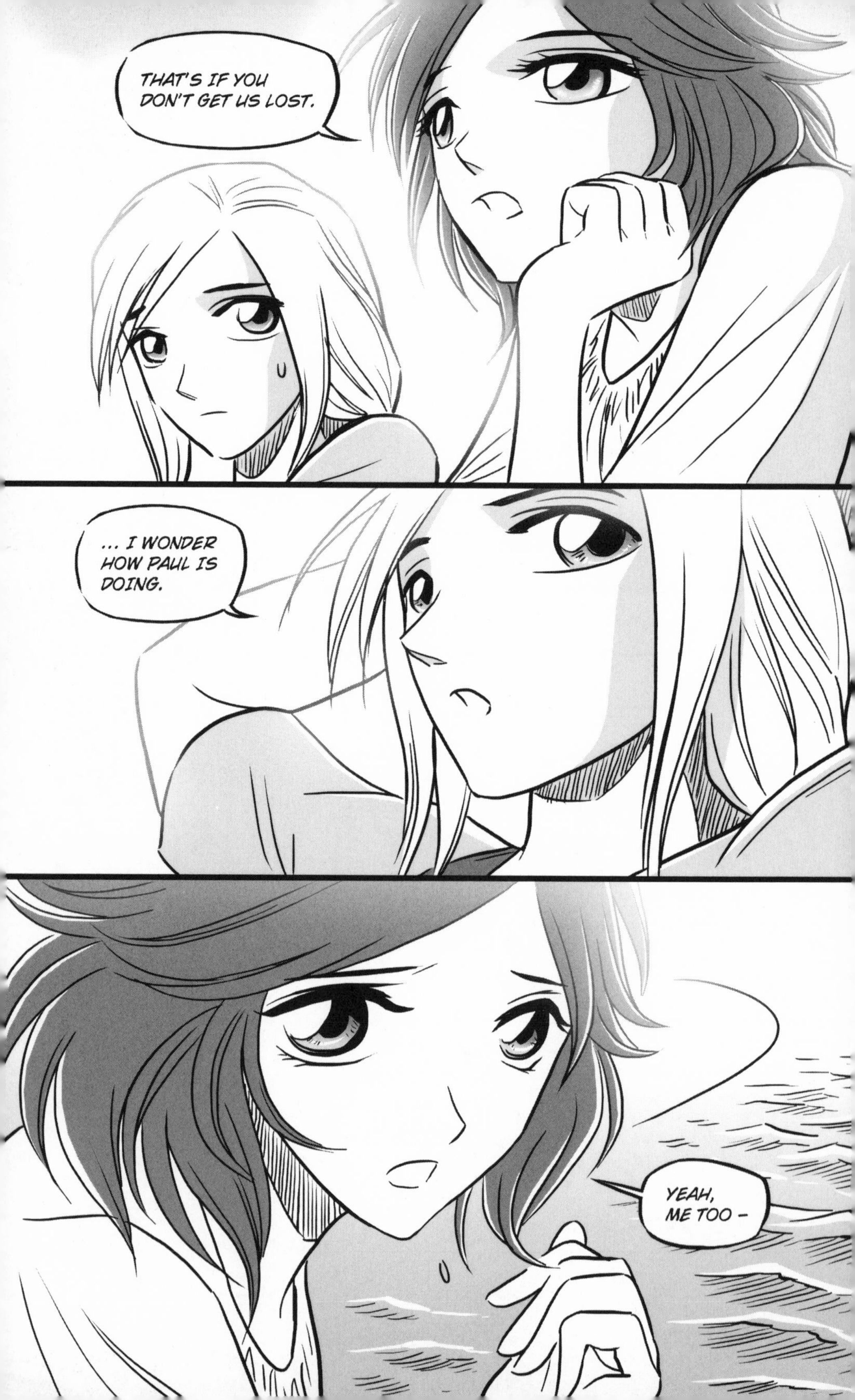
THAT'S IF YOU DON'T GET US LOST.
... I WONDER HOW PAUL IS DOING.
YEAH, ME TOO -

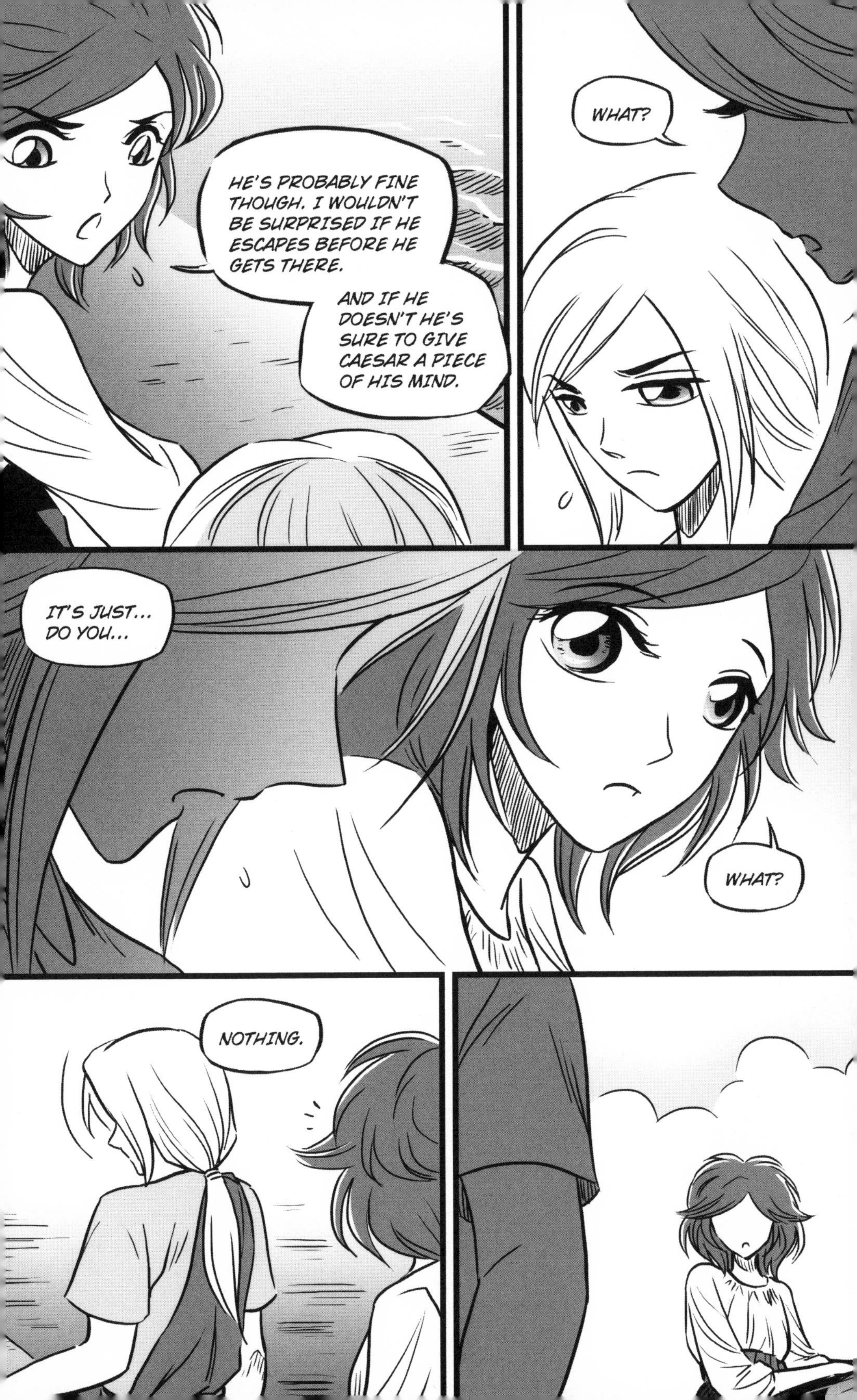
HE'S PROBABLY FINE THOUGH. I WOULDN'T BE SURPRISED IF HE ESCAPES BEFORE HE GETS THERE.
AND IF HE DOESN'T HE'S SURE TO GIVE CAESAR A PIECE OF HIS MIND.
WHAT?
IT'S JUST... DO YOU...
WHAT?
NOTHING.

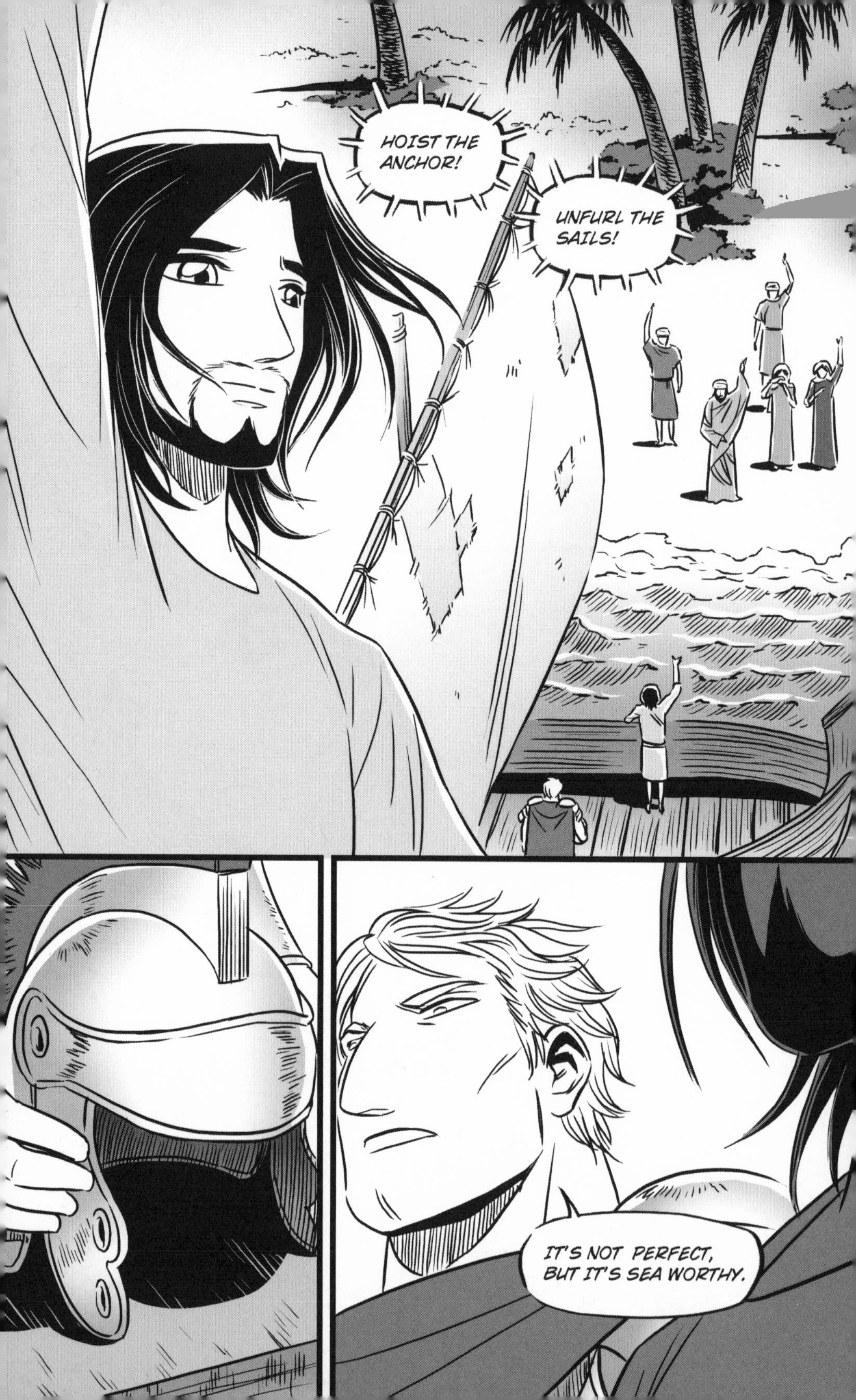
HOIST THE ANCHOR!
UNFURL THE SAILS!
IT'S NOT PERFECT, BUT IT'S SEA WORTHY.

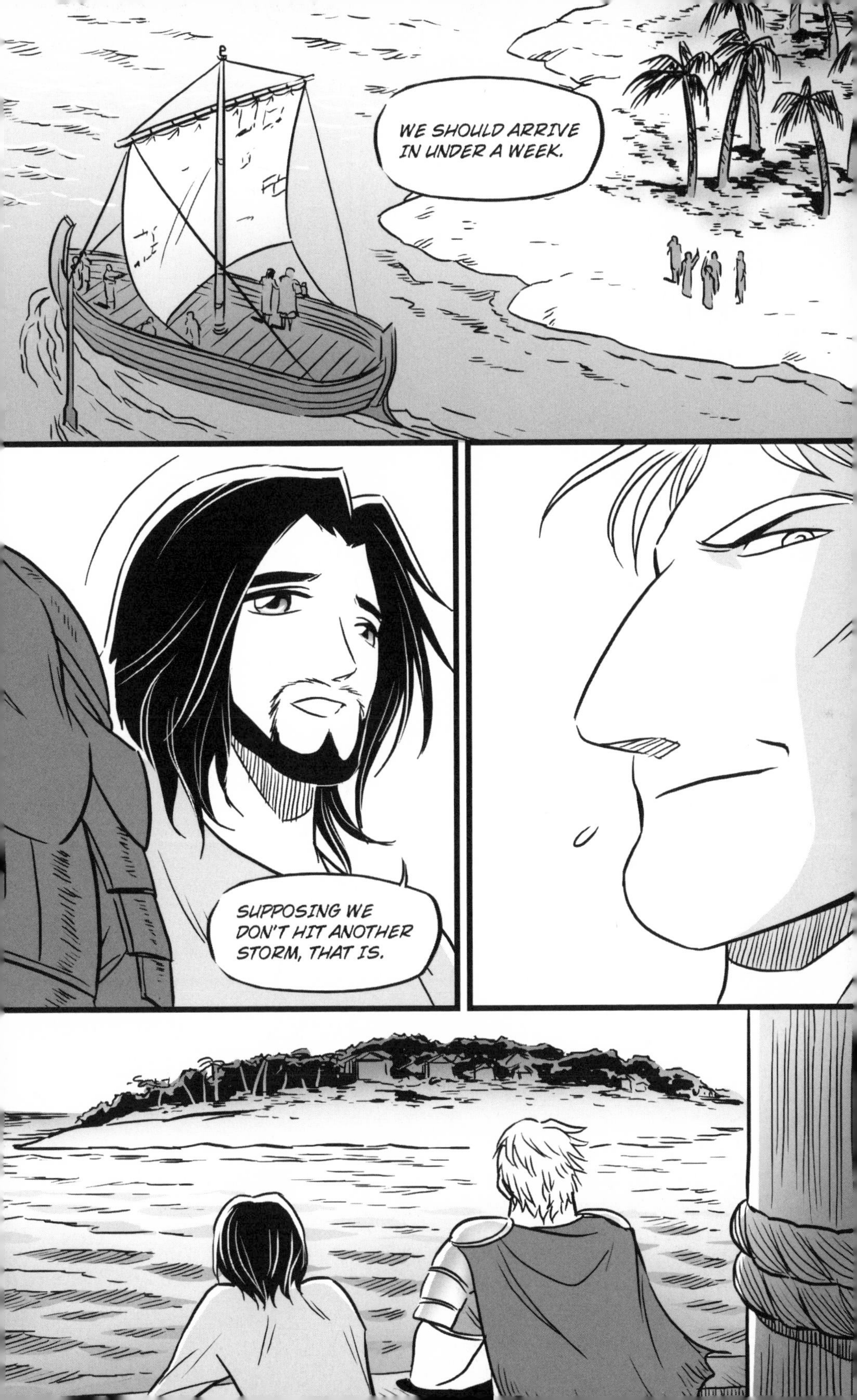
WE SHOULD ARRIVE IN UNDER A WEEK.
SUPPOSING WE DON'T HIT ANOTHER STORM, THAT IS.

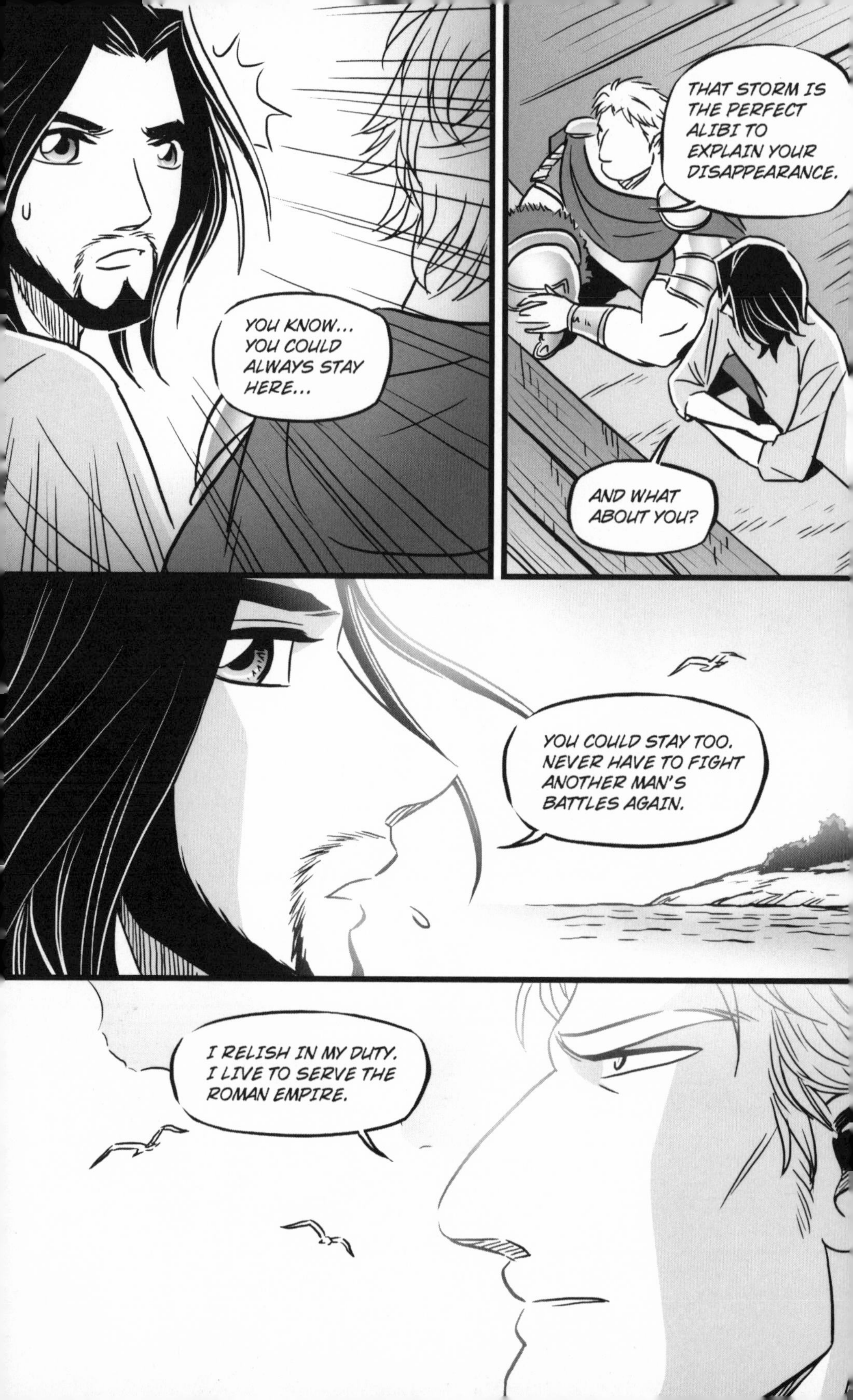
YOU KNOW... YOU COULD ALWAYS STAY HERE...
THAT STORM IS THE PERFECT ALIBI TO EXPLAIN YOUR DISAPPEARANCE.
AND WHAT ABOUT YOU?
YOU COULD STAY TOO. NEVER HAVE TO FIGHT ANOTHER MAN'S BATTLES AGAIN.
I RELISH IN MY DUTY. I LIVE TO SERVE THE ROMAN EMPIRE.

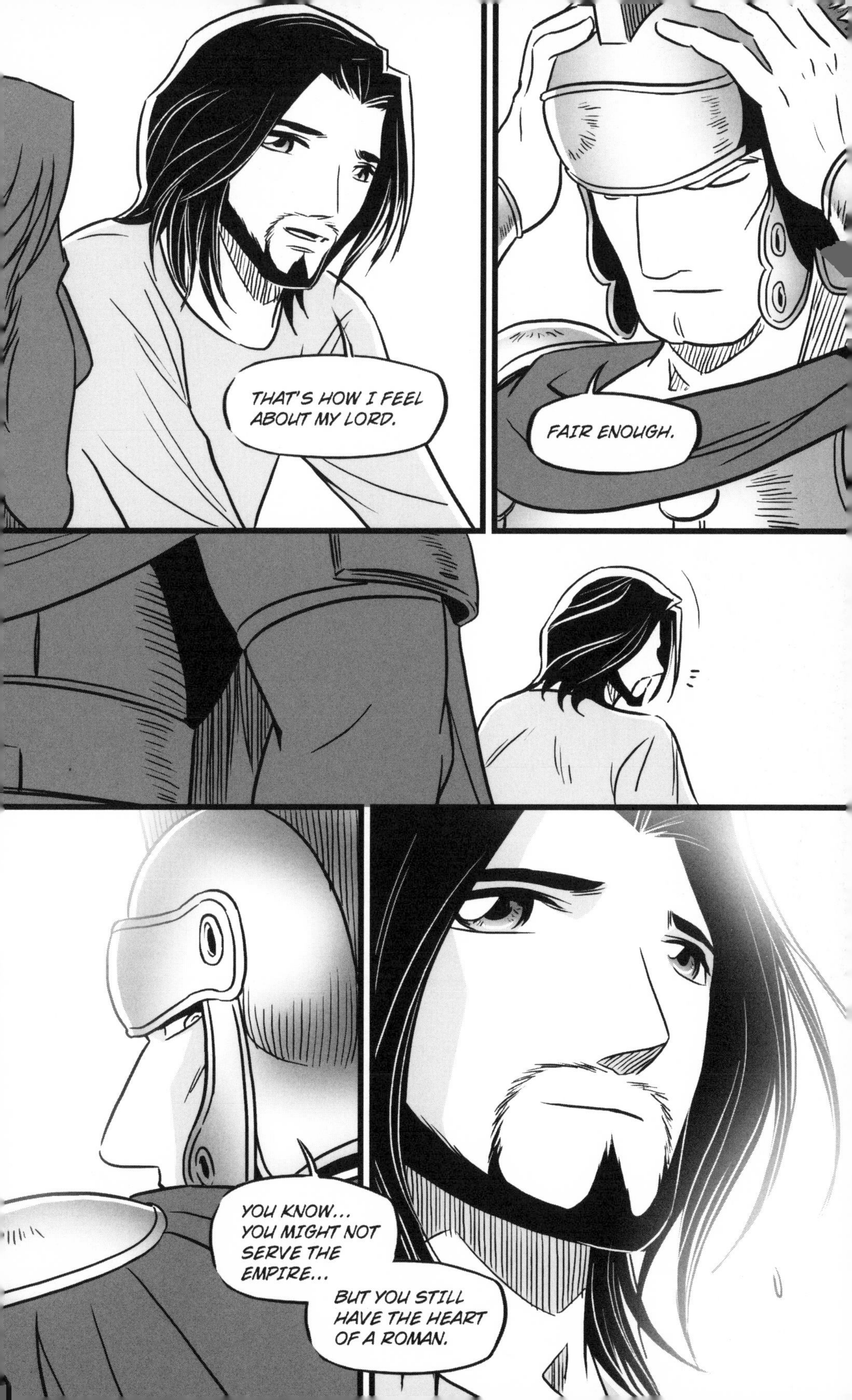
THAT'S HOW I FEEL ABOUT MY LORD.
FAIR ENOUGH.
YOU KNOW... YOU MIGHT NOT SERVE THE EMPIRE...
BUT YOU STILL HAVE THE HEART OF A ROMAN.

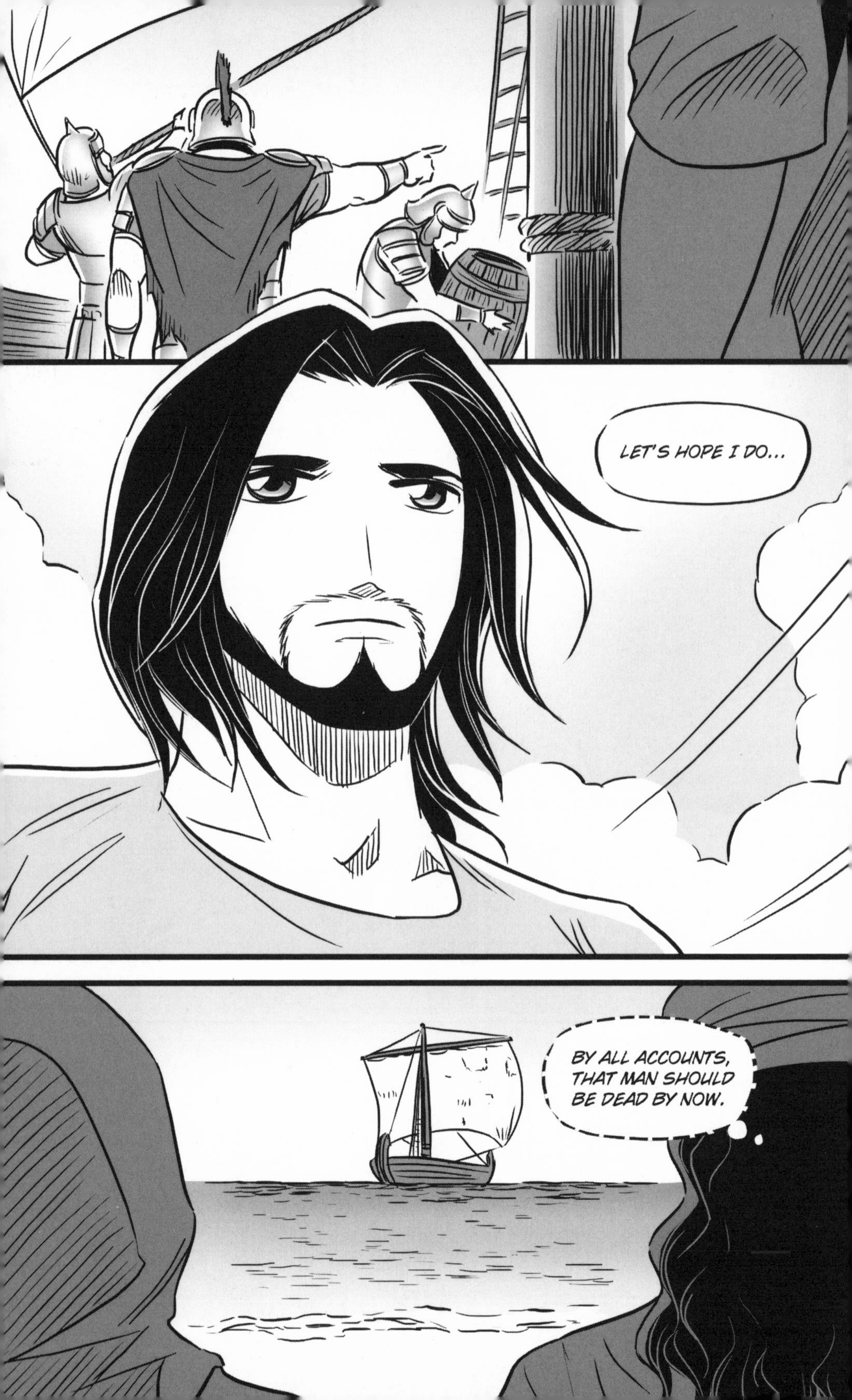
LET'S HOPE I DO...
BY ALL ACCOUNTS, THAT MAN SHOULD BE DEAD BY NOW.

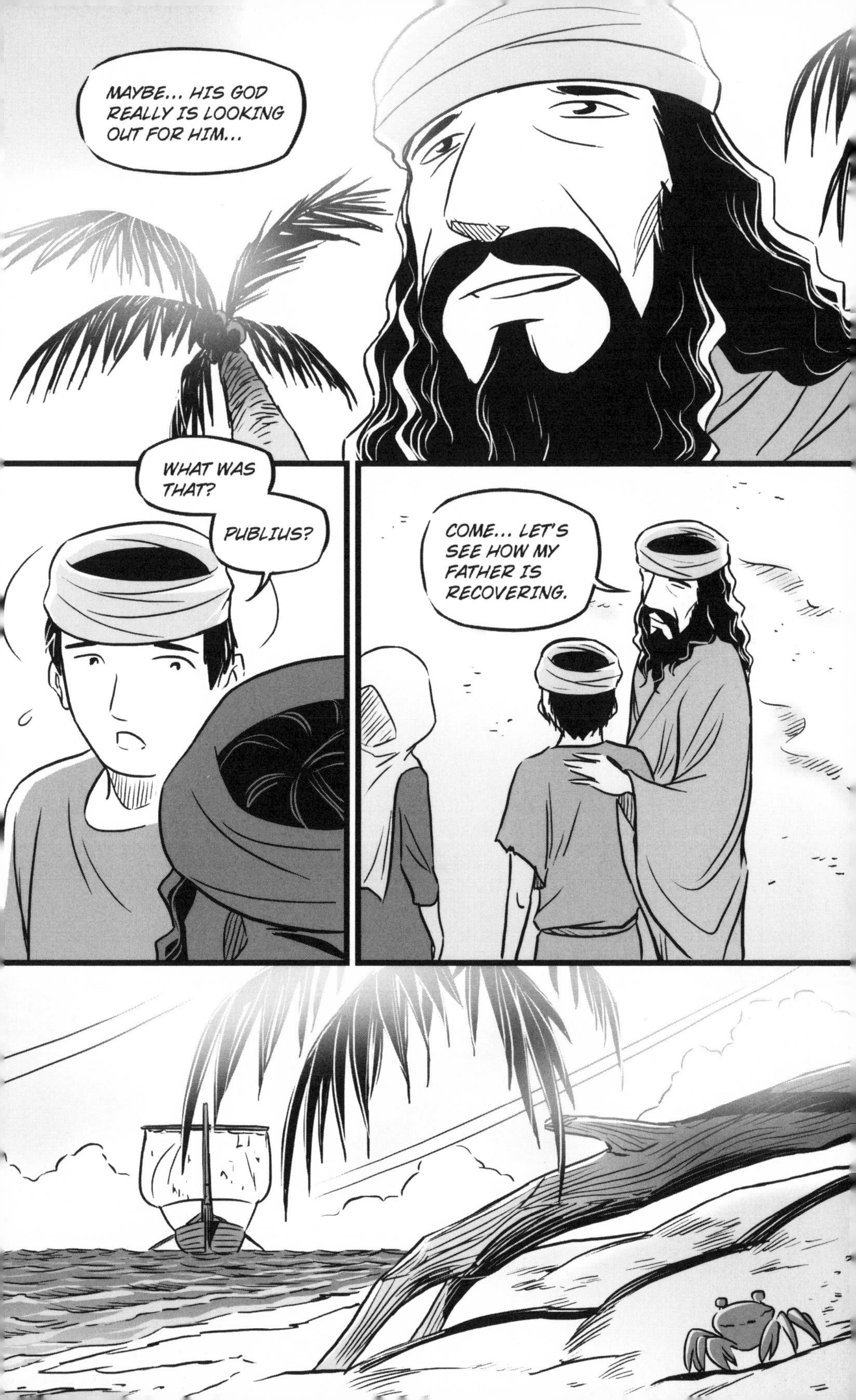
MAYBE... HIS GOD REALLY IS LOOKING OUT FOR HIM...
WHAT WAS THAT?
PUBLIUS?
COME... LET'S SEE HOW MY FATHER IS RECOVERING.

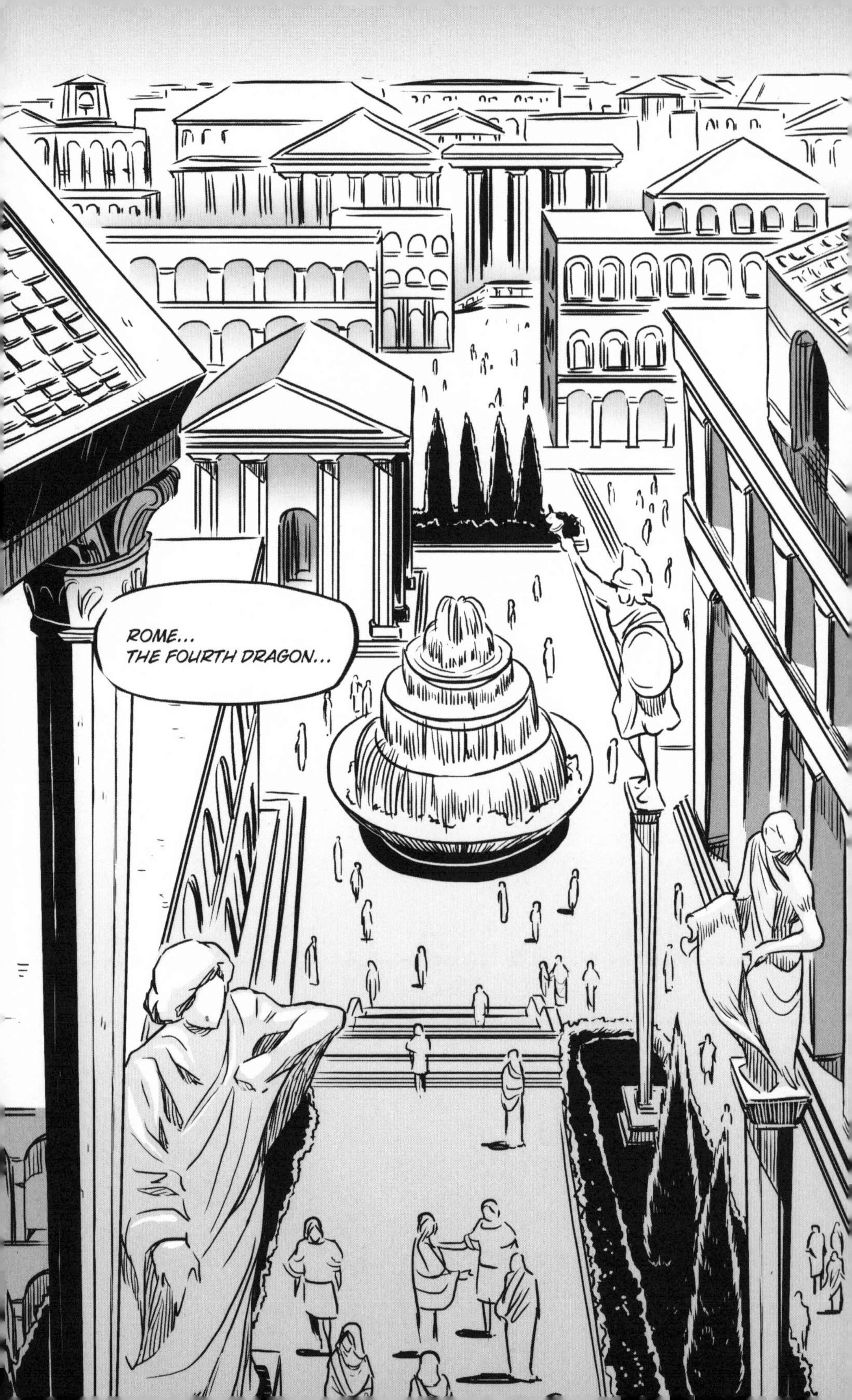
ROME...
THE FOURTH DRAGON...

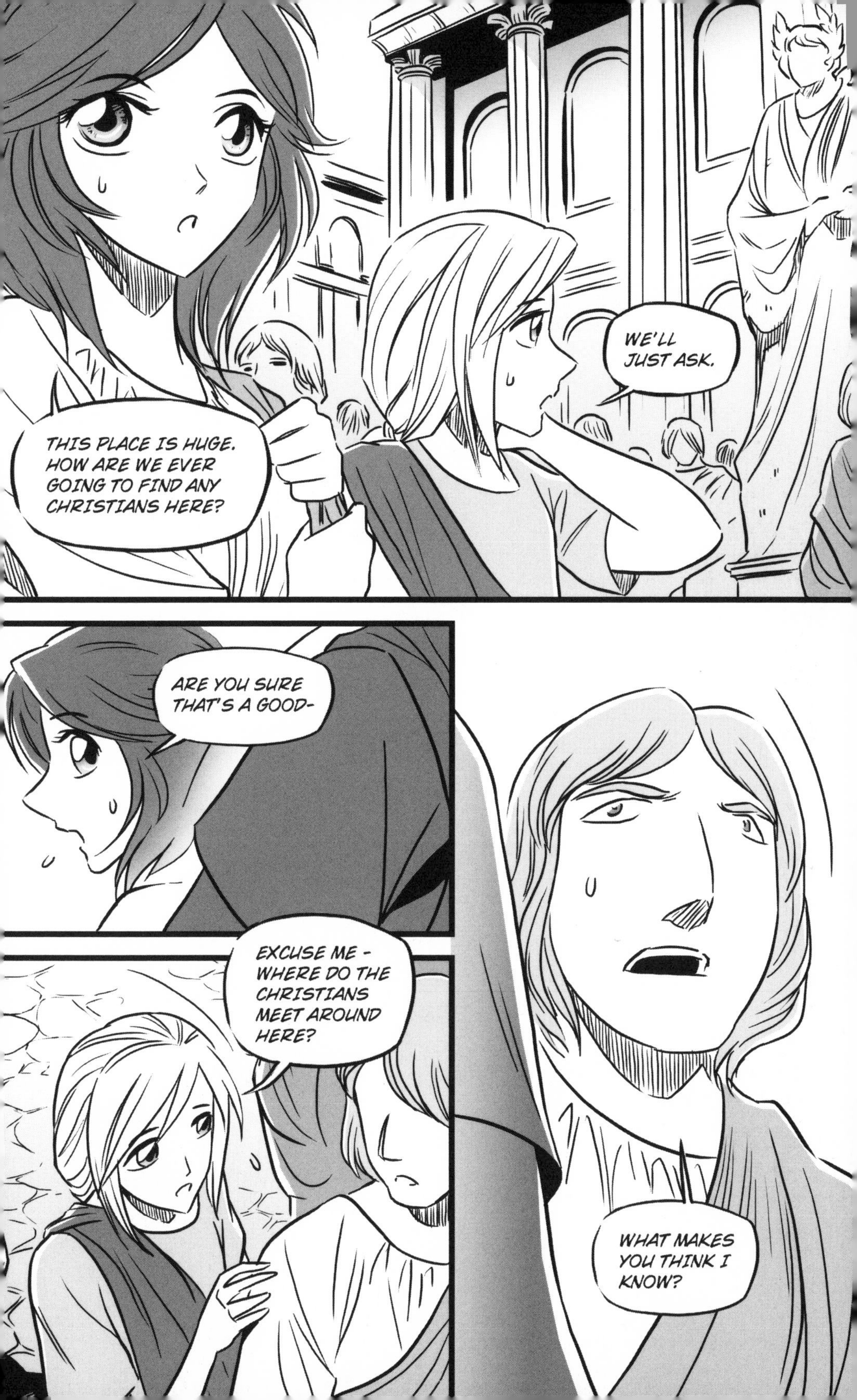
THIS PLACE IS HUGE. HOW ARE WE EVER GOING TO FIND ANY CHRISTIANS HERE?
WE'LL JUST ASK.
ARE YOU SURE THAT'S A GOOD-
EXCUSE ME - WHERE DO THE CHRISTIANS MEET AROUND HERE?
WHAT MAKES YOU THINK I KNOW?

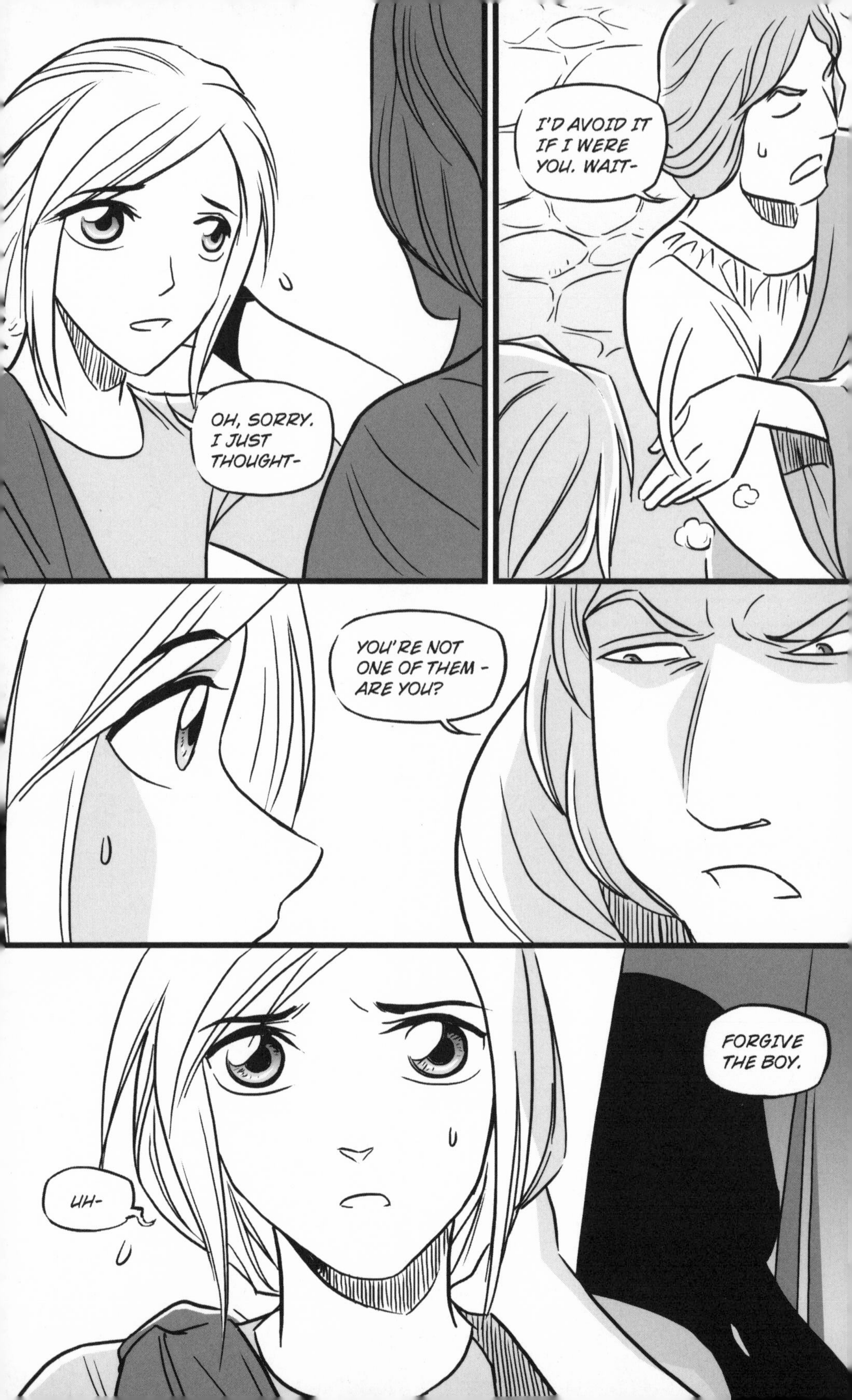
OH, SORRY.
I JUST
THOUGHT-
I'D AVOID IT
IF I WERE
YOU. WAIT-
YOU'RE NOT
ONE OF THEM -
ARE YOU?
FORGIVE
THE BOY.
UH-

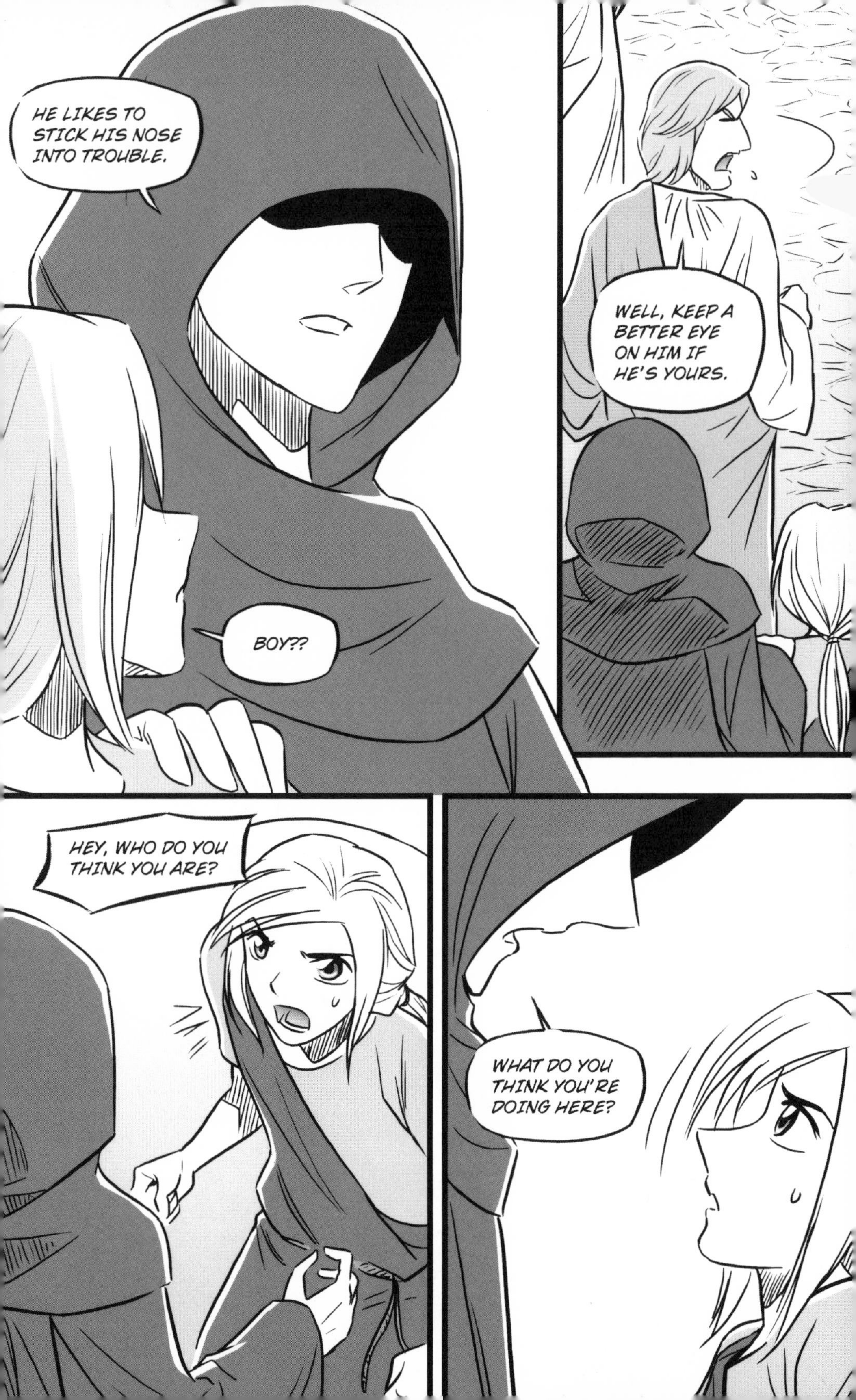
HE LIKES TO STICK HIS NOSE INTO TROUBLE.
WELL, KEEP A BETTER EYE ON HIM IF HE'S YOURS.
BOY??
HEY, WHO DO YOU THINK YOU ARE?
WHAT DO YOU THINK YOU'RE DOING HERE?

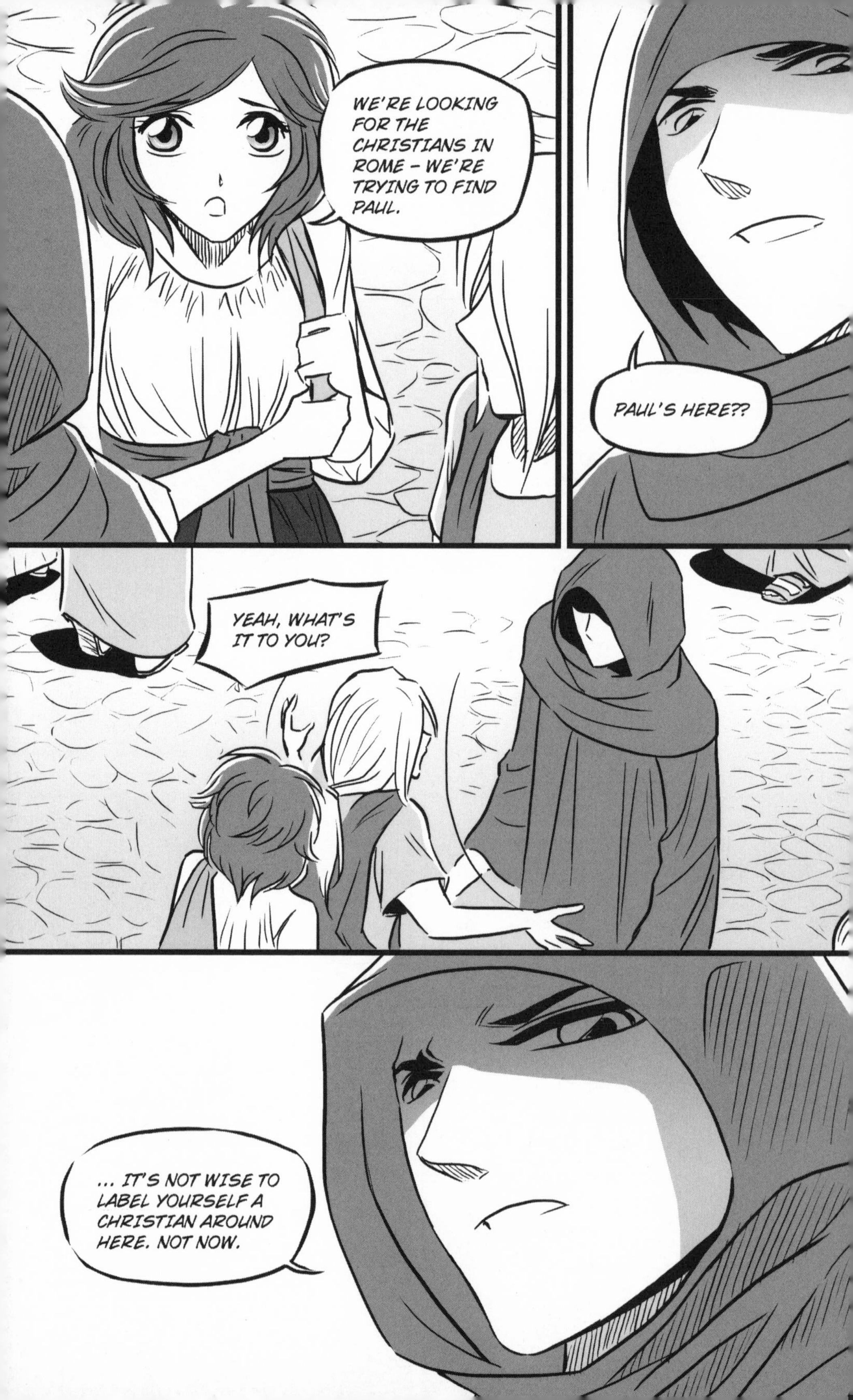
WE'RE LOOKING FOR THE CHRISTIANS IN ROME - WE'RE TRYING TO FIND PAUL.
PAUL'S HERE??
YEAH, WHAT'S IT TO YOU?
... IT'S NOT WISE TO LABEL YOURSELF A CHRISTIAN AROUND HERE. NOT NOW.

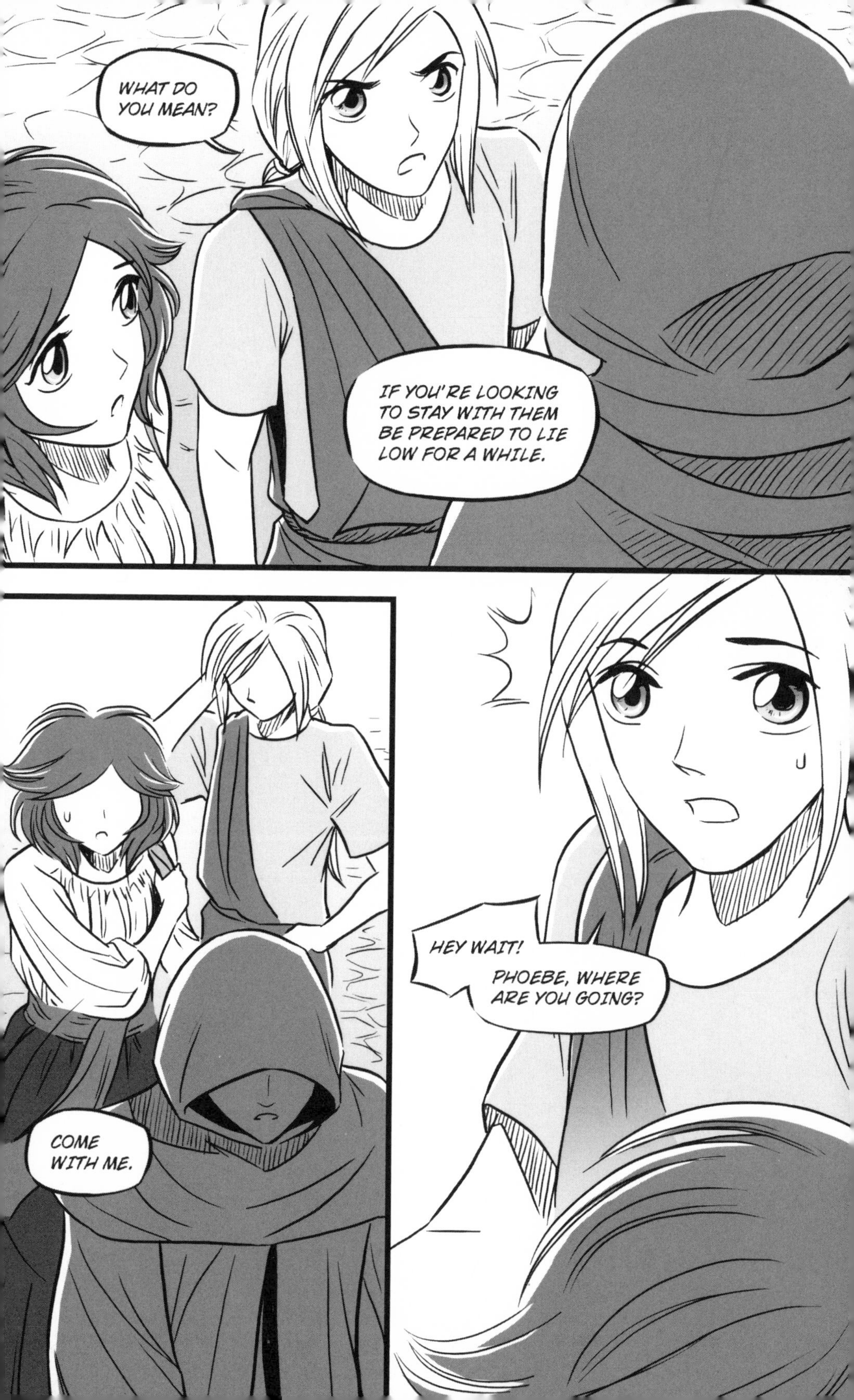
WHAT DO YOU MEAN?
IF YOU'RE LOOKING TO STAY WITH THEM BE PREPARED TO LIE LOW FOR A WHILE.
COME WITH ME.
HEY WAIT!
PHOEBE, WHERE ARE YOU GOING?

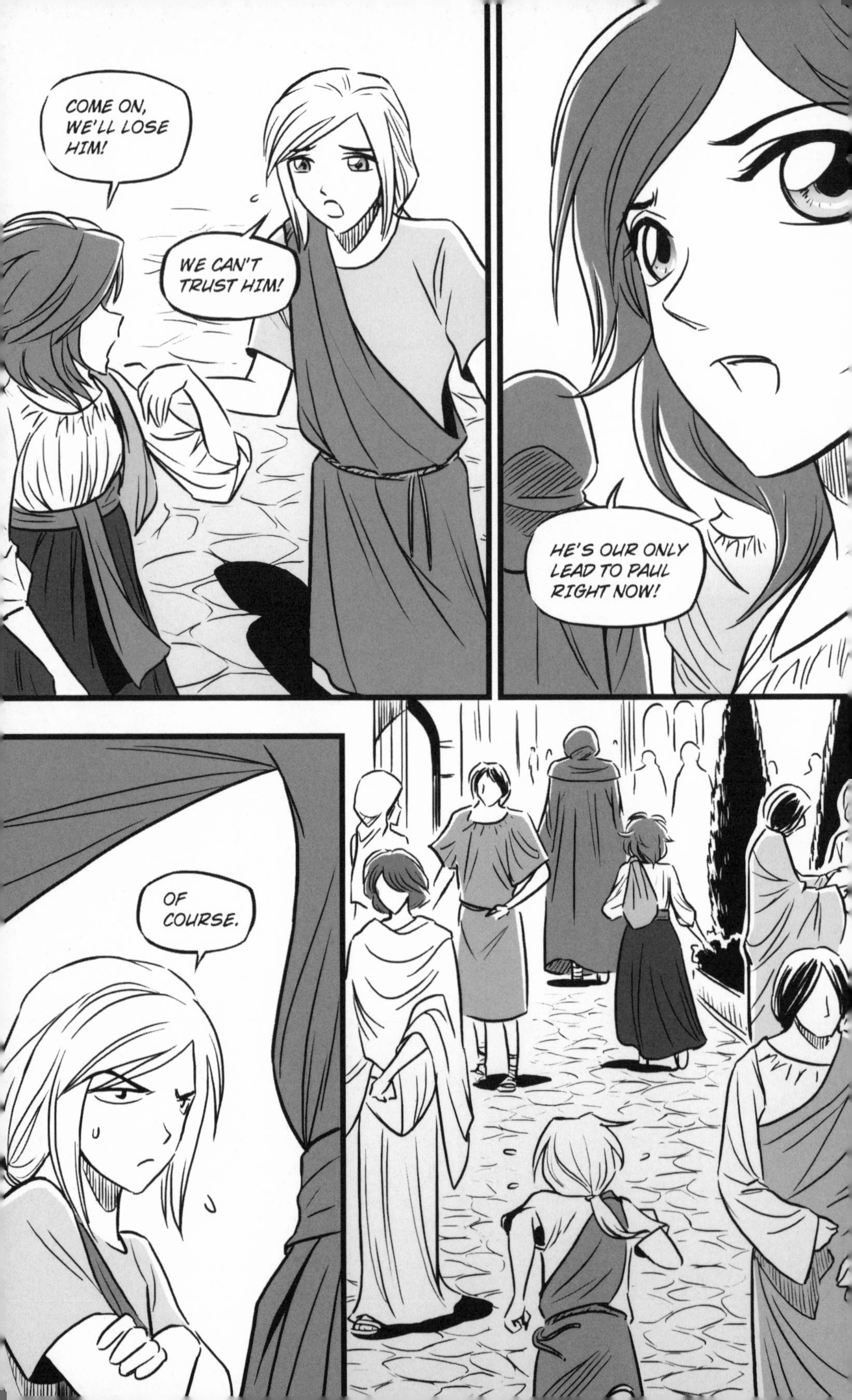
COME ON, WE'LL LOSE HIM!
WE CAN'T TRUST HIM!
HE'S OUR ONLY LEAD TO PAUL RIGHT NOW!
OF COURSE.

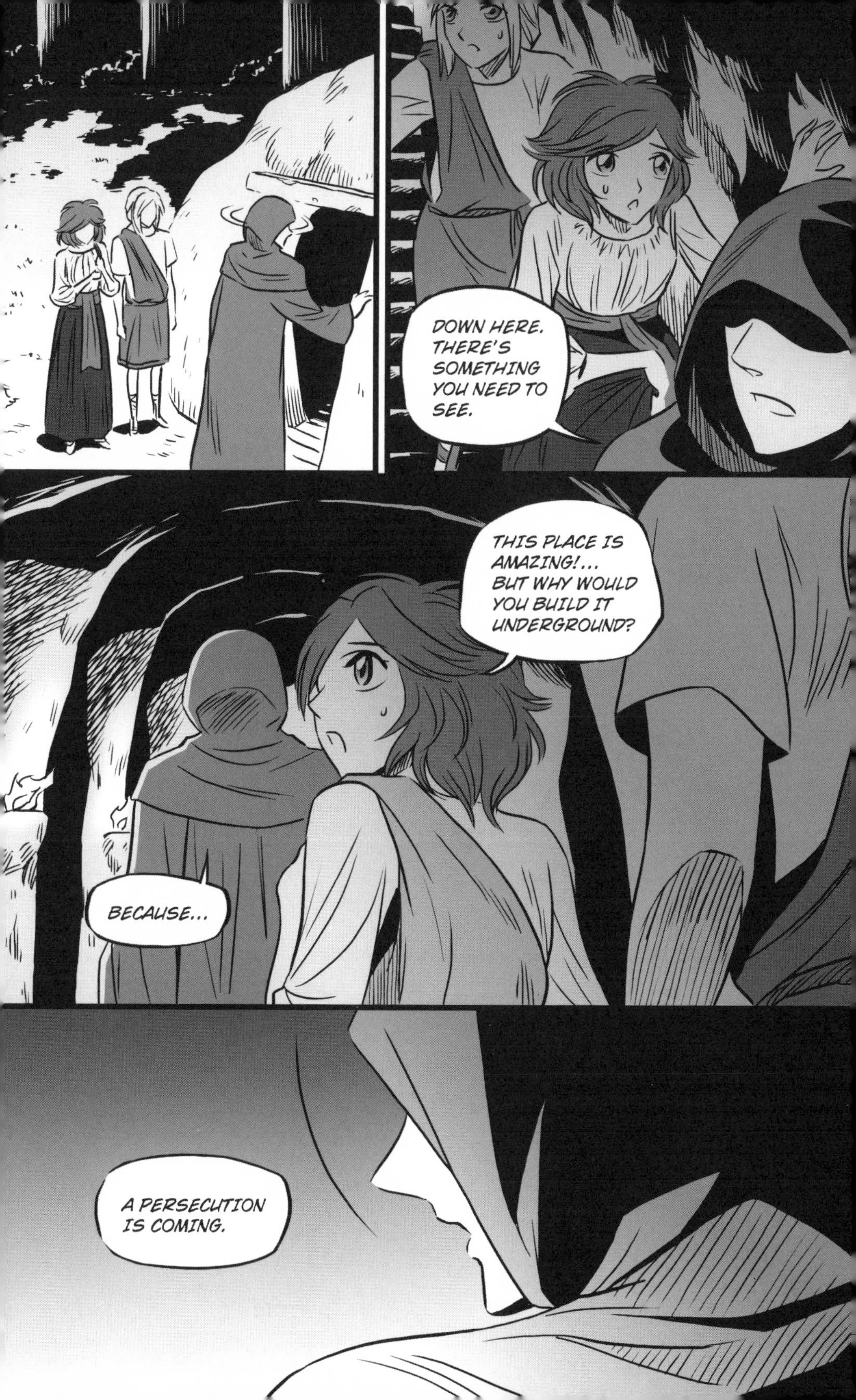
DOWN HERE. THERE'S SOMETHING YOU NEED TO SEE.
THIS PLACE IS AMAZING!... BUT WHY WOULD YOU BUILD IT UNDERGROUND?
BECAUSE...
A PERSECUTION IS COMING.

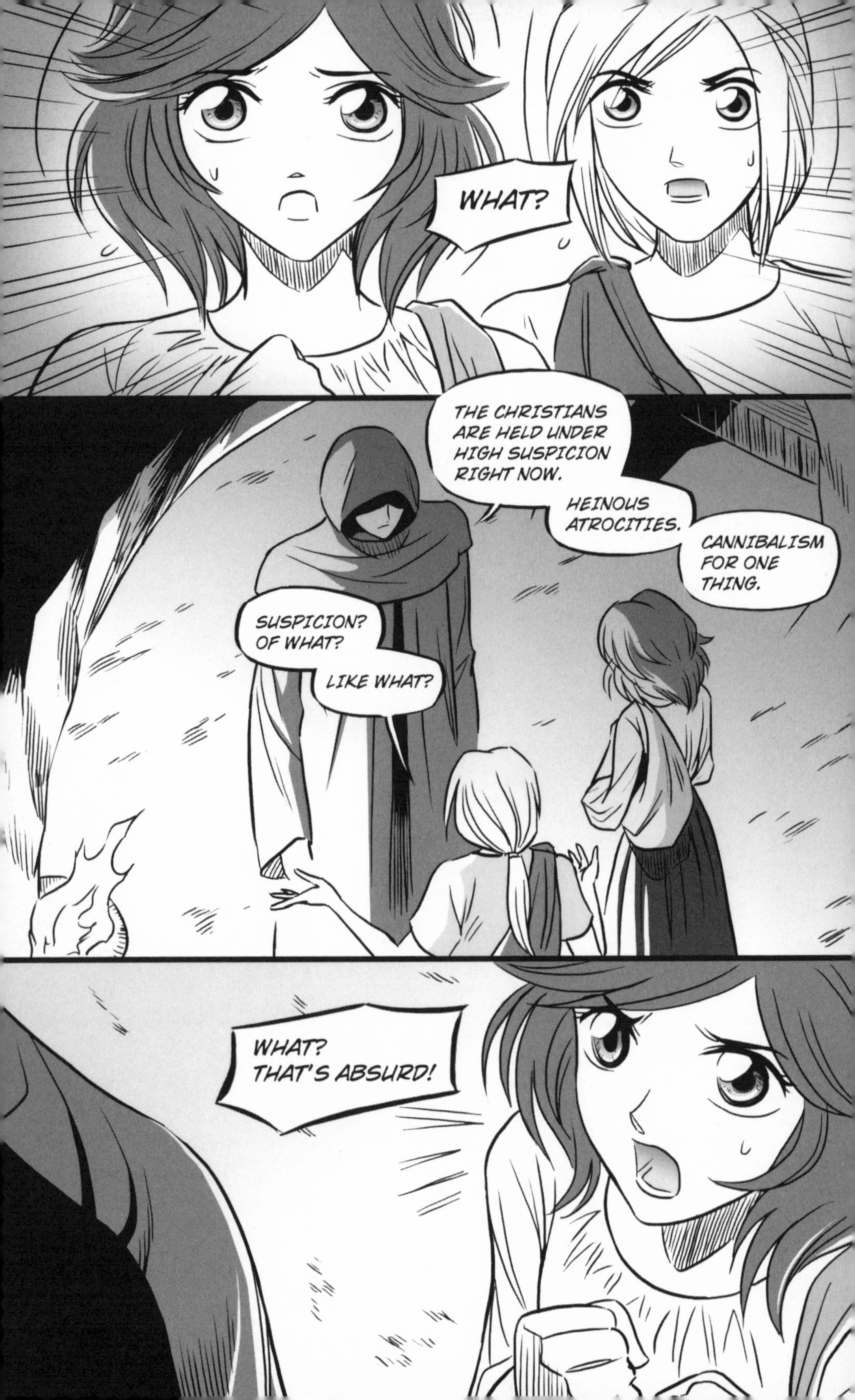
WHAT?
THE CHRISTIANS ARE HELD UNDER HIGH SUSPICION RIGHT NOW.
HEINOUS ATROCITIES.
CANNIBALISM FOR ONE THING.
SUSPICION? OF WHAT?
LIKE WHAT?
WHAT? THAT'S ABSURD!

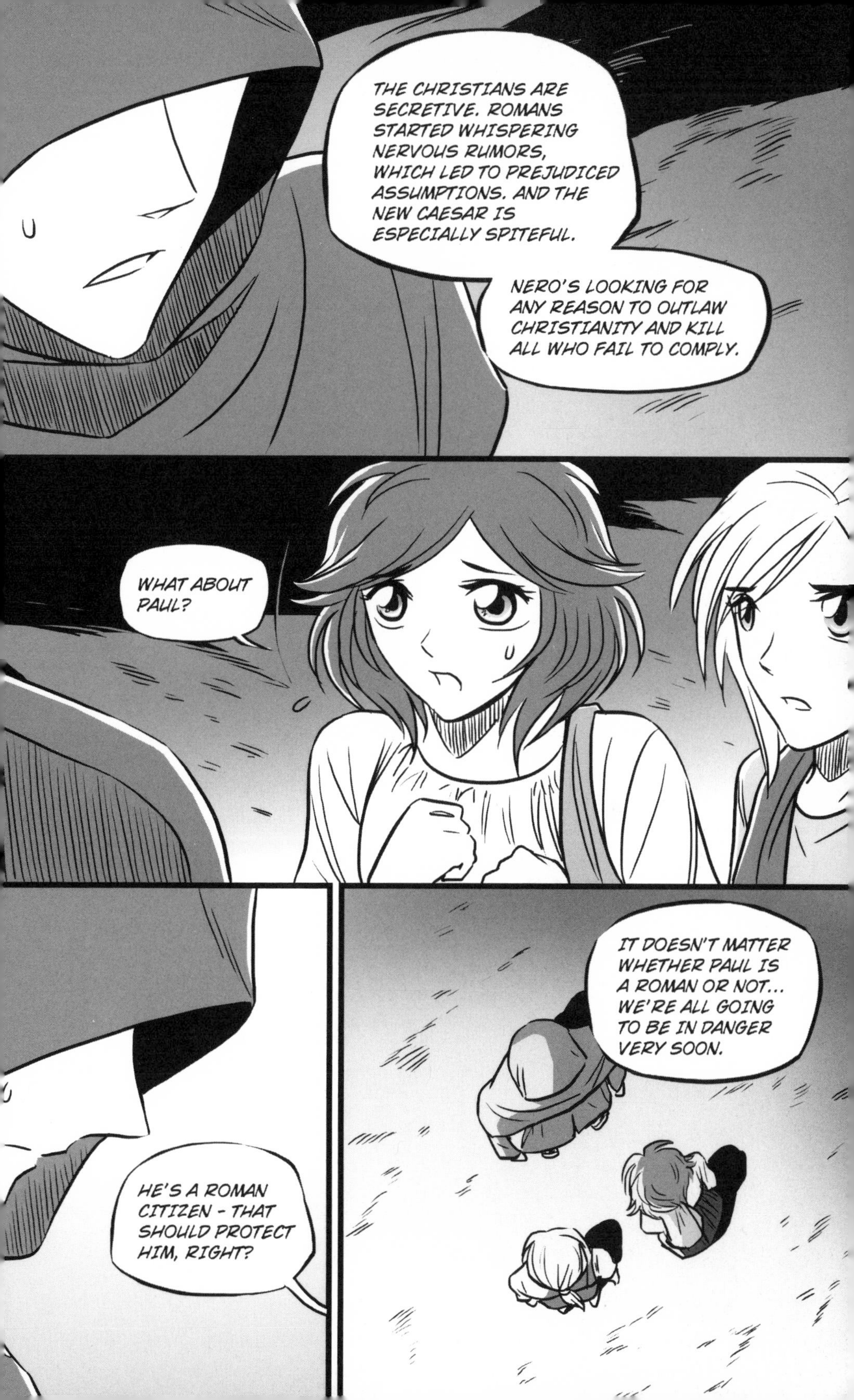
THE CHRISTIANS ARE SECRETIVE. ROMANS STARTED WHISPERING NERVOUS RUMORS, WHICH LED TO PREJUDICED ASSUMPTIONS. AND THE NEW CAESAR IS ESPECIALLY SPITEFUL.
NERO'S LOOKING FOR ANY REASON TO OUTLAW CHRISTIANITY AND KILL ALL WHO FAIL TO COMPLY.
WHAT ABOUT PAUL?
HE'S A ROMAN CITIZEN - THAT SHOULD PROTECT HIM, RIGHT?
IT DOESN'T MATTER WHETHER PAUL IS A ROMAN OR NOT... WE'RE ALL GOING TO BE IN DANGER VERY SOON.

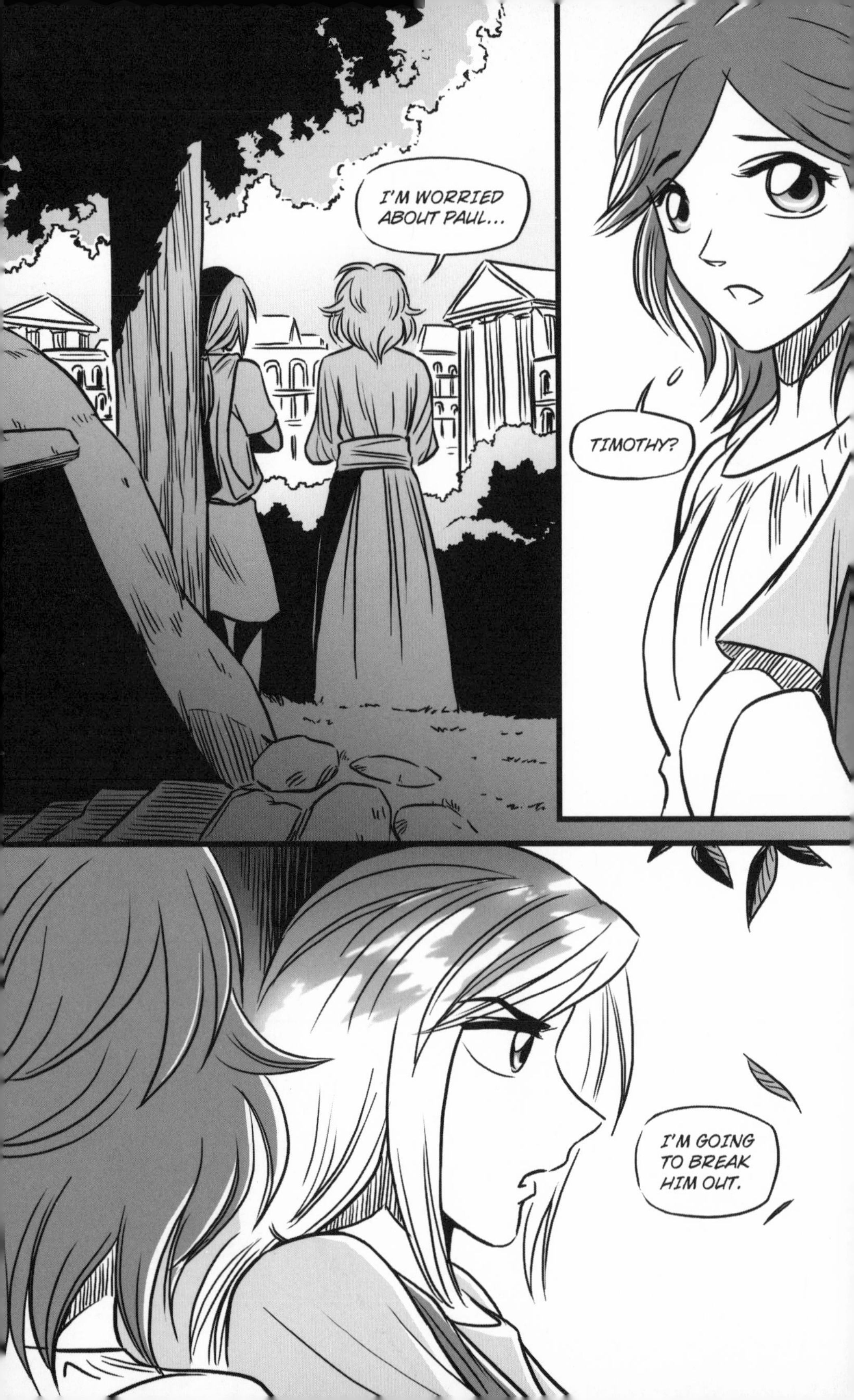
I'M WORRIED ABOUT PAUL...
TIMOTHY?
I'M GOING TO BREAK HIM OUT.

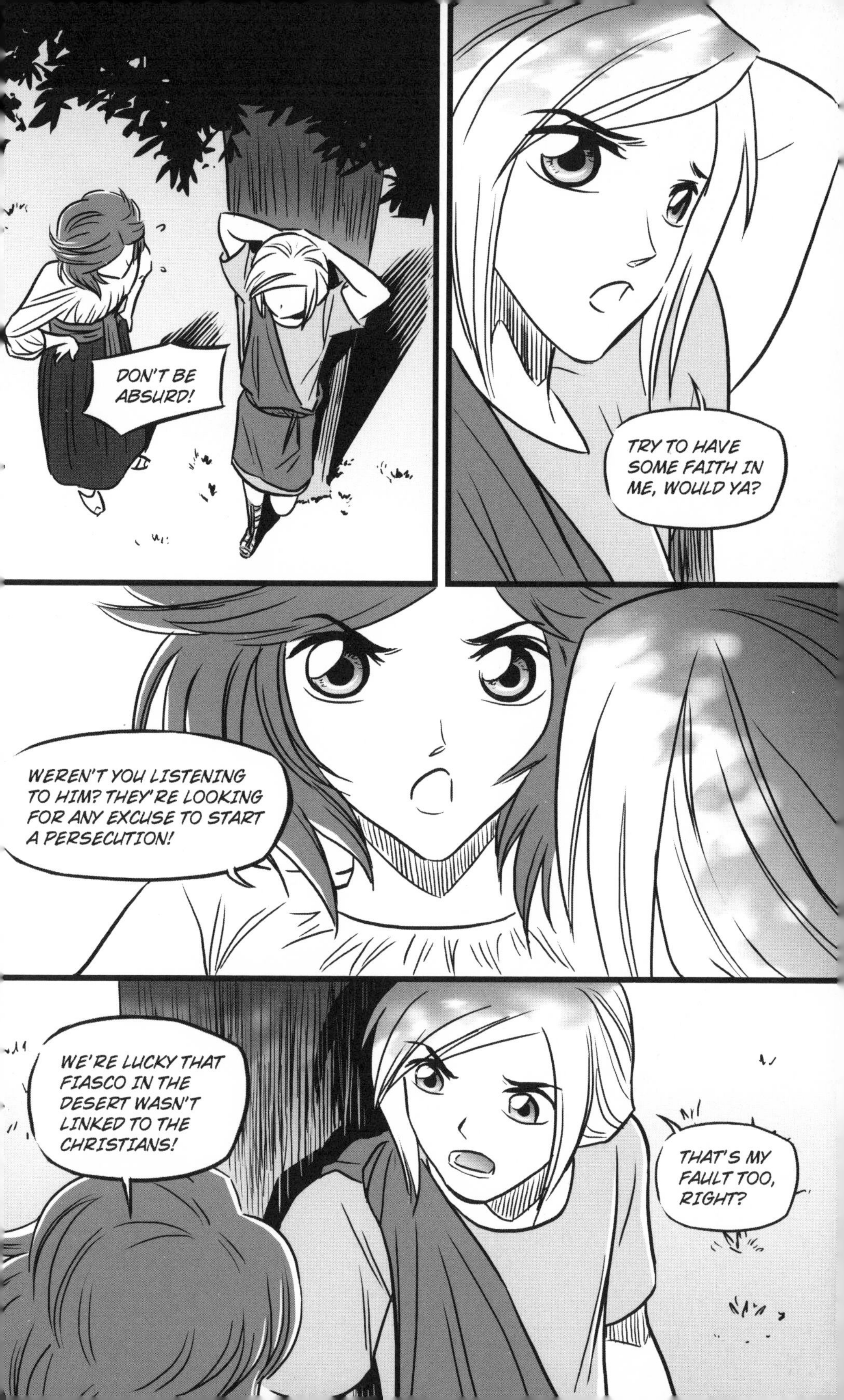
DON'T BE ABSURD!
TRY TO HAVE SOME FAITH IN ME, WOULD YA?
WEREN'T YOU LISTENING TO HIM? THEY'RE LOOKING FOR ANY EXCUSE TO START A PERSECUTION!
WE'RE LUCKY THAT FIASCO IN THE DESERT WASN'T LINKED TO THE CHRISTIANS!
THAT'S MY FAULT TOO, RIGHT?

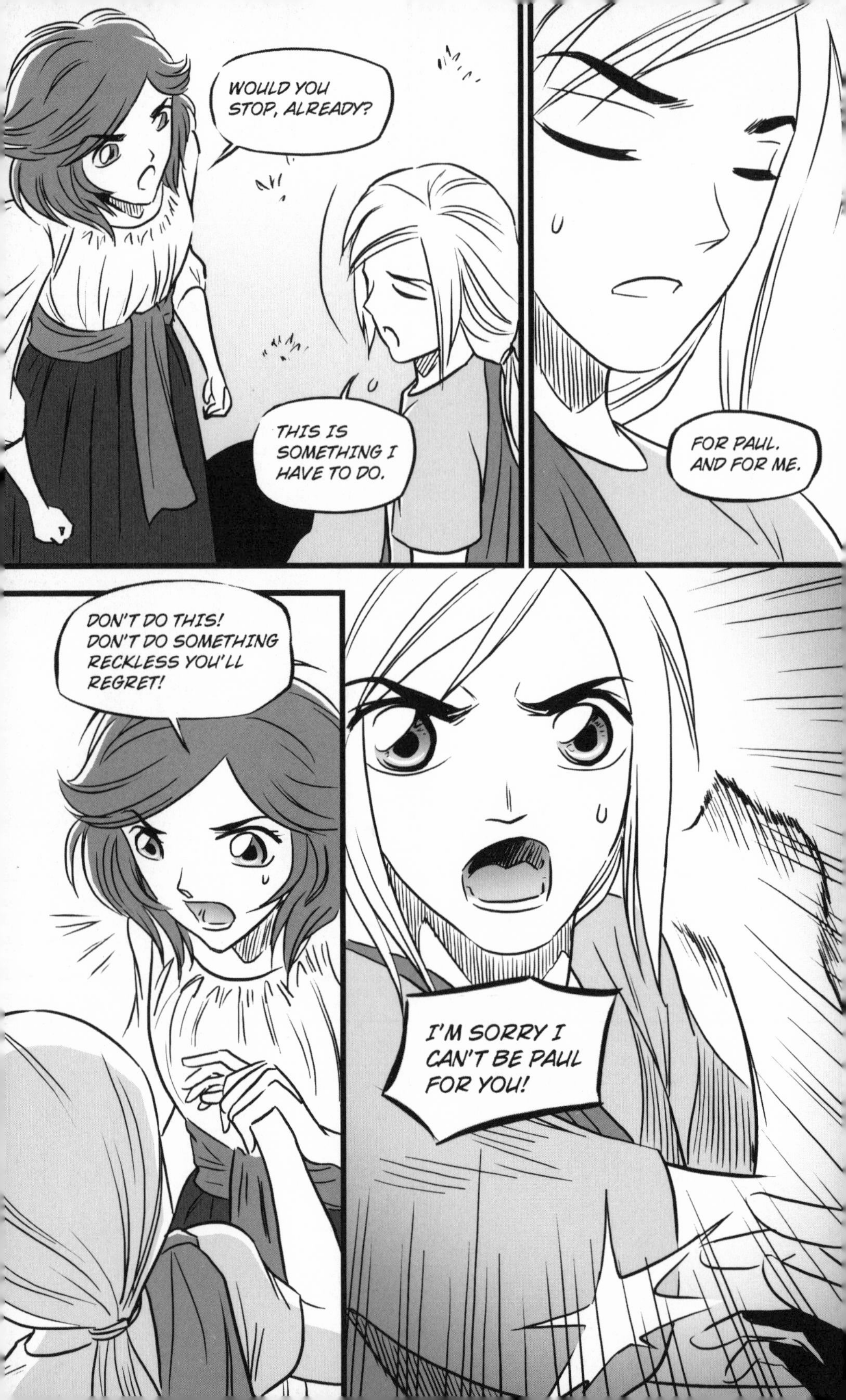
WOULD YOU STOP, ALREADY?
THIS IS SOMETHING I HAVE TO DO.
FOR PAUL. AND FOR ME.
DON'T DO THIS! DON'T DO SOMETHING RECKLESS YOU'LL REGRET!
I'M SORRY I CAN'T BE PAUL FOR YOU!

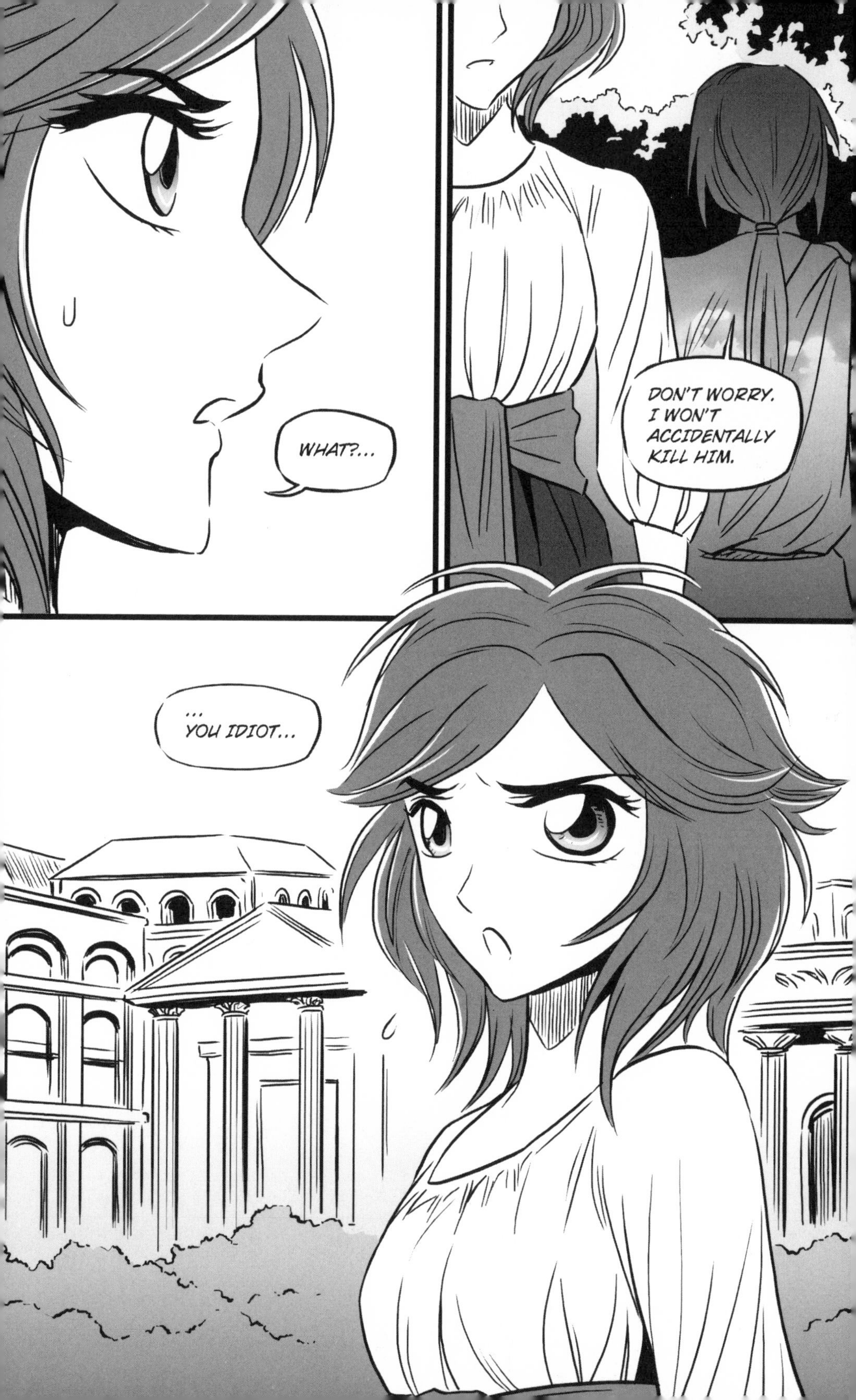
WHAT?...
DON'T WORRY. I WON'T ACCIDENTALLY KILL HIM.
... YOU IDIOT...

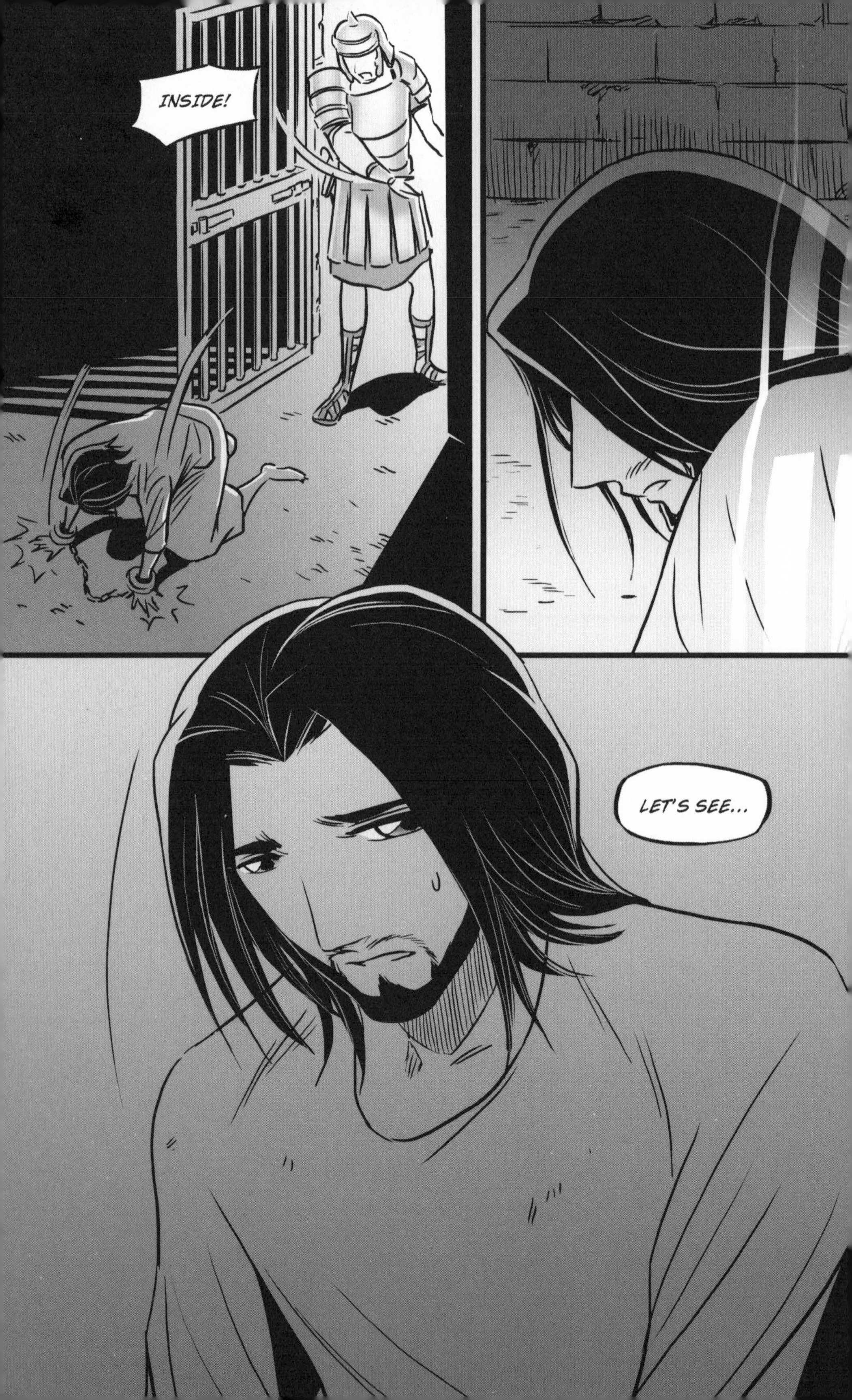
INSIDE!
LET'S SEE...

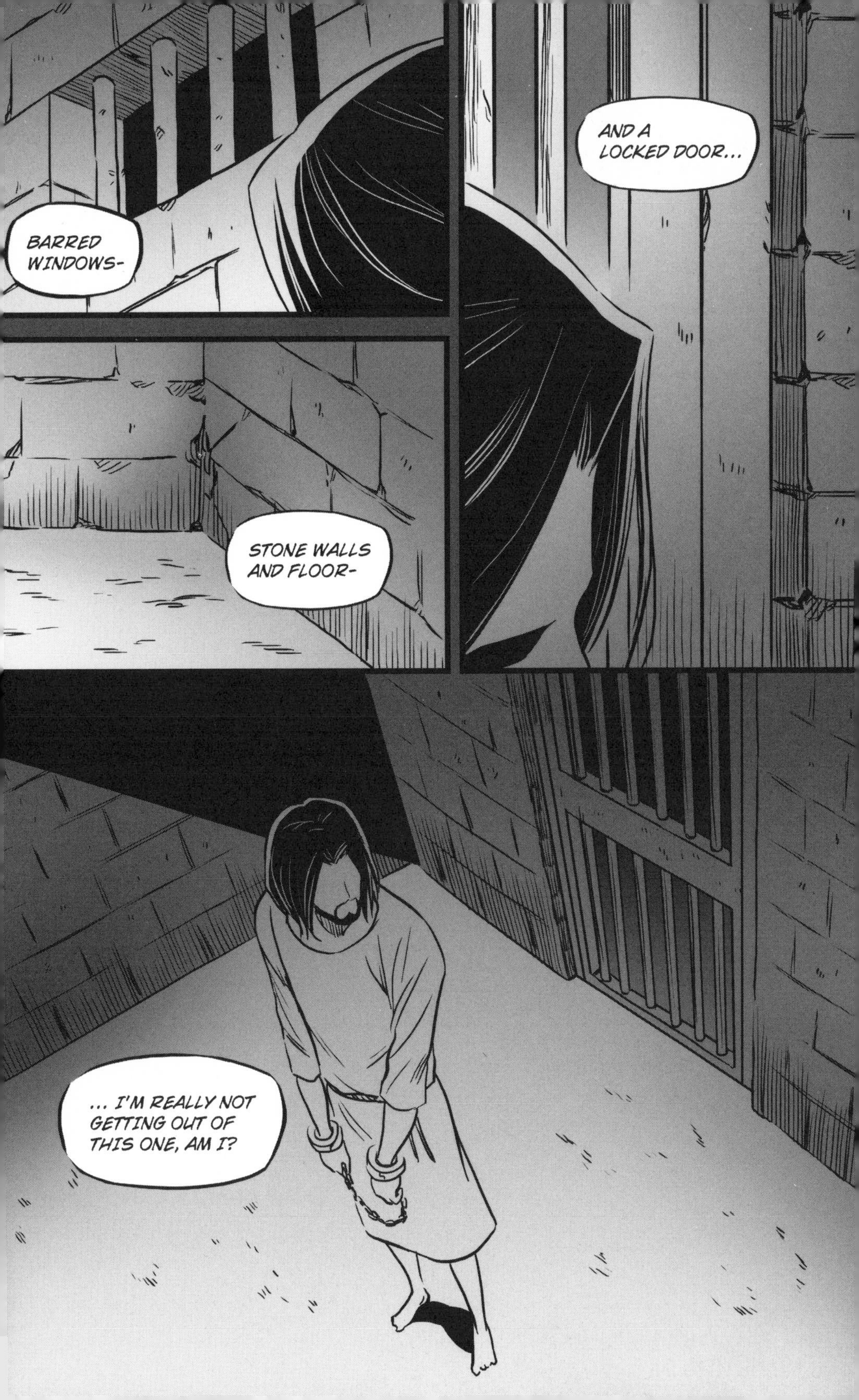
BARRED WINDOWS-
AND A LOCKED DOOR...
STONE WALLS AND FLOOR-
... I'M REALLY NOT GETTING OUT OF THIS ONE, AM I?

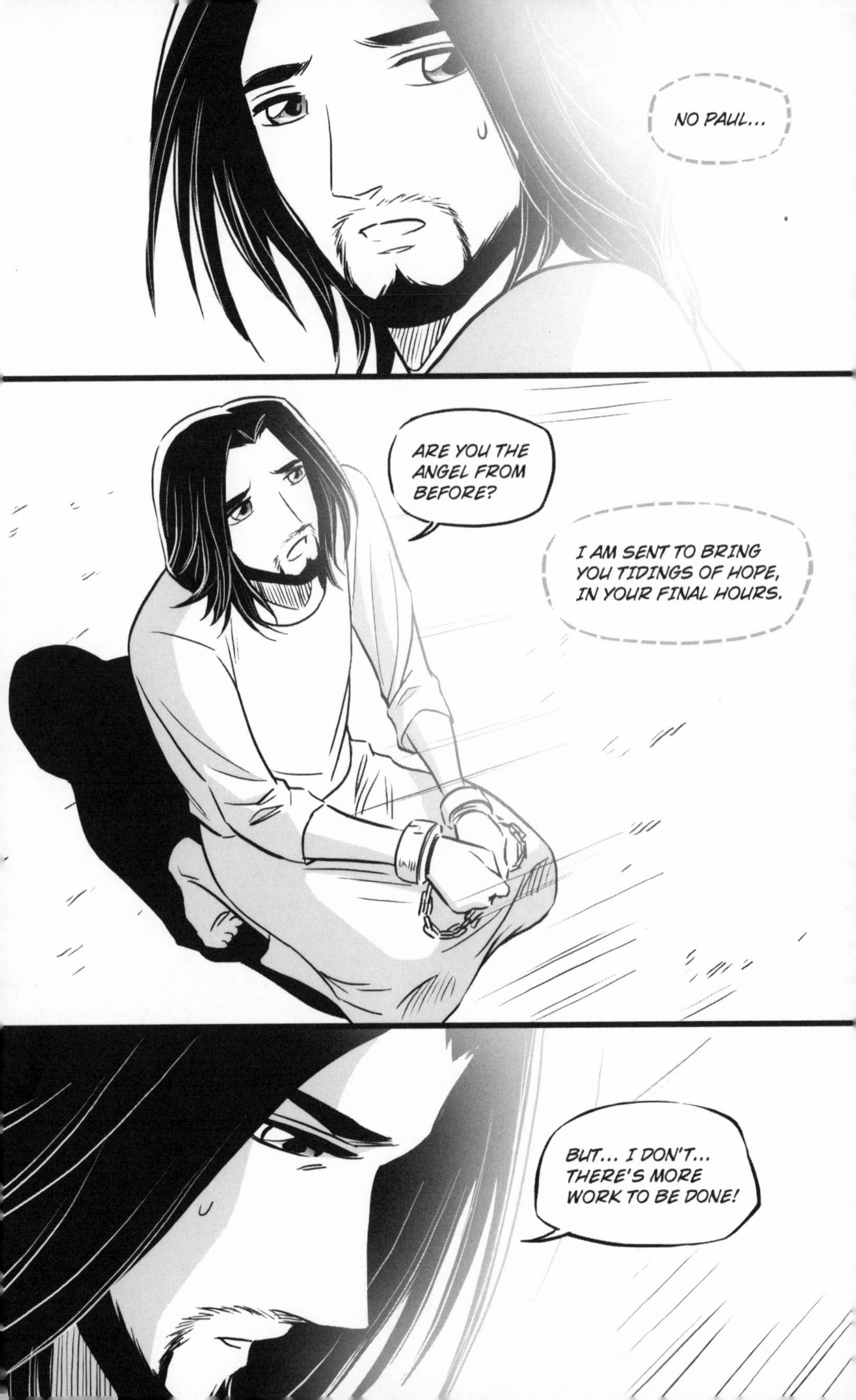
NO PAUL...
ARE YOU THE ANGEL FROM BEFORE?
I AM SENT TO BRING YOU TIDINGS OF HOPE, IN YOUR FINAL HOURS.
BUT... I DON'T... THERE'S MORE WORK TO BE DONE!

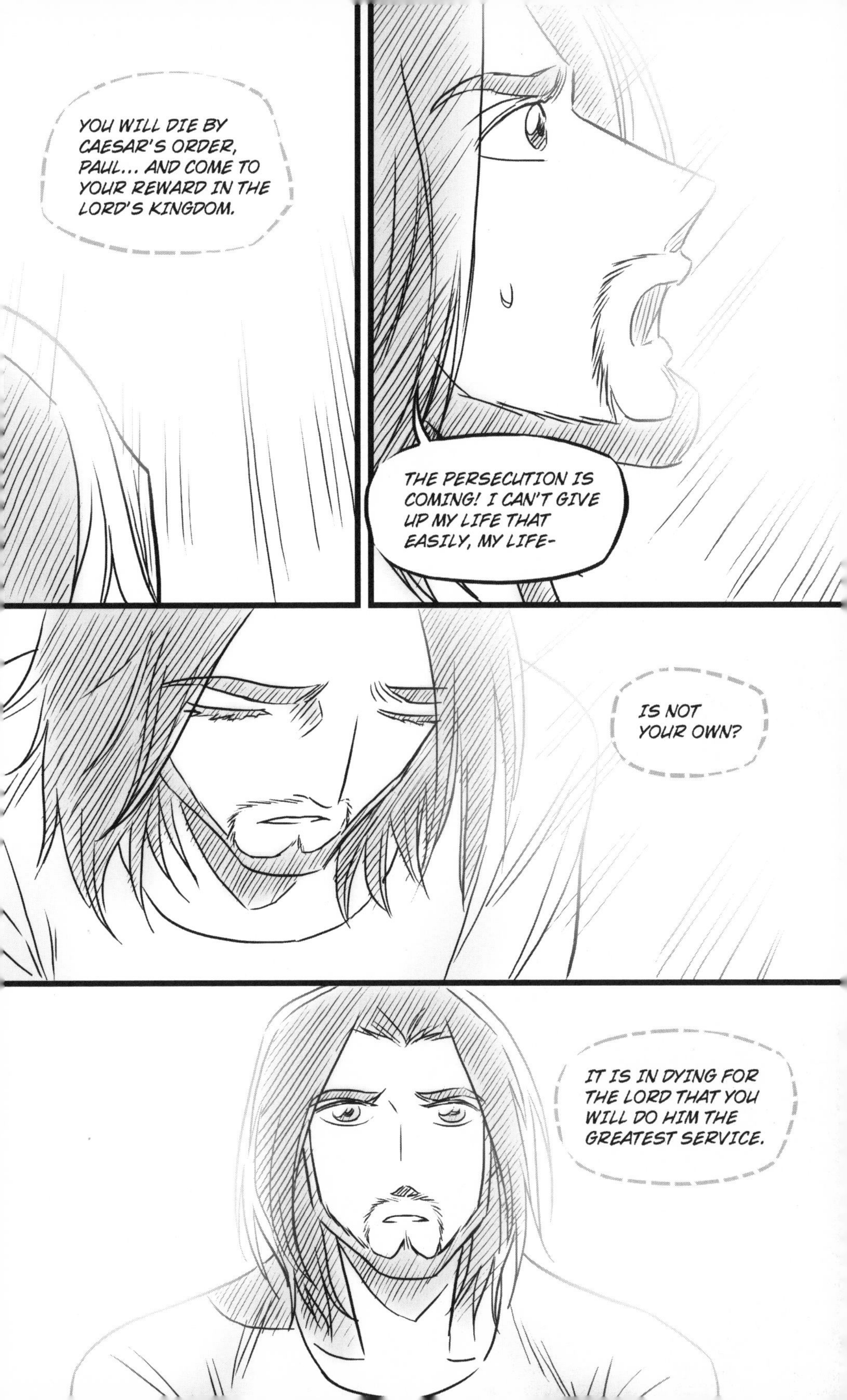
YOU WILL DIE BY CAESAR'S ORDER, PAUL... AND COME TO YOUR REWARD IN THE LORD'S KINGDOM.
THE PERSECUTION IS COMING! I CAN'T GIVE UP MY LIFE THAT EASILY, MY LIFE-
IS NOT YOUR OWN?
IT IS IN DYING FOR THE LORD THAT YOU WILL DO HIM THE GREATEST SERVICE.

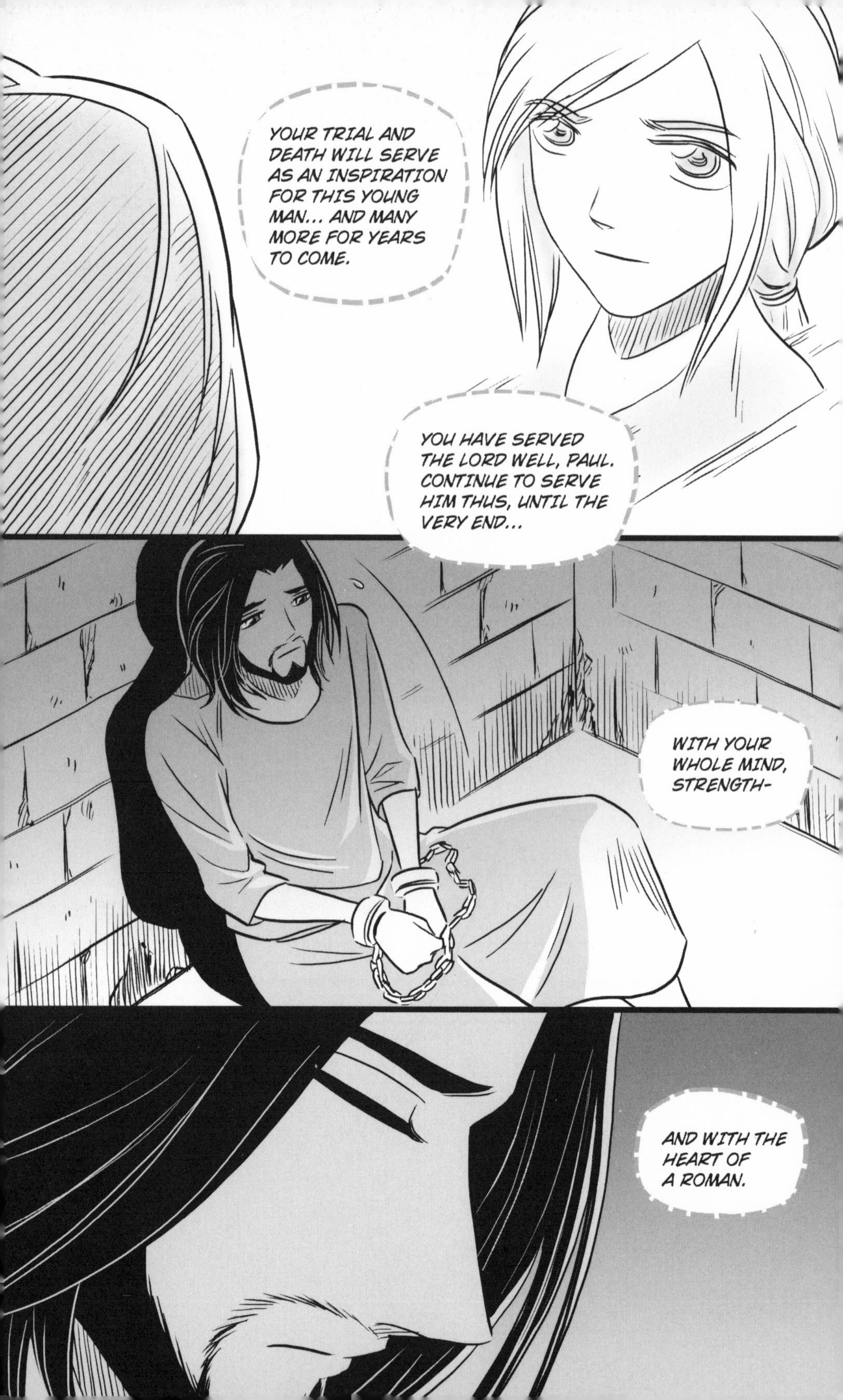
YOUR TRIAL AND DEATH WILL SERVE AS AN INSPIRATION FOR THIS YOUNG MAN... AND MANY MORE FOR YEARS TO COME.
YOU HAVE SERVED THE LORD WELL, PAUL. CONTINUE TO SERVE HIM THUS, UNTIL THE VERY END...
WITH YOUR WHOLE MIND, STRENGTH-
AND WITH THE HEART OF A ROMAN.

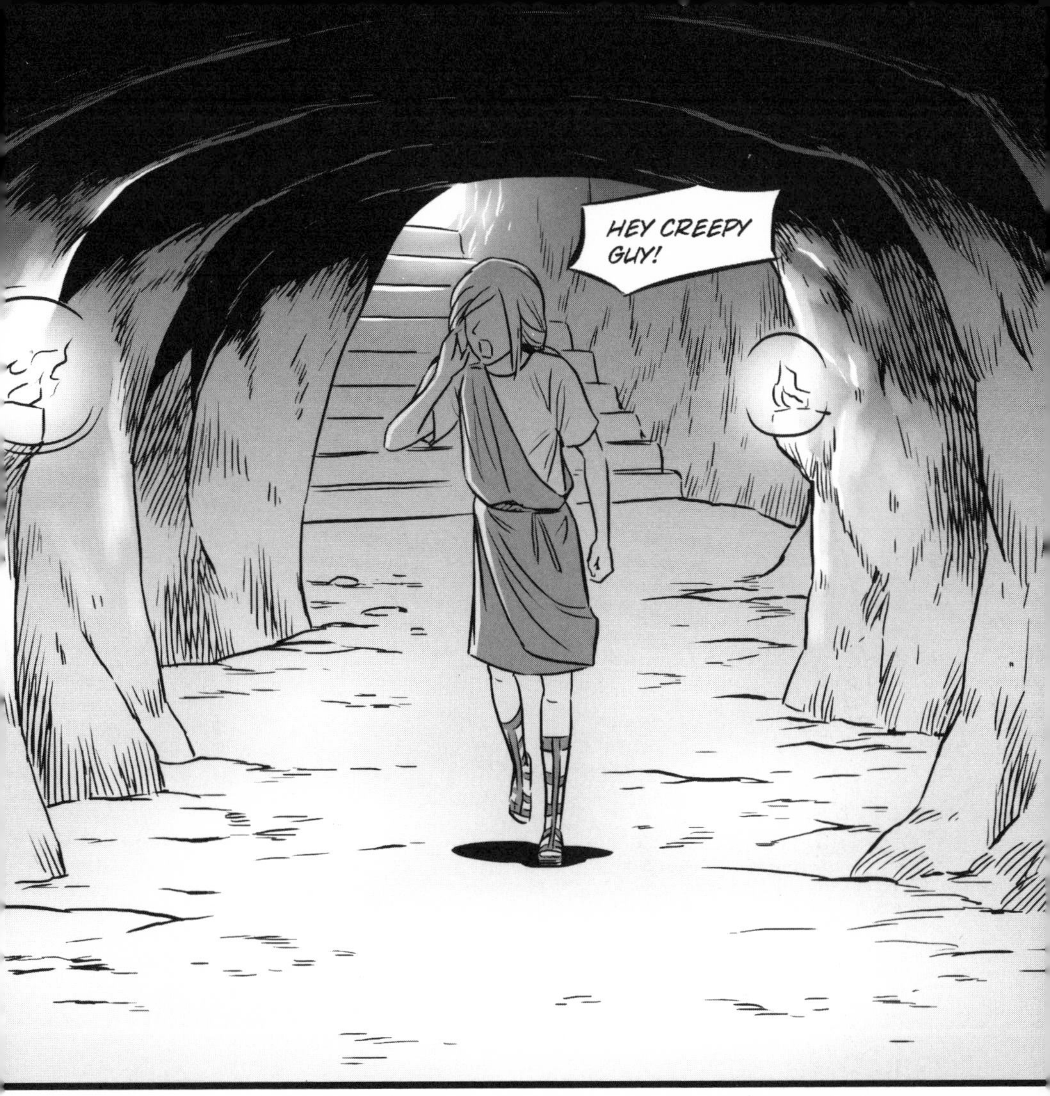
HEY CREEPY GUY!

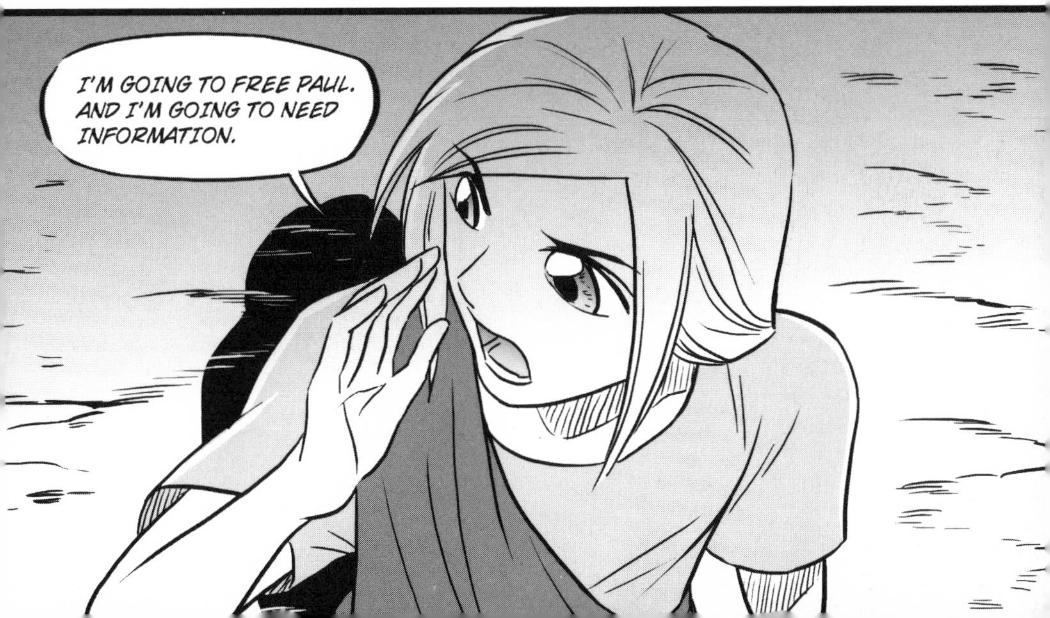
I'M GOING TO FREE PAUL. AND I'M GOING TO NEED INFORMATION.

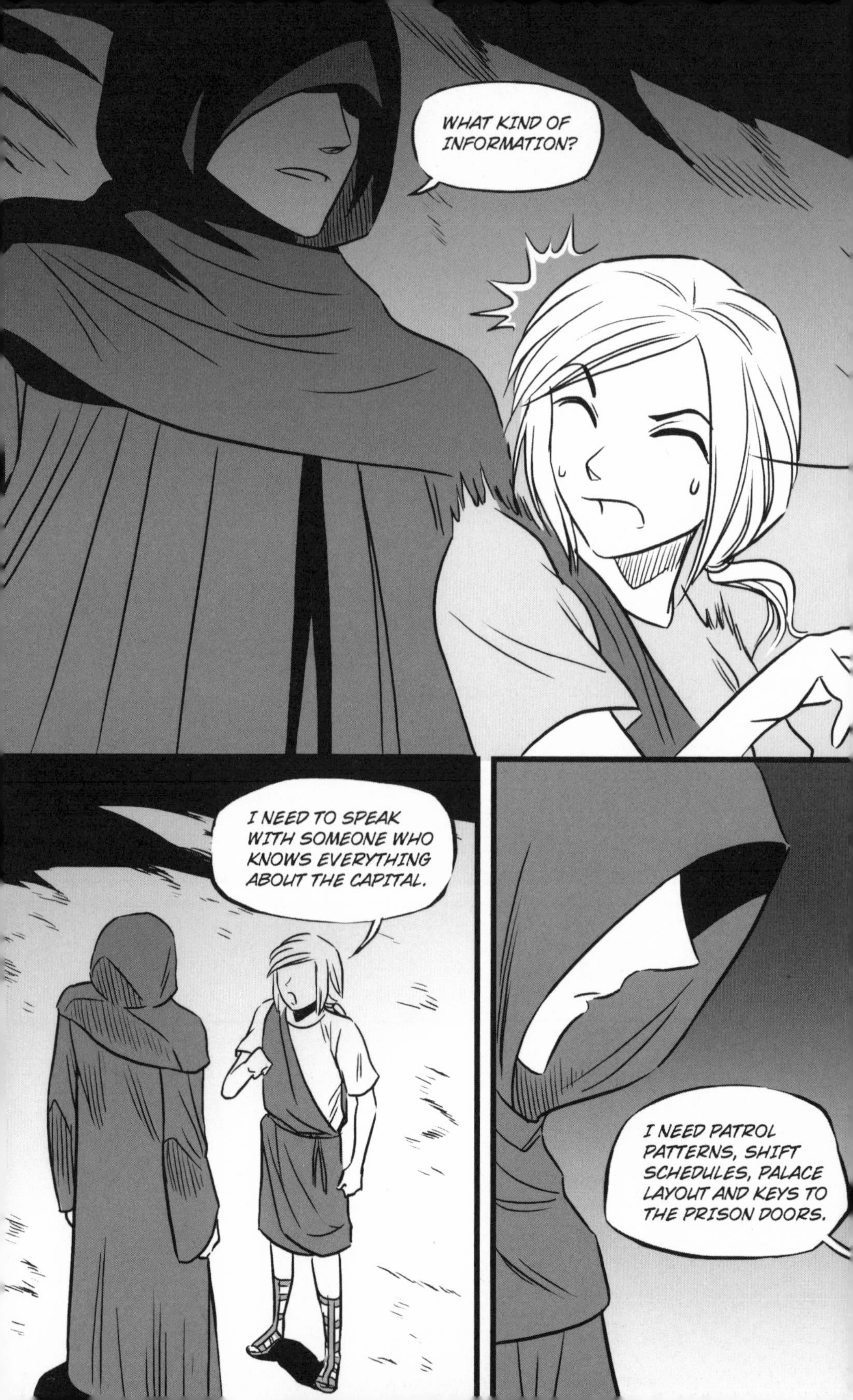
WHAT KIND OF INFORMATION?
I NEED TO SPEAK WITH SOMEONE WHO KNOWS EVERYTHING ABOUT THE CAPITAL.
I NEED PATROL PATTERNS, SHIFT SCHEDULES, PALACE LAYOUT AND KEYS TO THE PRISON DOORS.

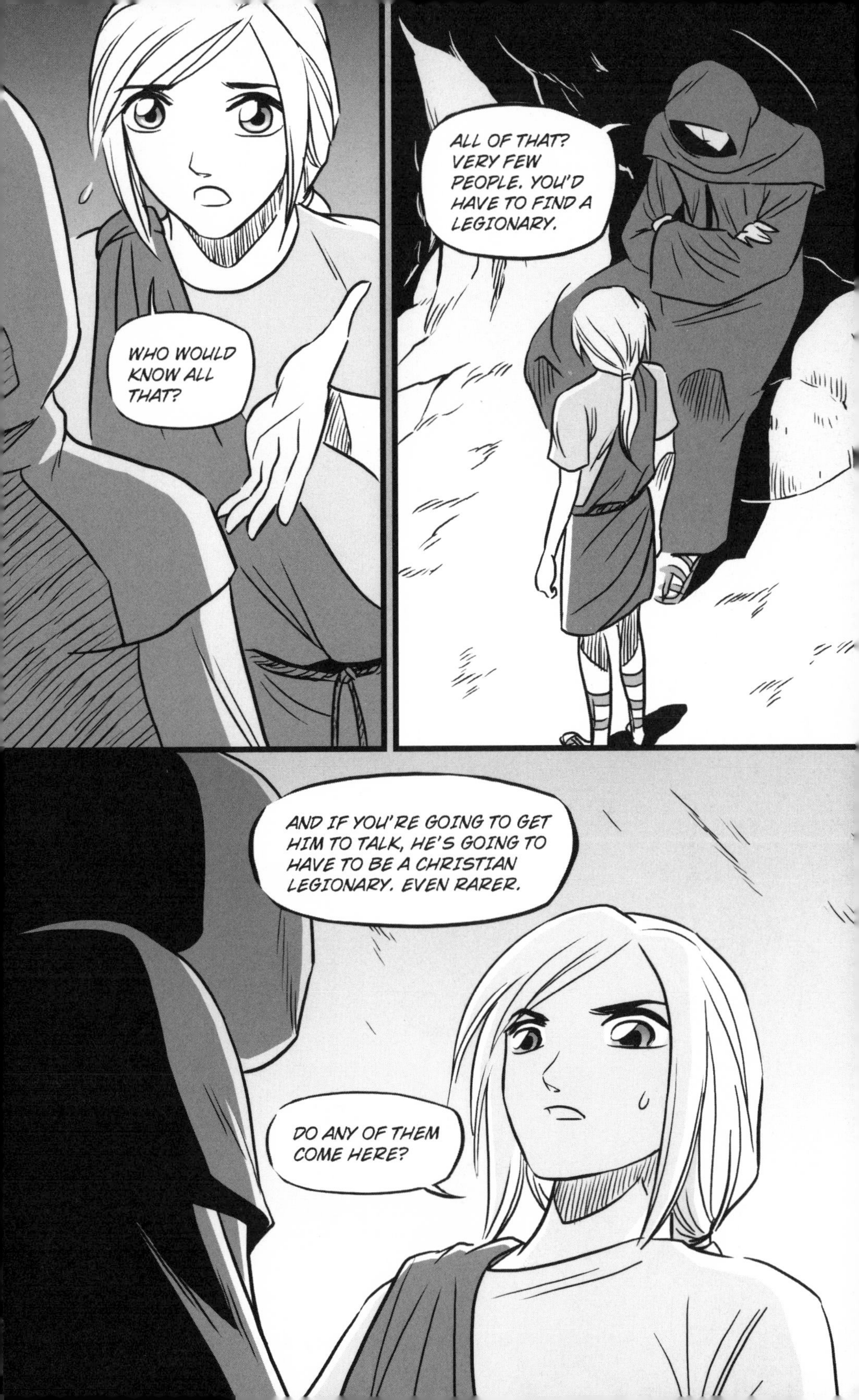
WHO WOULD KNOW ALL THAT?
ALL OF THAT? VERY FEW PEOPLE. YOU'D HAVE TO FIND A LEGIONARY.
AND IF YOU'RE GOING TO GET HIM TO TALK, HE'S GOING TO HAVE TO BE A CHRISTIAN LEGIONARY. EVEN RARER.
DO ANY OF THEM COME HERE?

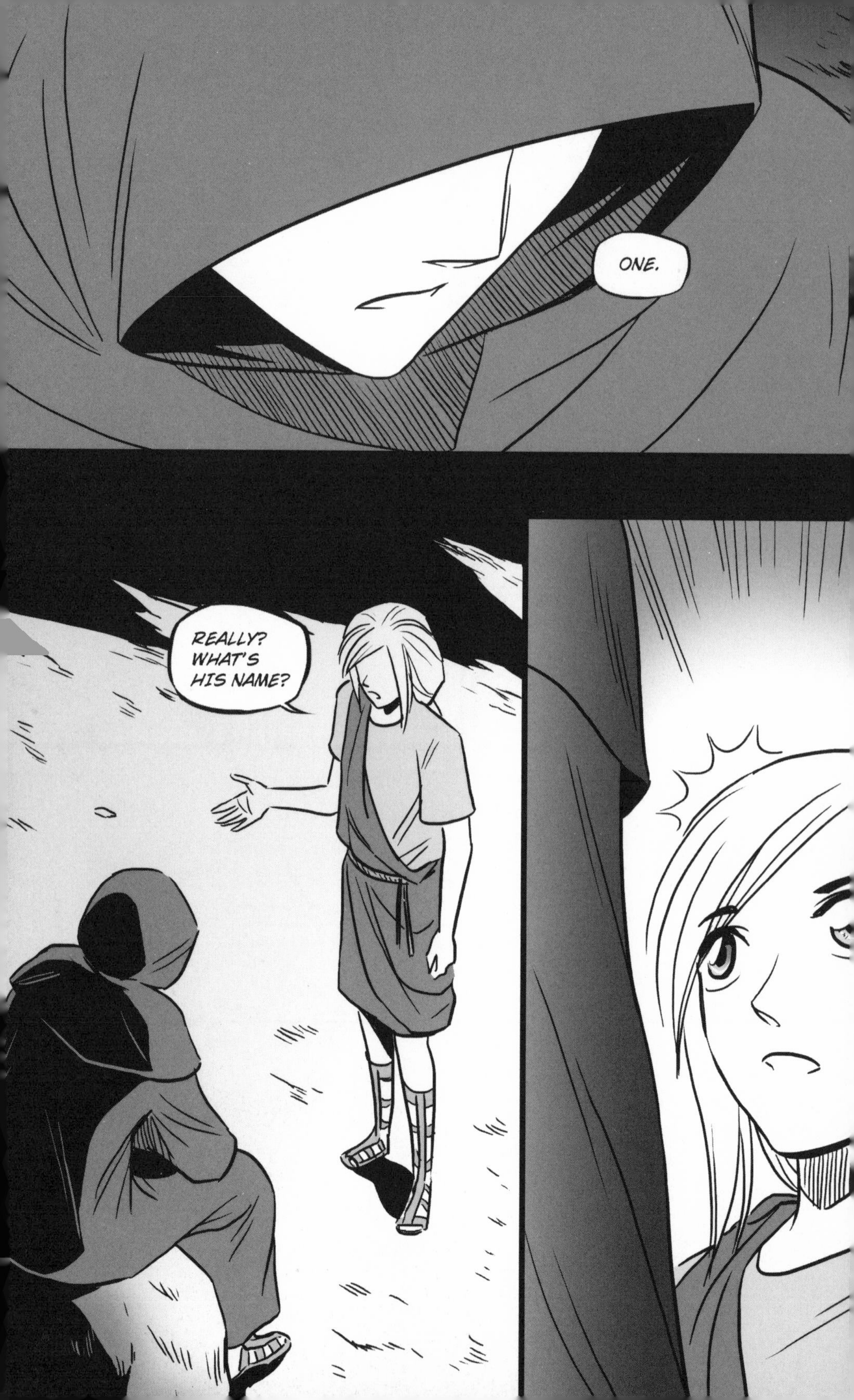
ONE.
REALLY? WHAT'S HIS NAME?

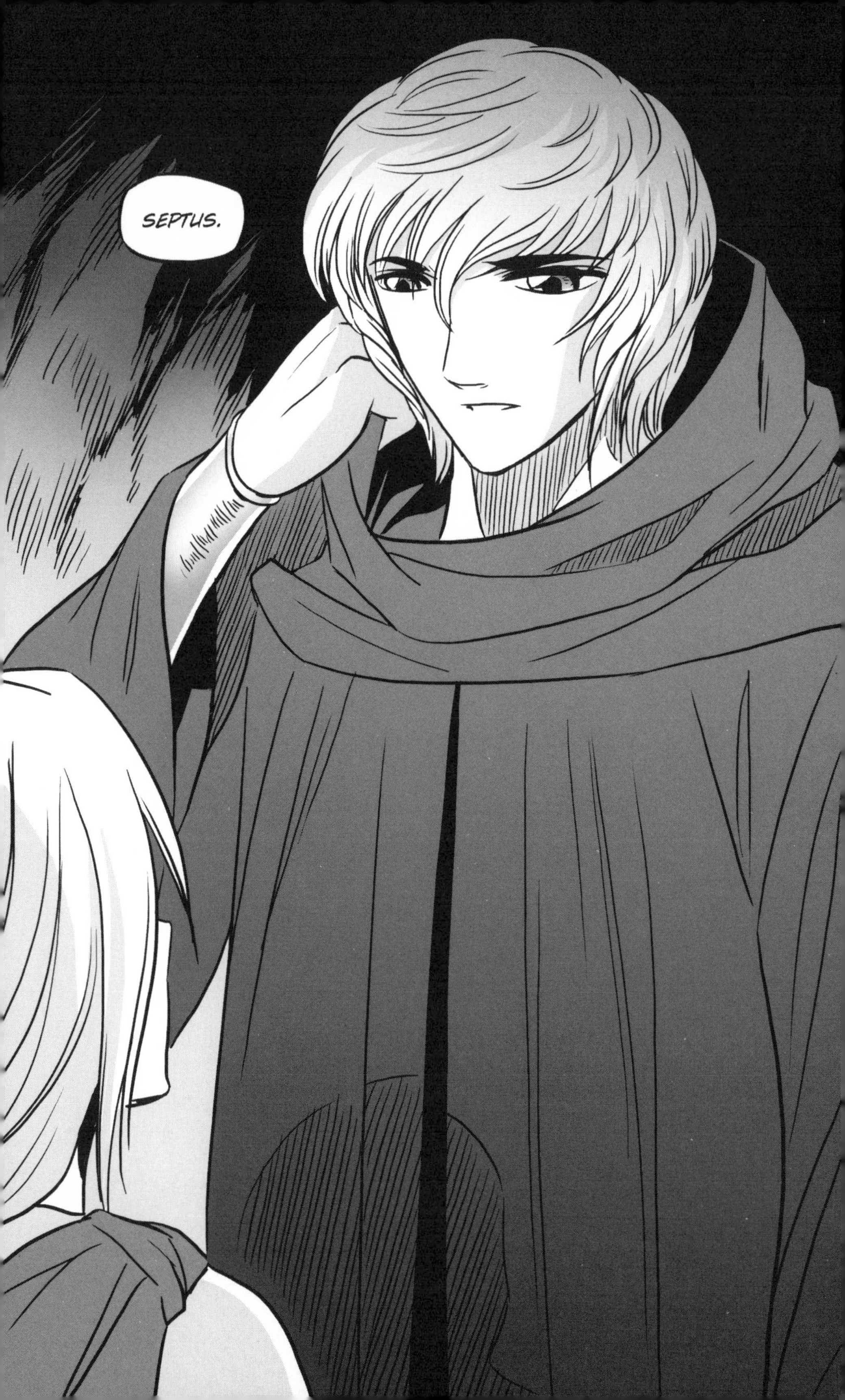
SEPTUS.

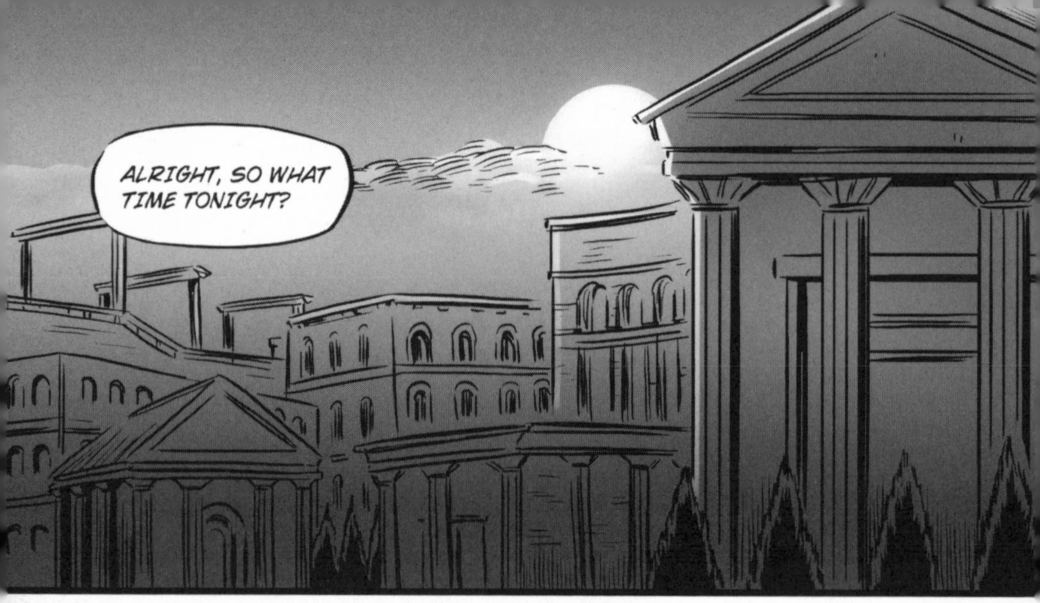
ALRIGHT, SO WHAT TIME TONIGHT?

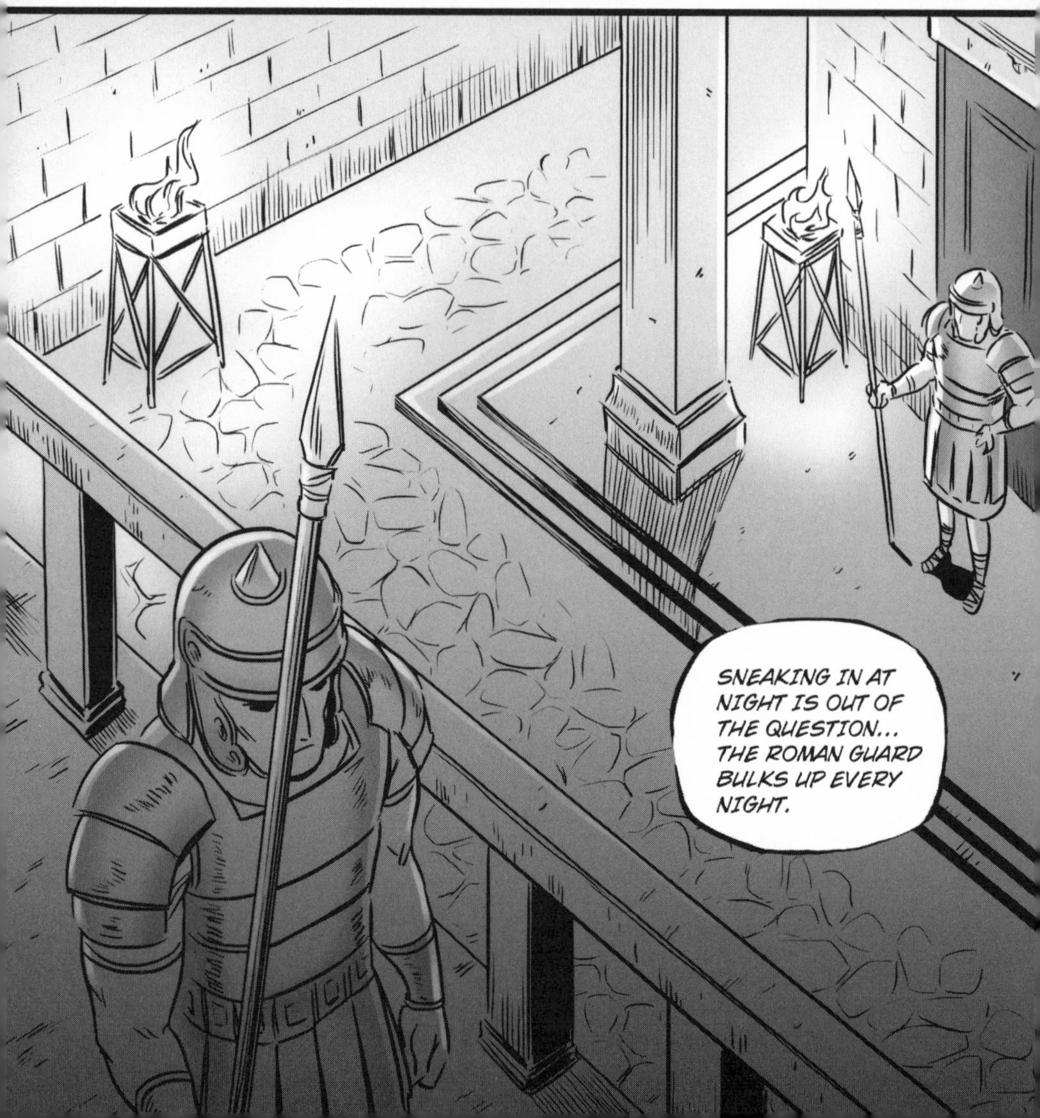
SNEAKING IN AT NIGHT IS OUT OF THE QUESTION... THE ROMAN GUARD BULKS UP EVERY NIGHT.

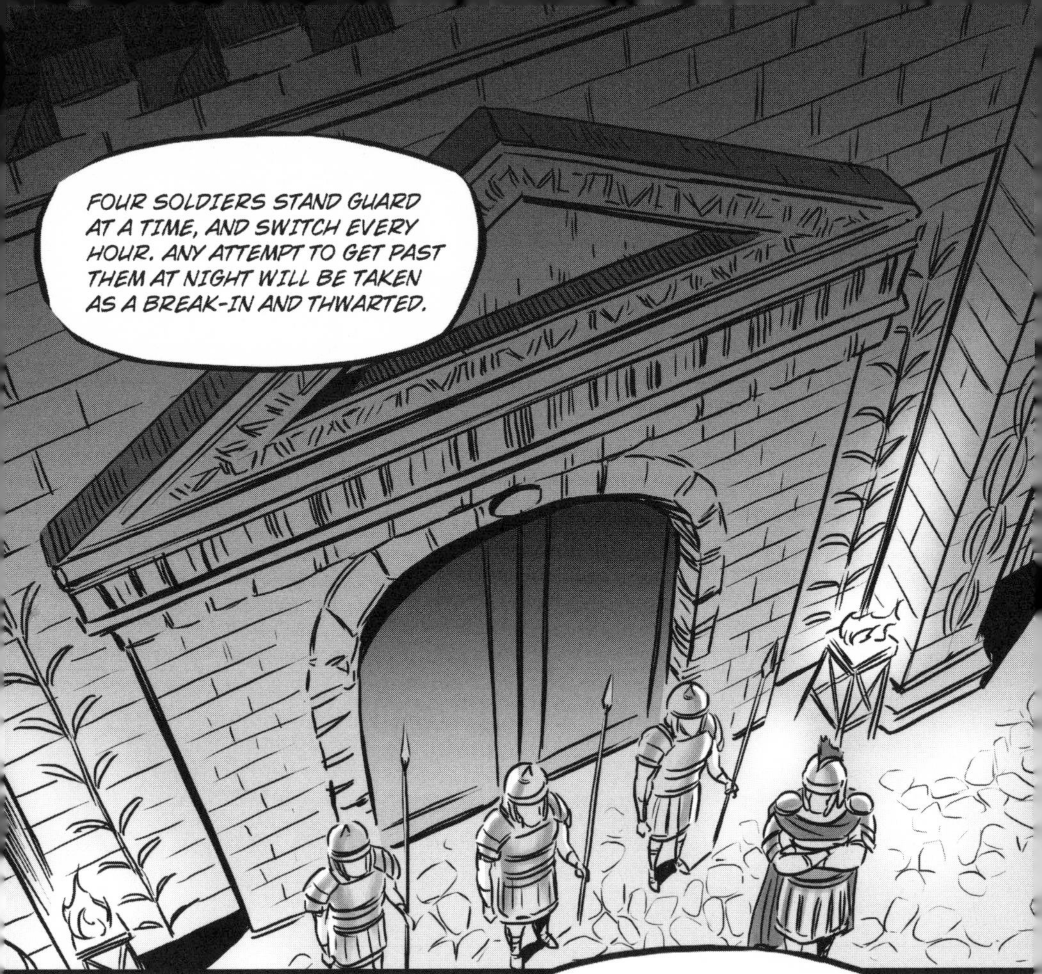
FOUR SOLDIERS STAND GUARD AT A TIME, AND SWITCH EVERY HOUR. ANY ATTEMPT TO GET PAST THEM AT NIGHT WILL BE TAKEN AS A BREAK-IN AND THWARTED.

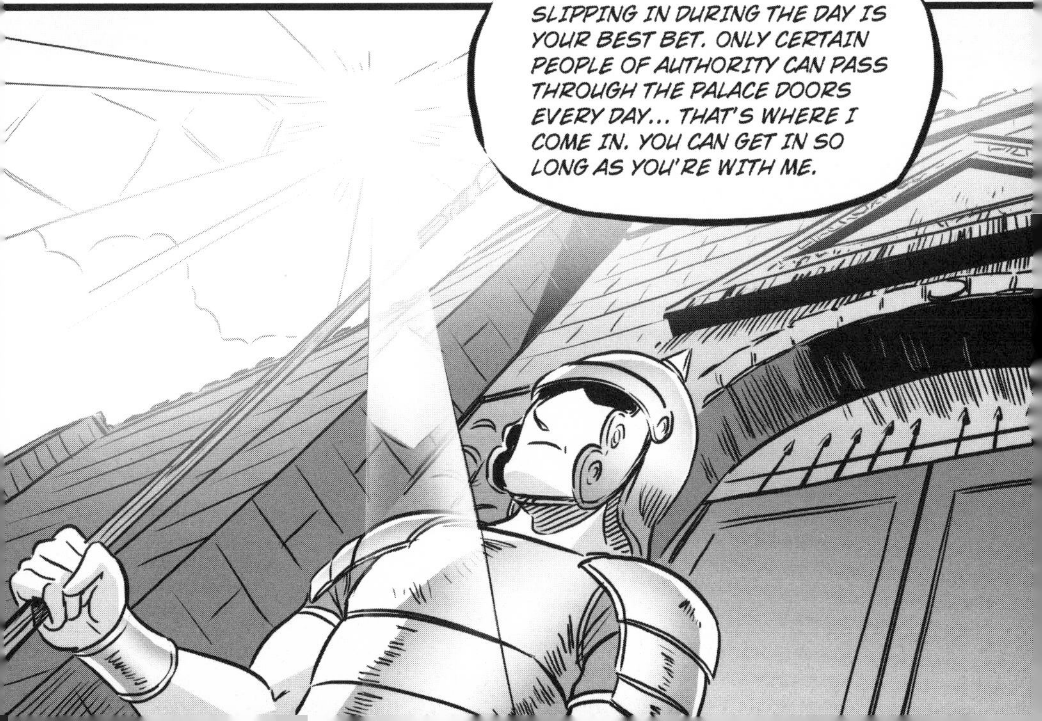
SLIPPING IN DURING THE DAY IS YOUR BEST BET. ONLY CERTAIN PEOPLE OF AUTHORITY CAN PASS THROUGH THE PALACE DOORS EVERY DAY... THAT'S WHERE I COME IN. YOU CAN GET IN SO LONG AS YOU'RE WITH ME.

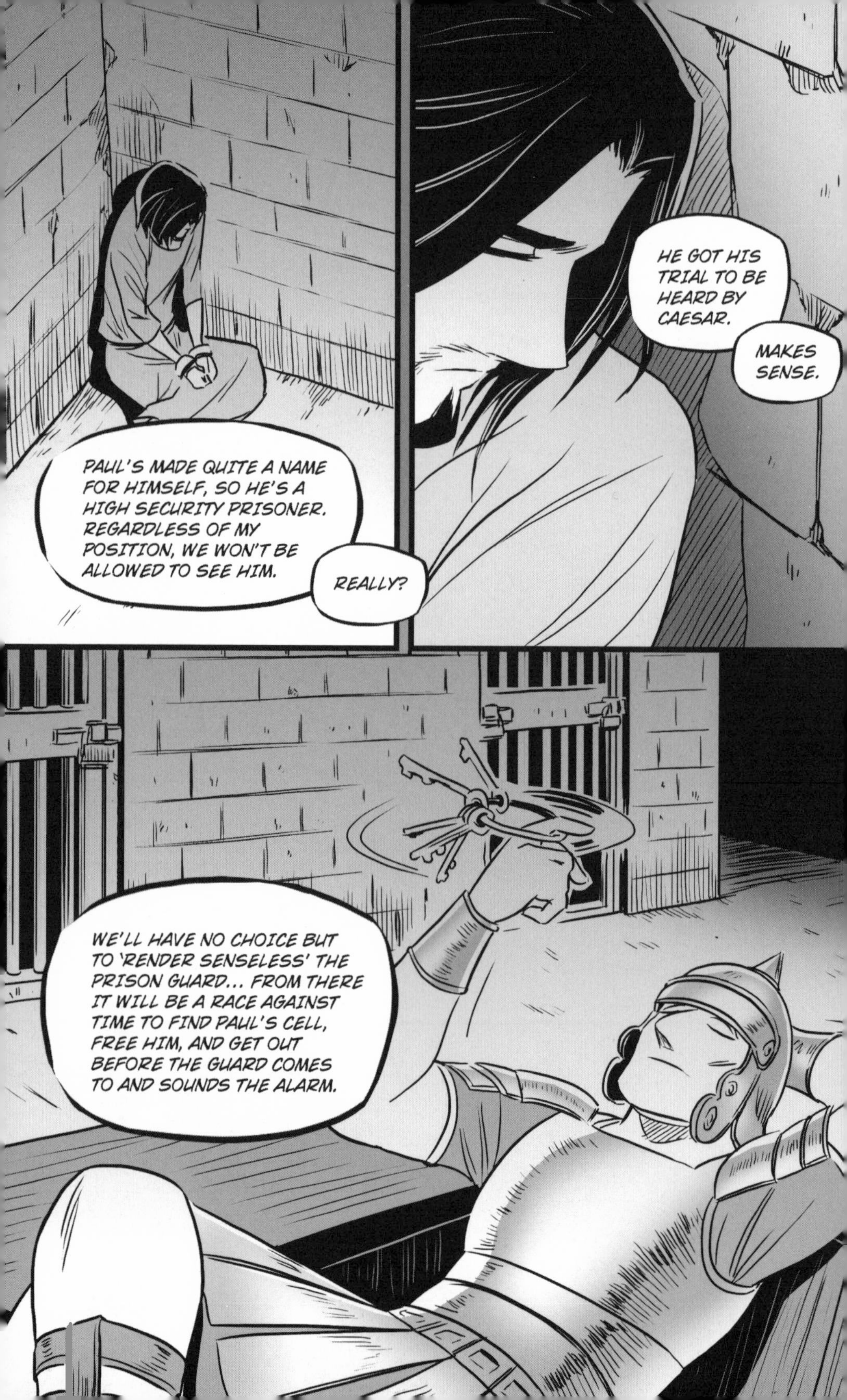
PAUL'S MADE QUITE A NAME FOR HIMSELF, SO HE'S A HIGH SECURITY PRISONER. REGARDLESS OF MY POSITION, WE WON'T BE ALLOWED TO SEE HIM.
REALLY?
HE GOT HIS TRIAL TO BE HEARD BY CAESAR.
MAKES SENSE.
WE'LL HAVE NO CHOICE BUT TO 'RENDER SENSELESS' THE PRISON GUARD... FROM THERE IT WILL BE A RACE AGAINST TIME TO FIND PAUL'S CELL, FREE HIM, AND GET OUT BEFORE THE GUARD COMES TO AND SOUNDS THE ALARM.

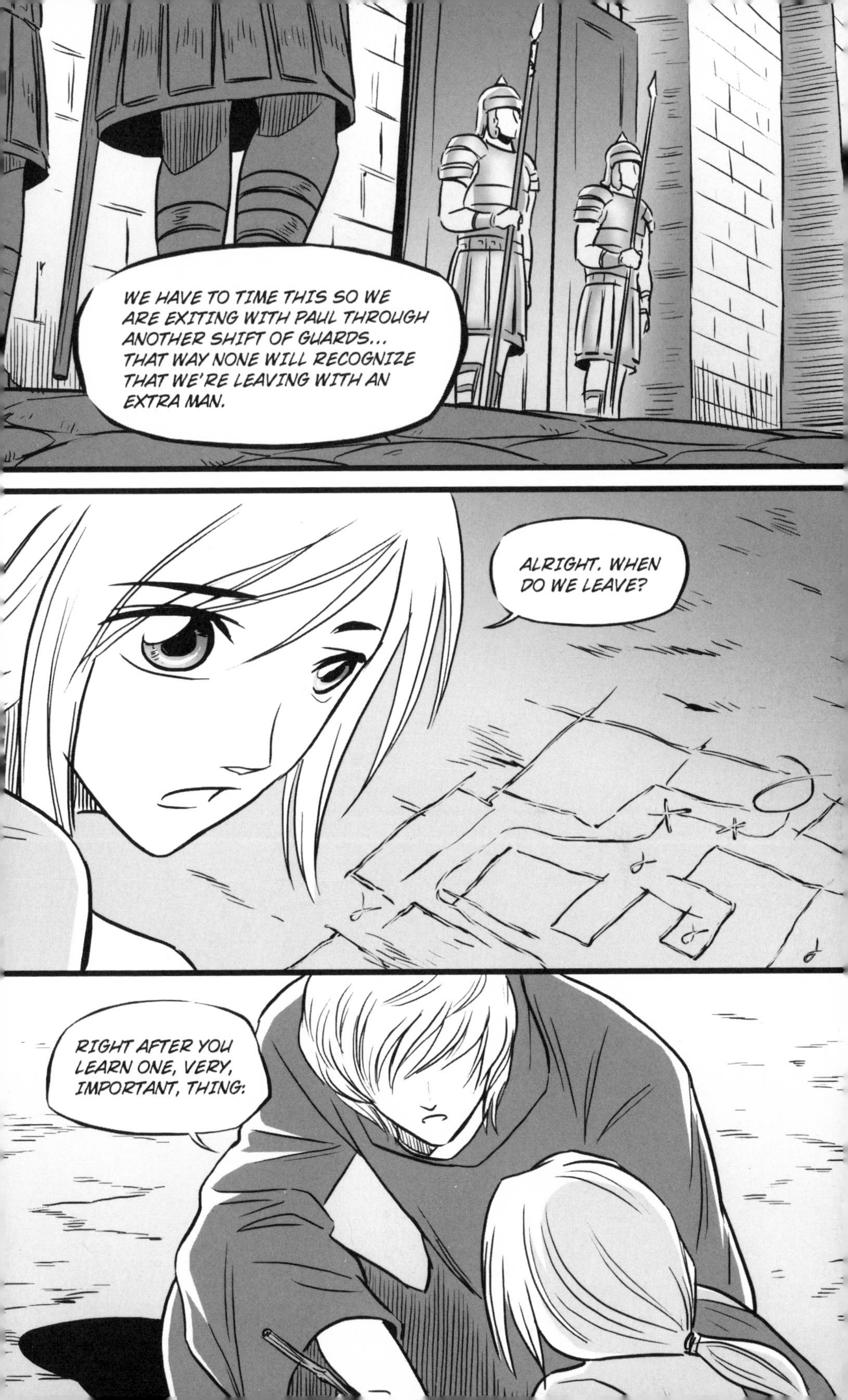
WE HAVE TO TIME THIS SO WE ARE EXITING WITH PAUL THROUGH ANOTHER SHIFT OF GUARDS... THAT WAY NONE WILL RECOGNIZE THAT WE'RE LEAVING WITH AN EXTRA MAN.
ALRIGHT. WHEN DO WE LEAVE?
RIGHT AFTER YOU LEARN ONE, VERY, IMPORTANT, THING:

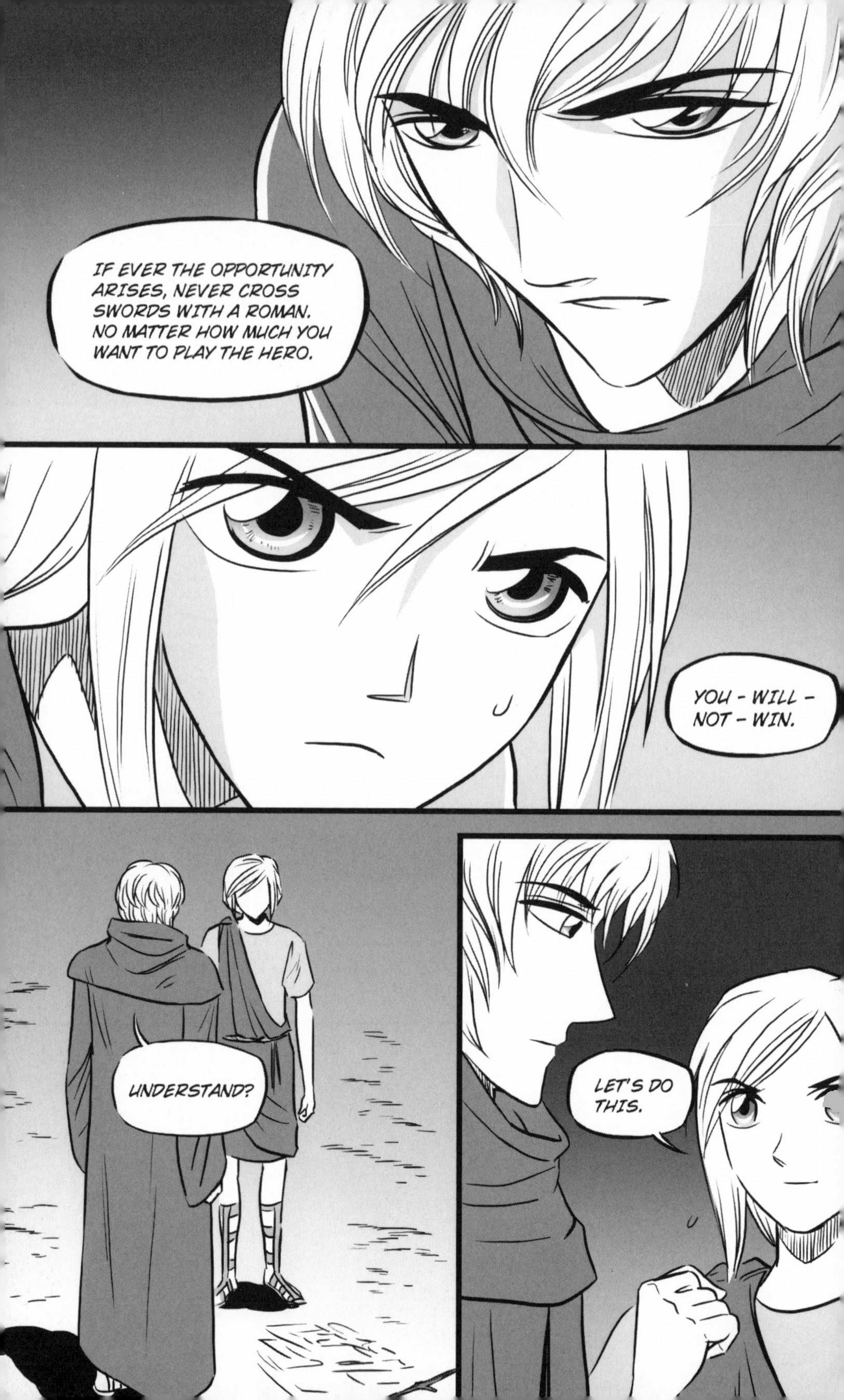
IF EVER THE OPPORTUNITY ARISES, NEVER CROSS SWORDS WITH A ROMAN. NO MATTER HOW MUCH YOU WANT TO PLAY THE HERO.
YOU - WILL - NOT - WIN.
UNDERSTAND?
LET'S DO THIS.

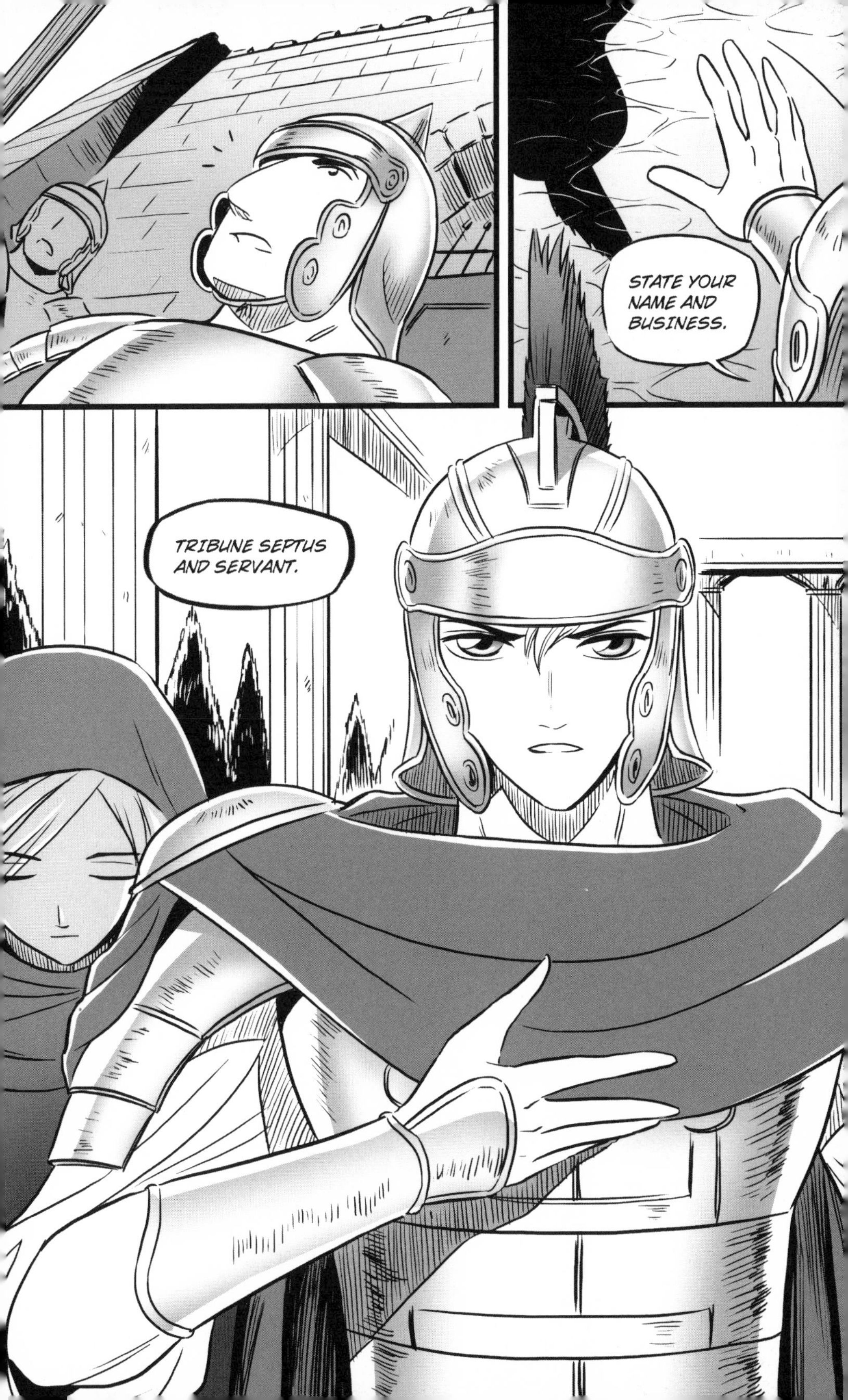
STATE YOUR NAME AND BUSINESS.
TRIBUNE SEPTUS AND SERVANT.

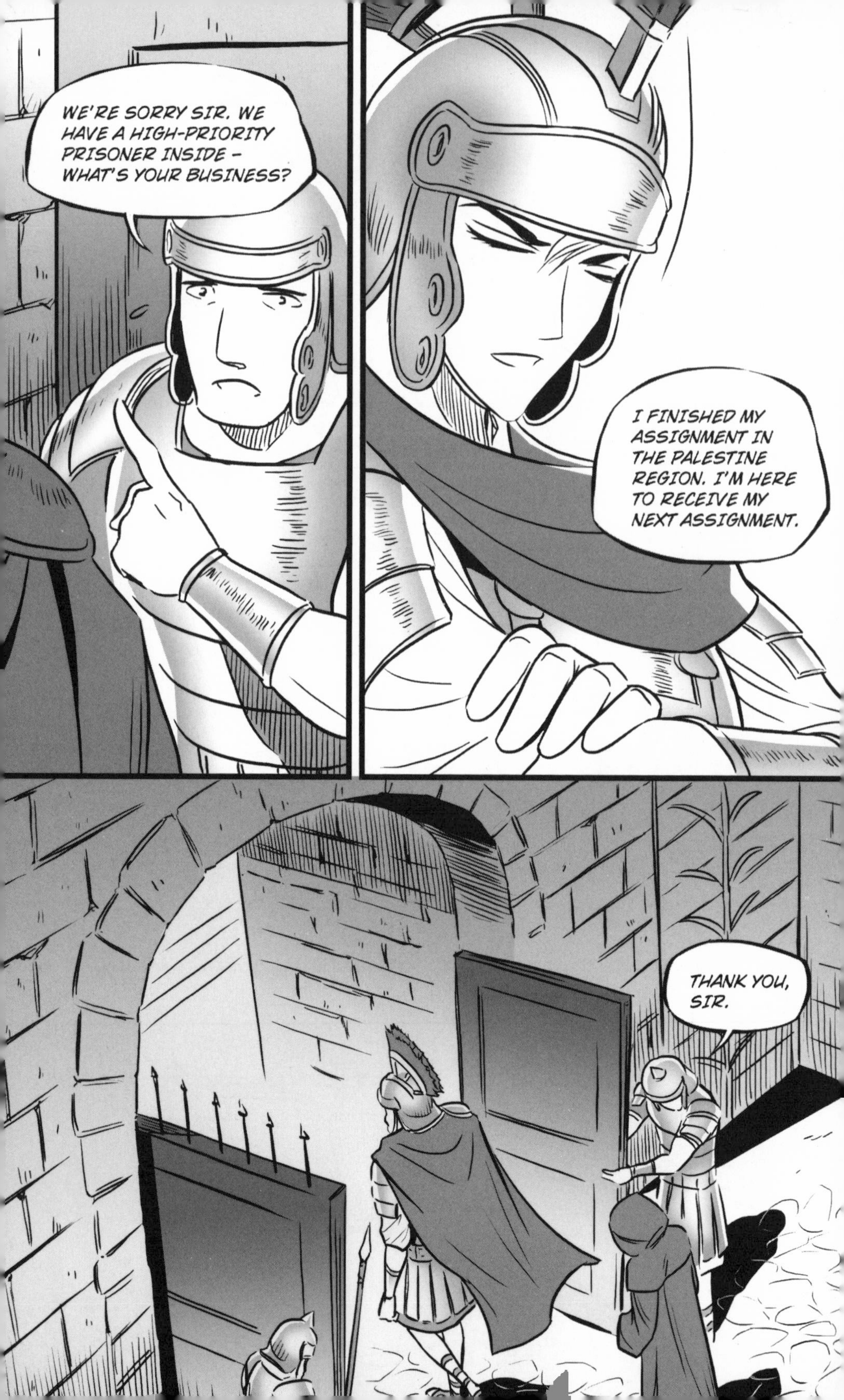
WE'RE SORRY SIR. WE HAVE A HIGH-PRIORITY PRISONER INSIDE – WHAT'S YOUR BUSINESS?
I FINISHED MY ASSIGNMENT IN THE PALESTINE REGION. I'M HERE TO RECEIVE MY NEXT ASSIGNMENT.
THANK YOU, SIR.

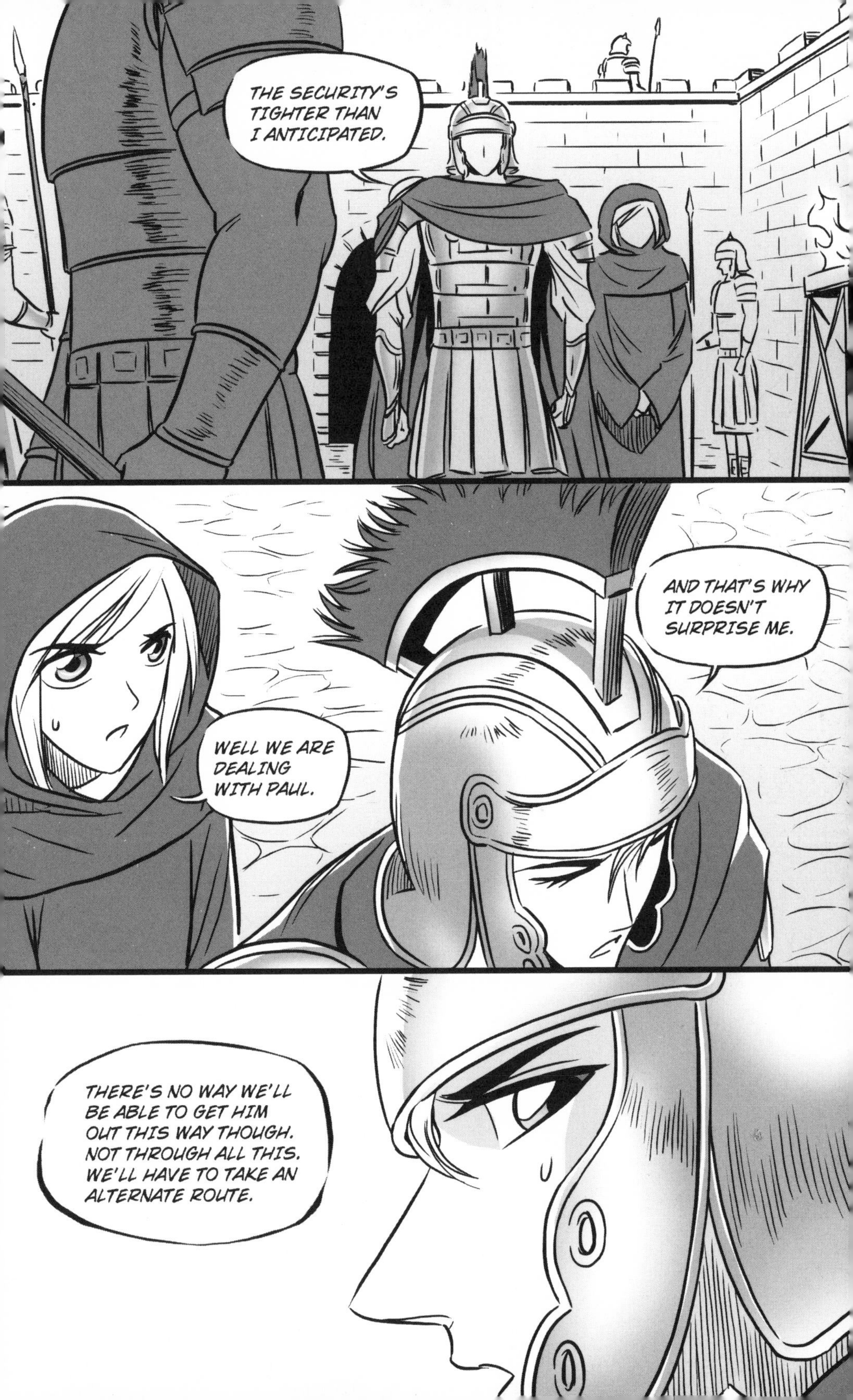
THE SECURITY'S TIGHTER THAN I ANTICIPATED.
AND THAT'S WHY IT DOESN'T SURPRISE ME.
WELL WE ARE DEALING WITH PAUL.
THERE'S NO WAY WE'LL BE ABLE TO GET HIM OUT THIS WAY THOUGH. NOT THROUGH ALL THIS. WE'LL HAVE TO TAKE AN ALTERNATE ROUTE.

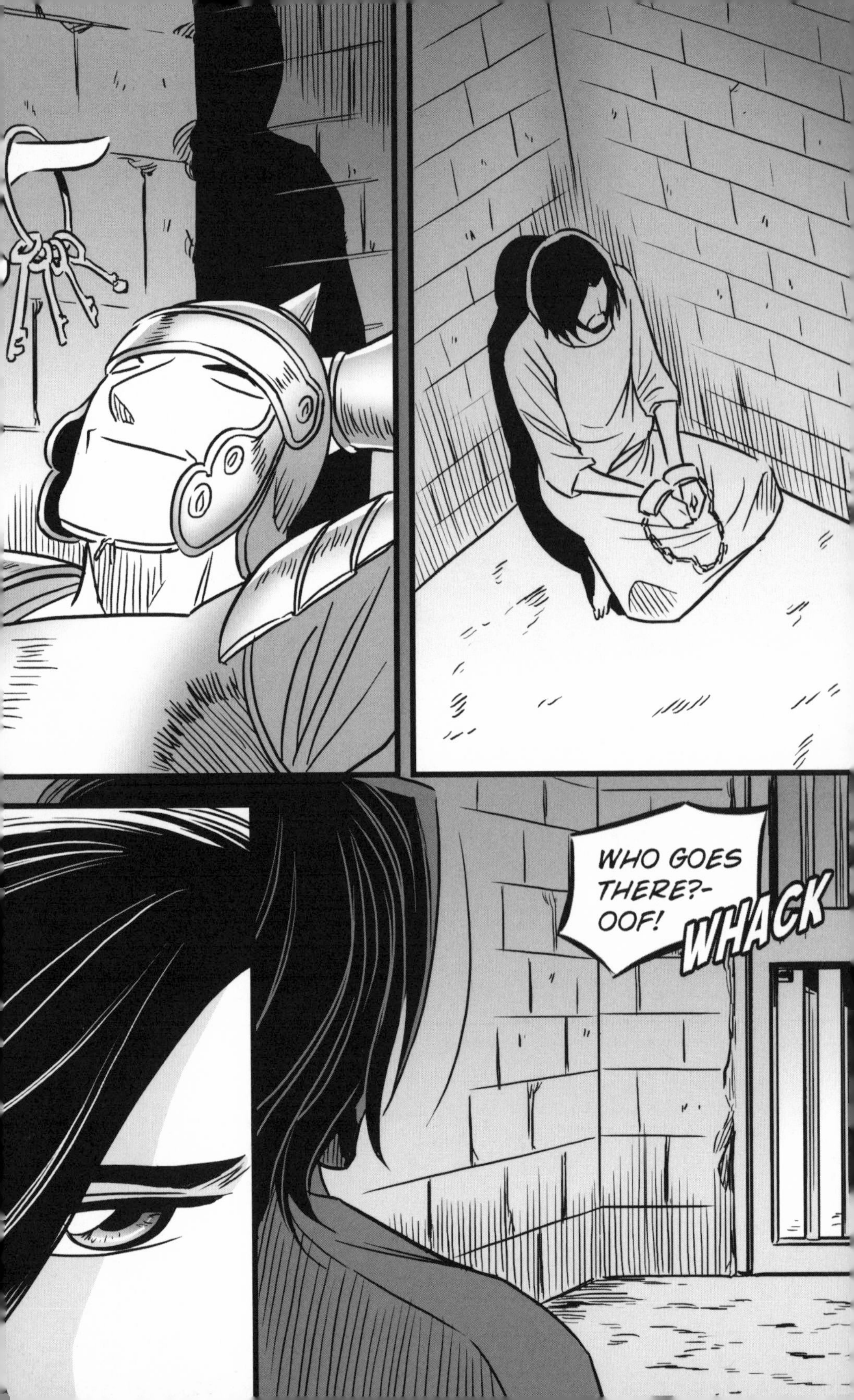
WHO GOES THERE?- OOF!
WHACK

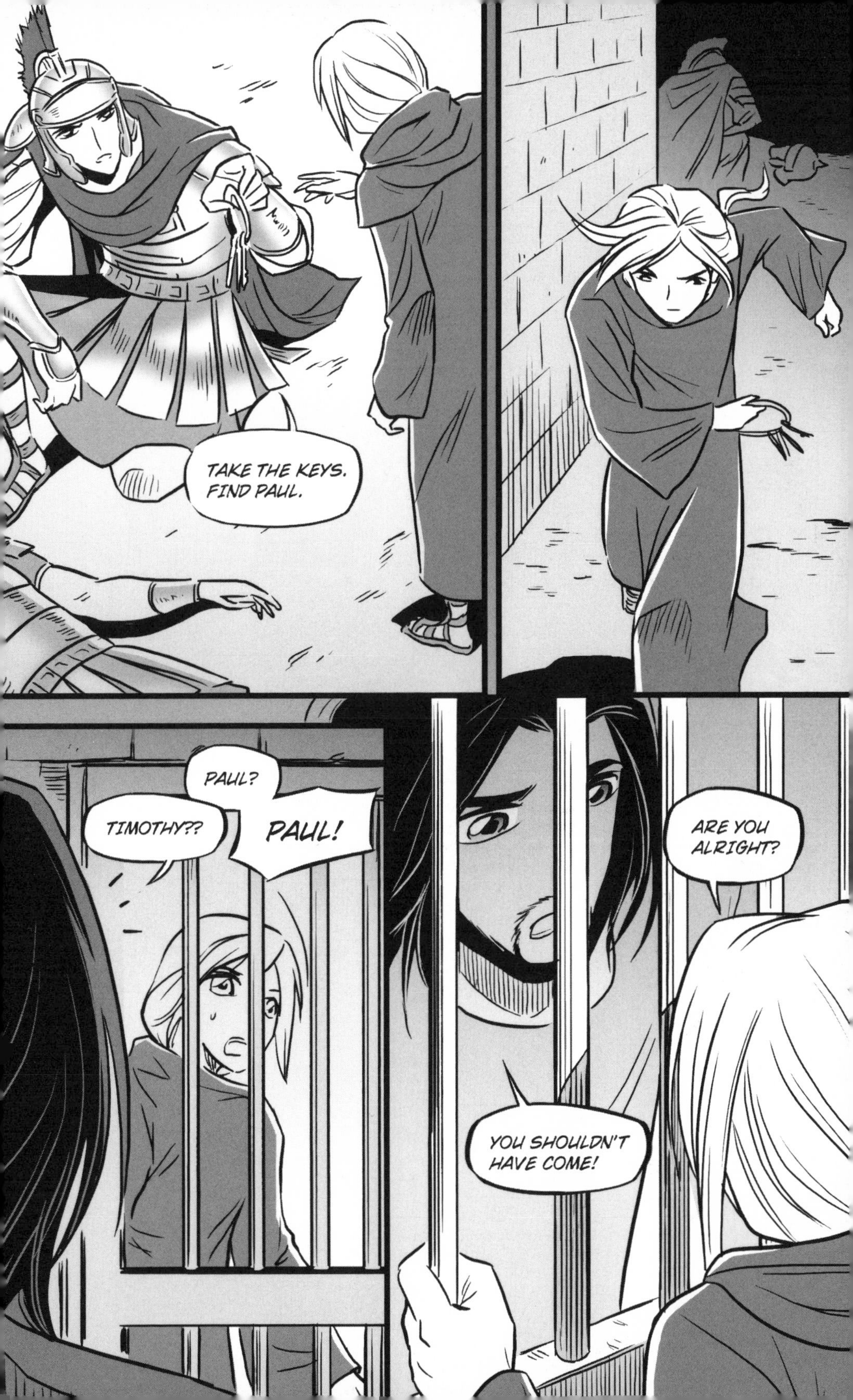
TAKE THE KEYS. FIND PAUL.
PAUL?
TIMOTHY??
PAUL!
ARE YOU ALRIGHT?
YOU SHOULDN'T HAVE COME!

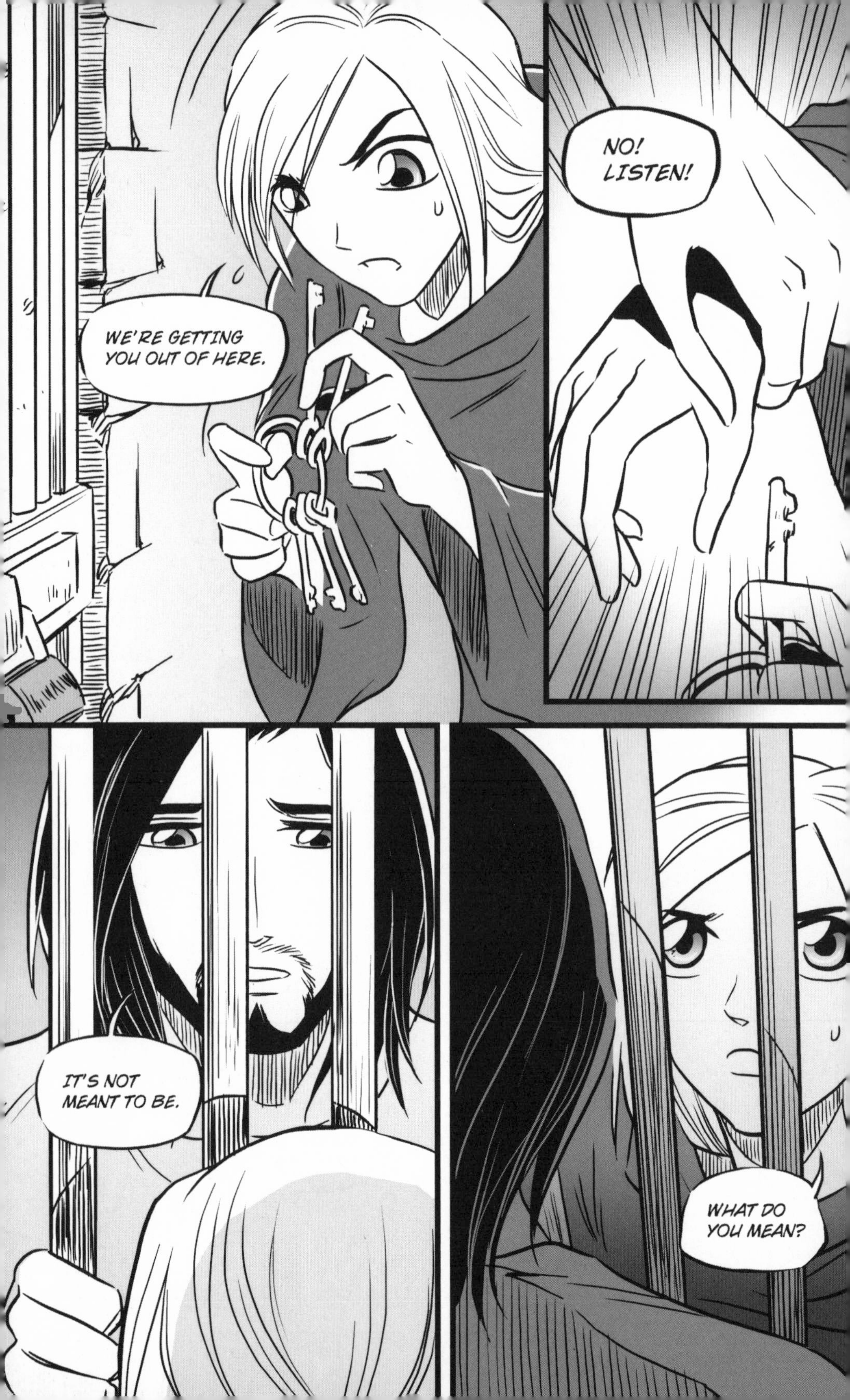
WE'RE GETTING YOU OUT OF HERE.
NO! LISTEN!
IT'S NOT MEANT TO BE.
WHAT DO YOU MEAN?

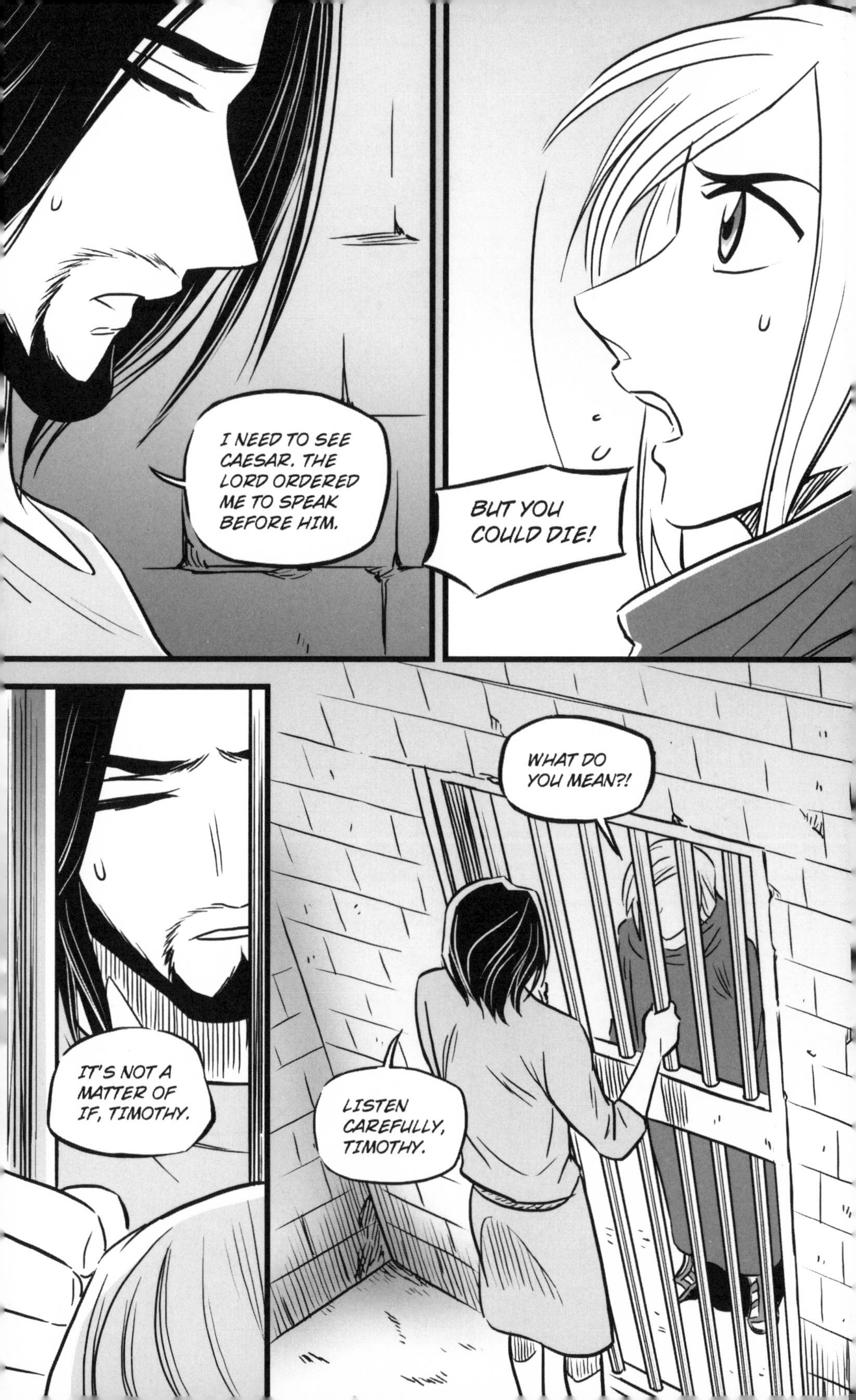
I NEED TO SEE CAESAR. THE LORD ORDERED ME TO SPEAK BEFORE HIM.
BUT YOU COULD DIE!
IT'S NOT A MATTER OF IF, TIMOTHY.
WHAT DO YOU MEAN?!
LISTEN CAREFULLY, TIMOTHY.

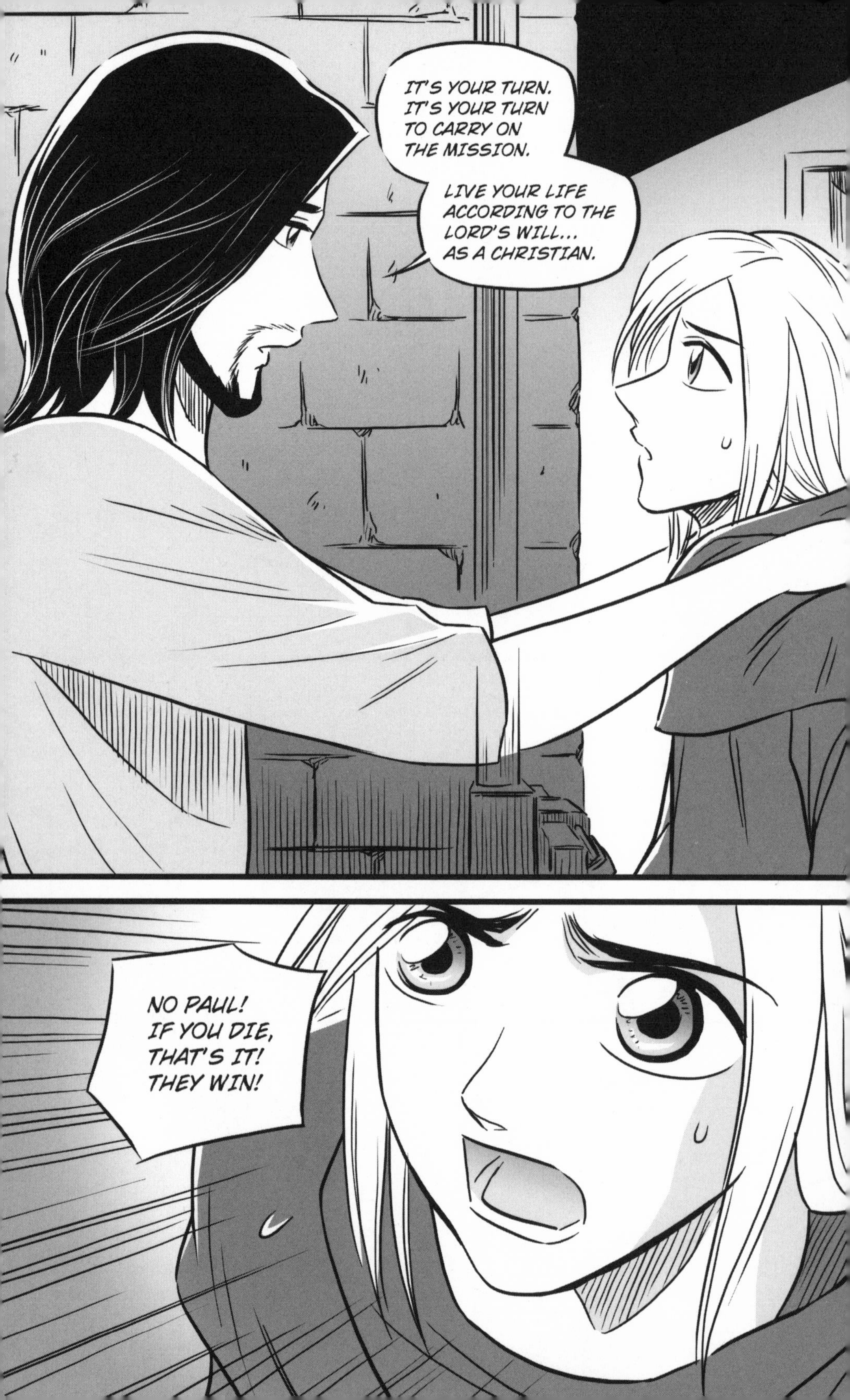
IT'S YOUR TURN. IT'S YOUR TURN TO CARRY ON THE MISSION.
LIVE YOUR LIFE ACCORDING TO THE LORD'S WILL... AS A CHRISTIAN.
NO PAUL! IF YOU DIE, THAT'S IT! THEY WIN!

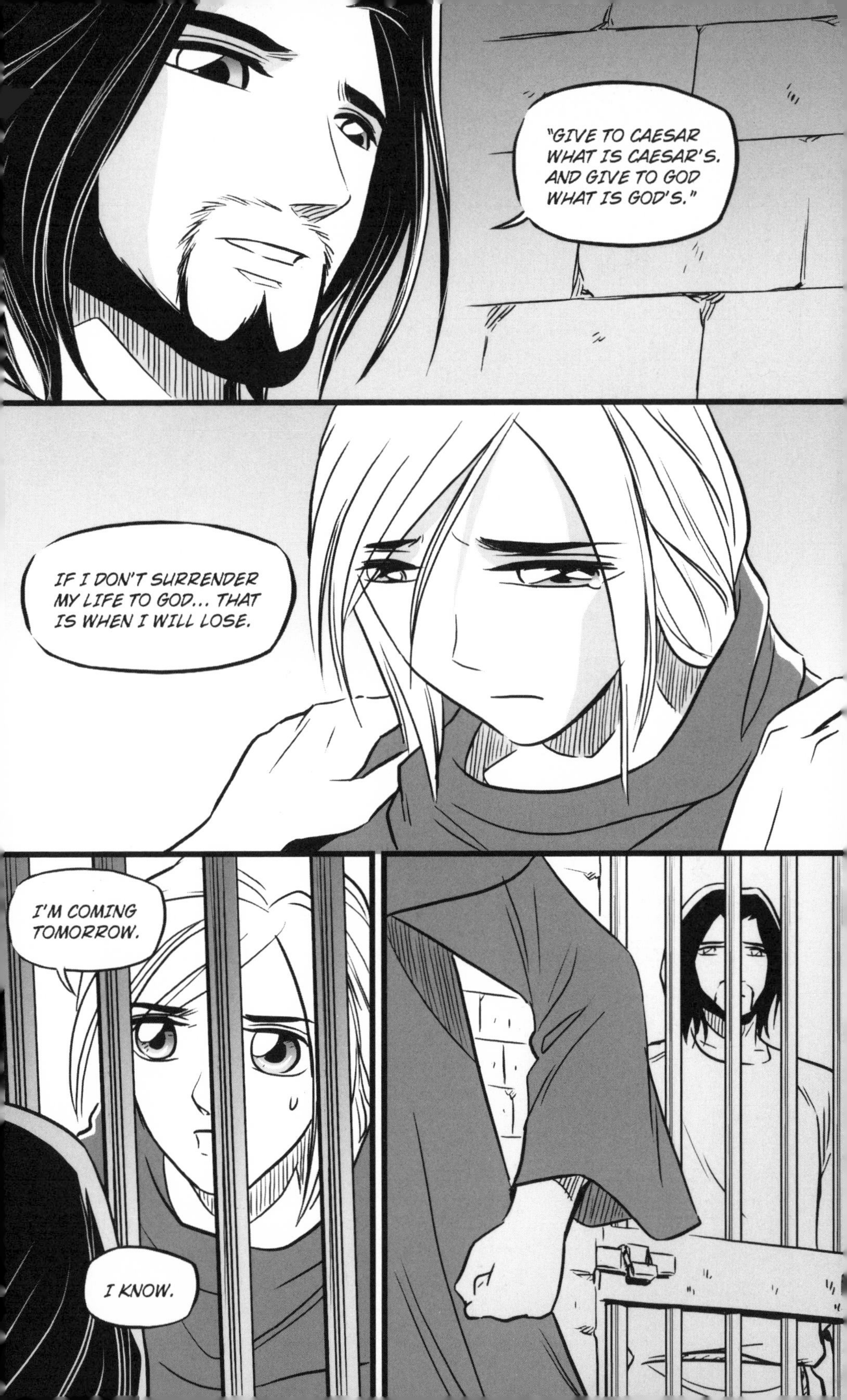
"GIVE TO CAESAR WHAT IS CAESAR'S. AND GIVE TO GOD WHAT IS GOD'S."
IF I DON'T SURRENDER MY LIFE TO GOD... THAT IS WHEN I WILL LOSE.
I'M COMING TOMORROW.
I KNOW.

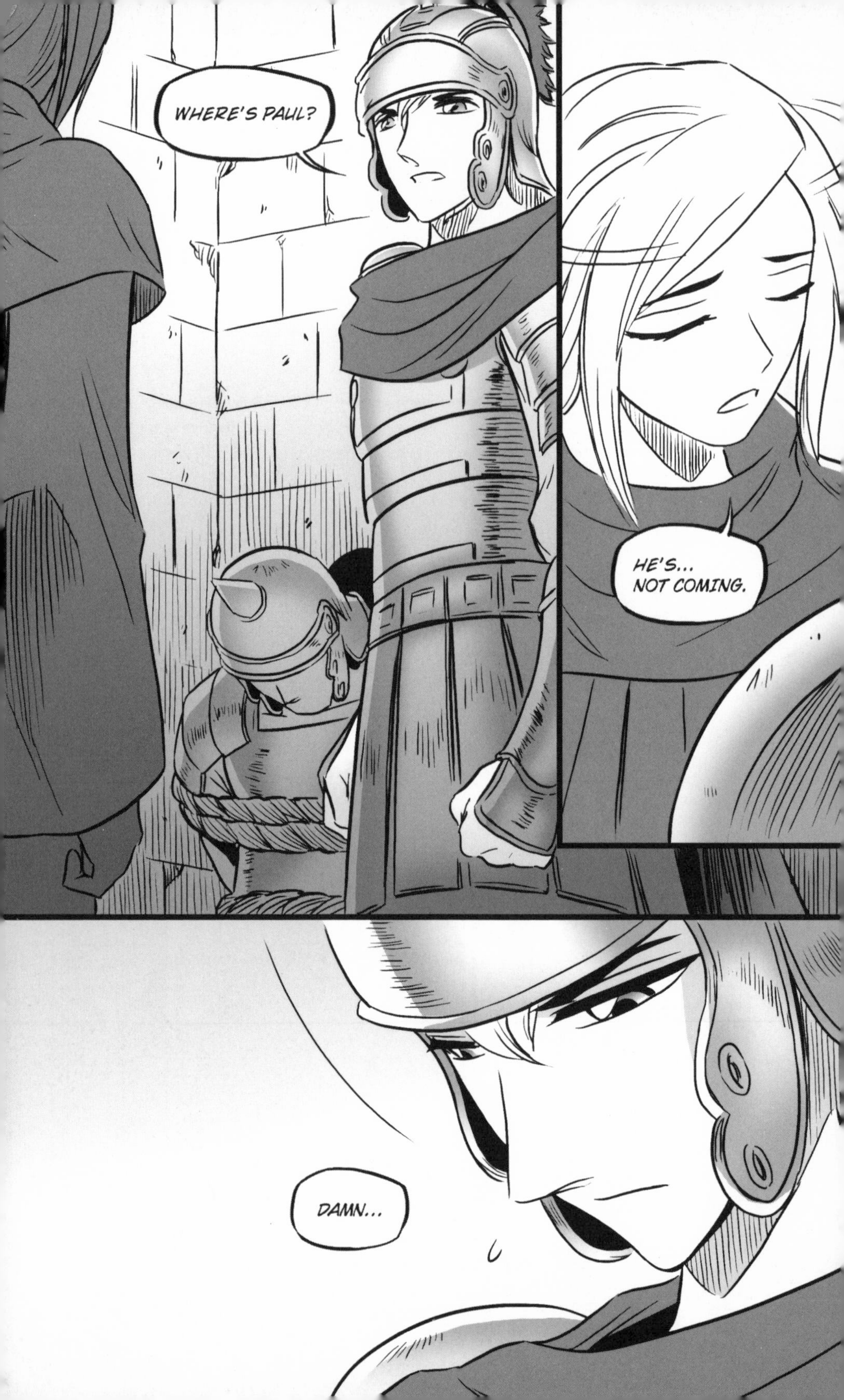
WHERE'S PAUL?
HE'S... NOT COMING.
DAMN...

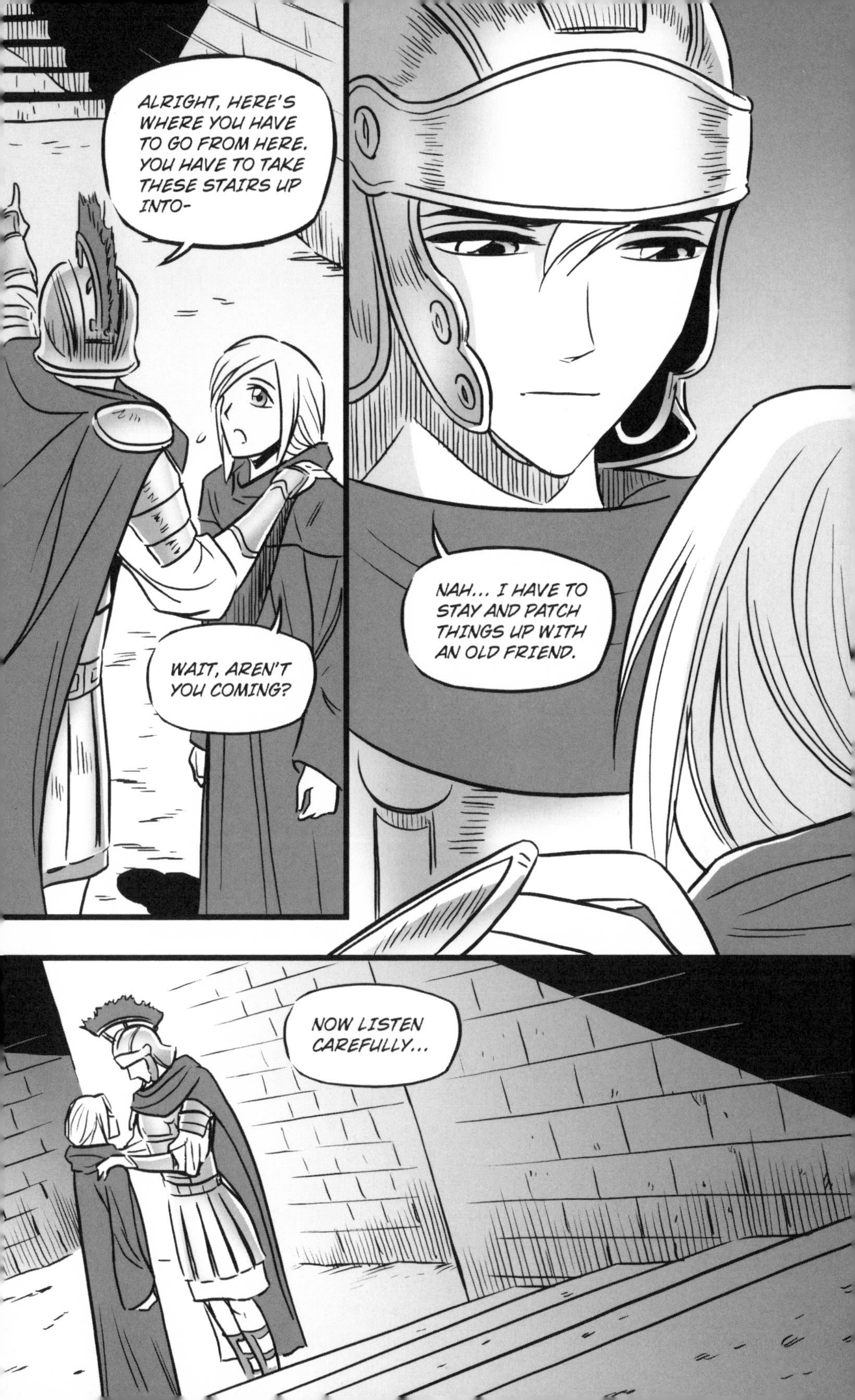
ALRIGHT, HERE'S WHERE YOU HAVE TO GO FROM HERE. YOU HAVE TO TAKE THESE STAIRS UP INTO-
WAIT, AREN'T YOU COMING?
NAH... I HAVE TO STAY AND PATCH THINGS UP WITH AN OLD FRIEND.
NOW LISTEN CAREFULLY...

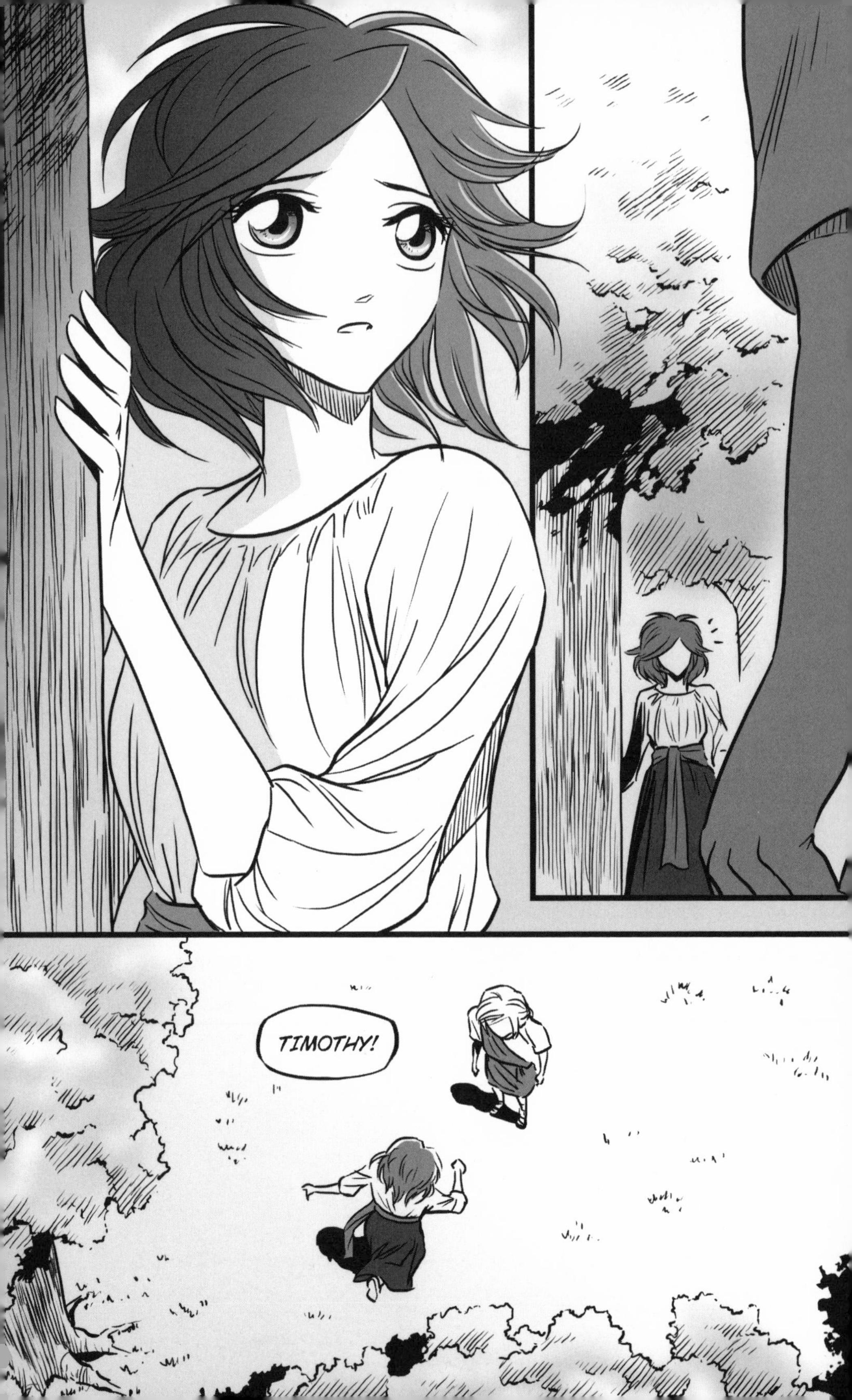
TIMOTHY!

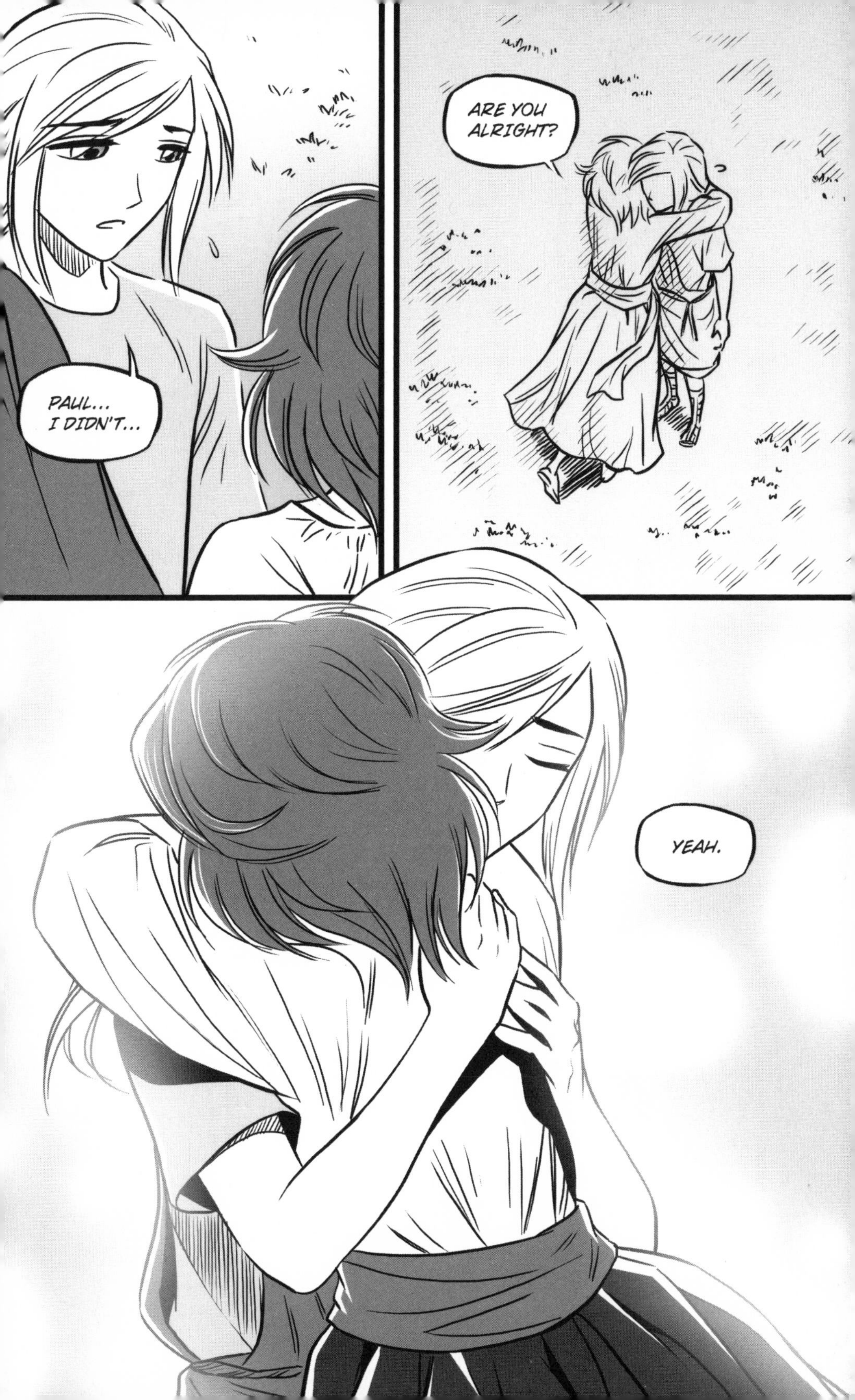
PAUL...
I DIDN'T...
ARE YOU
ALRIGHT?
YEAH.

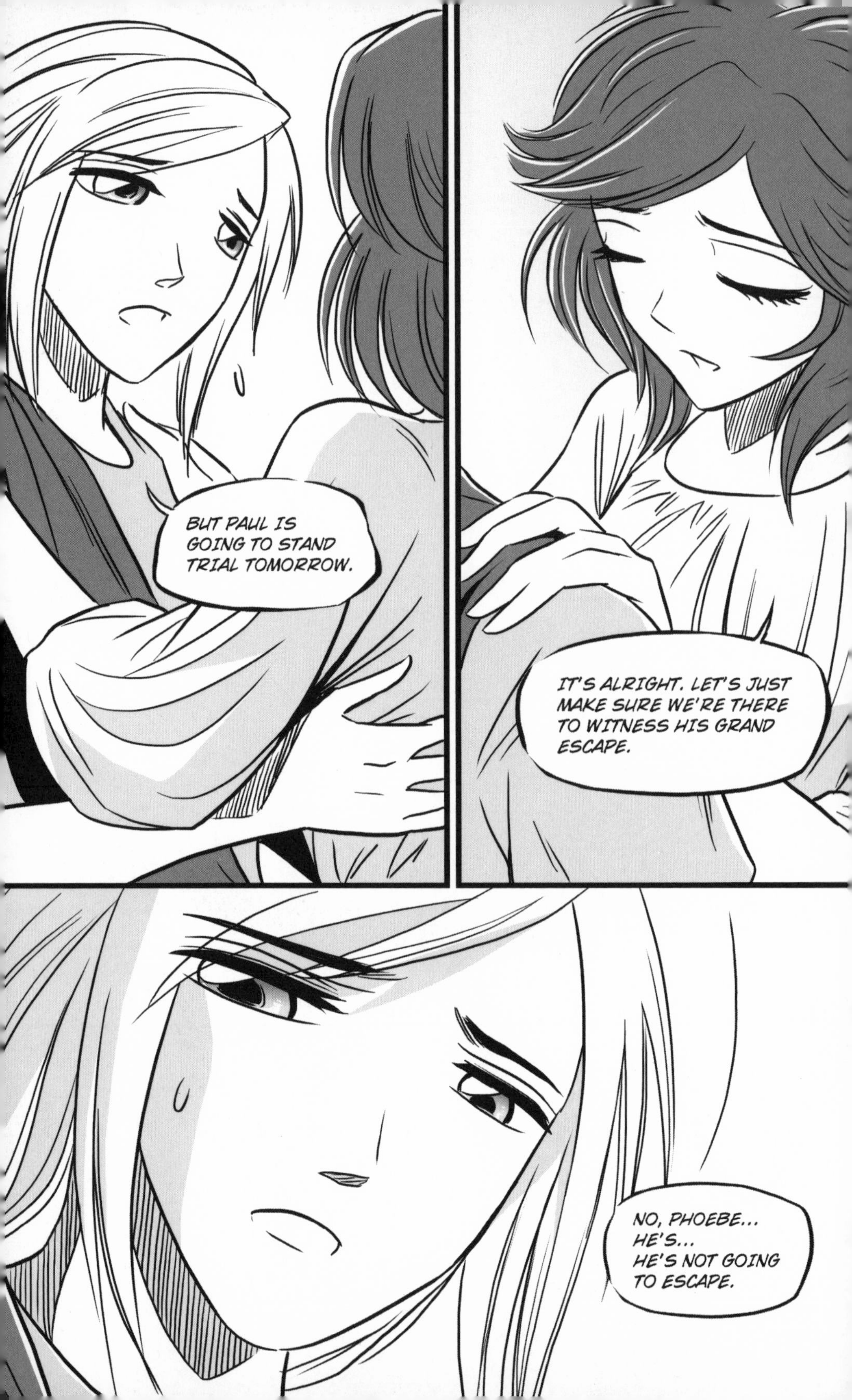
BUT PAUL IS GOING TO STAND TRIAL TOMORROW.
IT'S ALRIGHT. LET'S JUST MAKE SURE WE'RE THERE TO WITNESS HIS GRAND ESCAPE.
NO, PHOEBE... HE'S... HE'S NOT GOING TO ESCAPE.

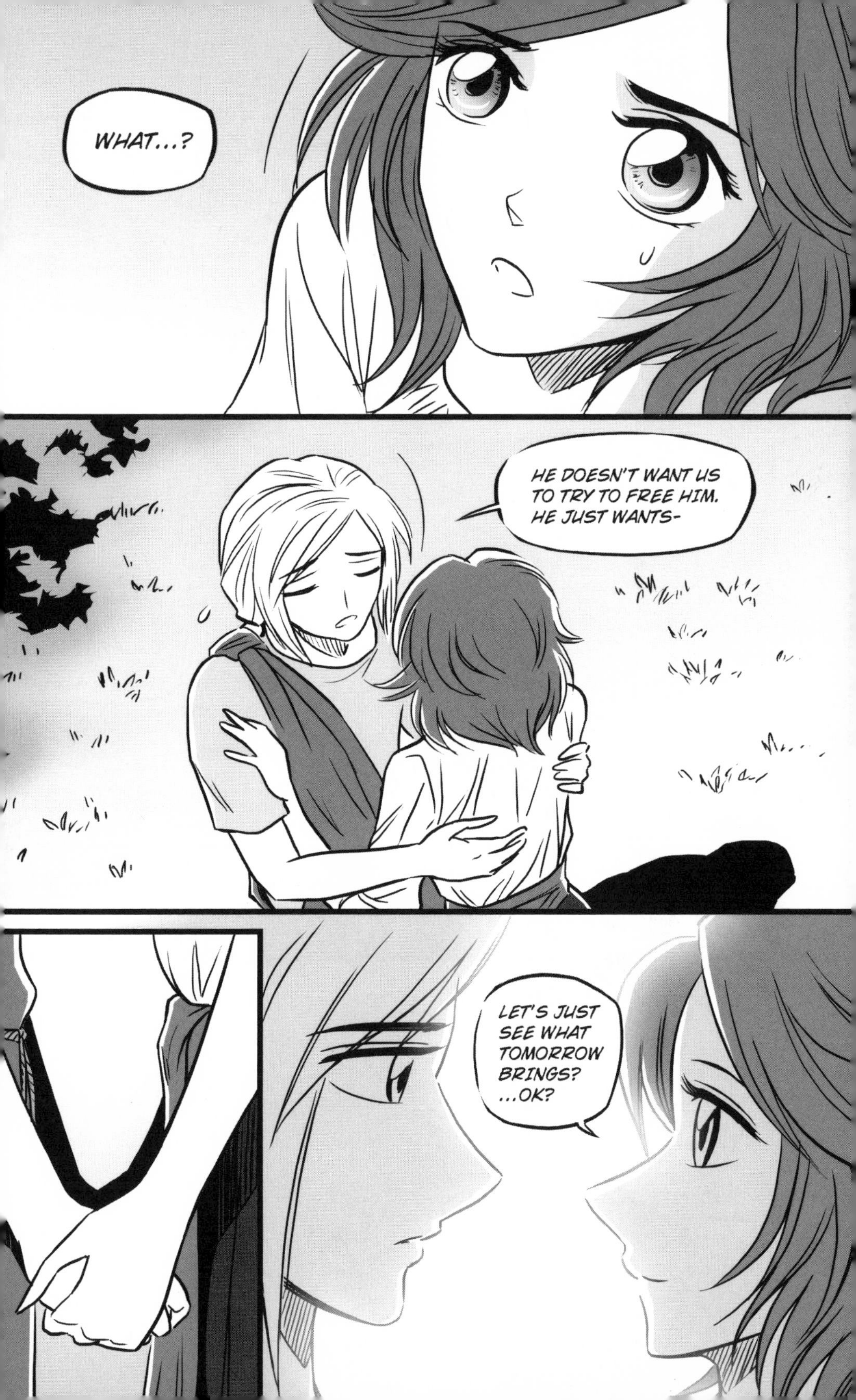
WHAT...?
HE DOESN'T WANT US TO TRY TO FREE HIM. HE JUST WANTS-
LET'S JUST SEE WHAT TOMORROW BRINGS? ...OK?

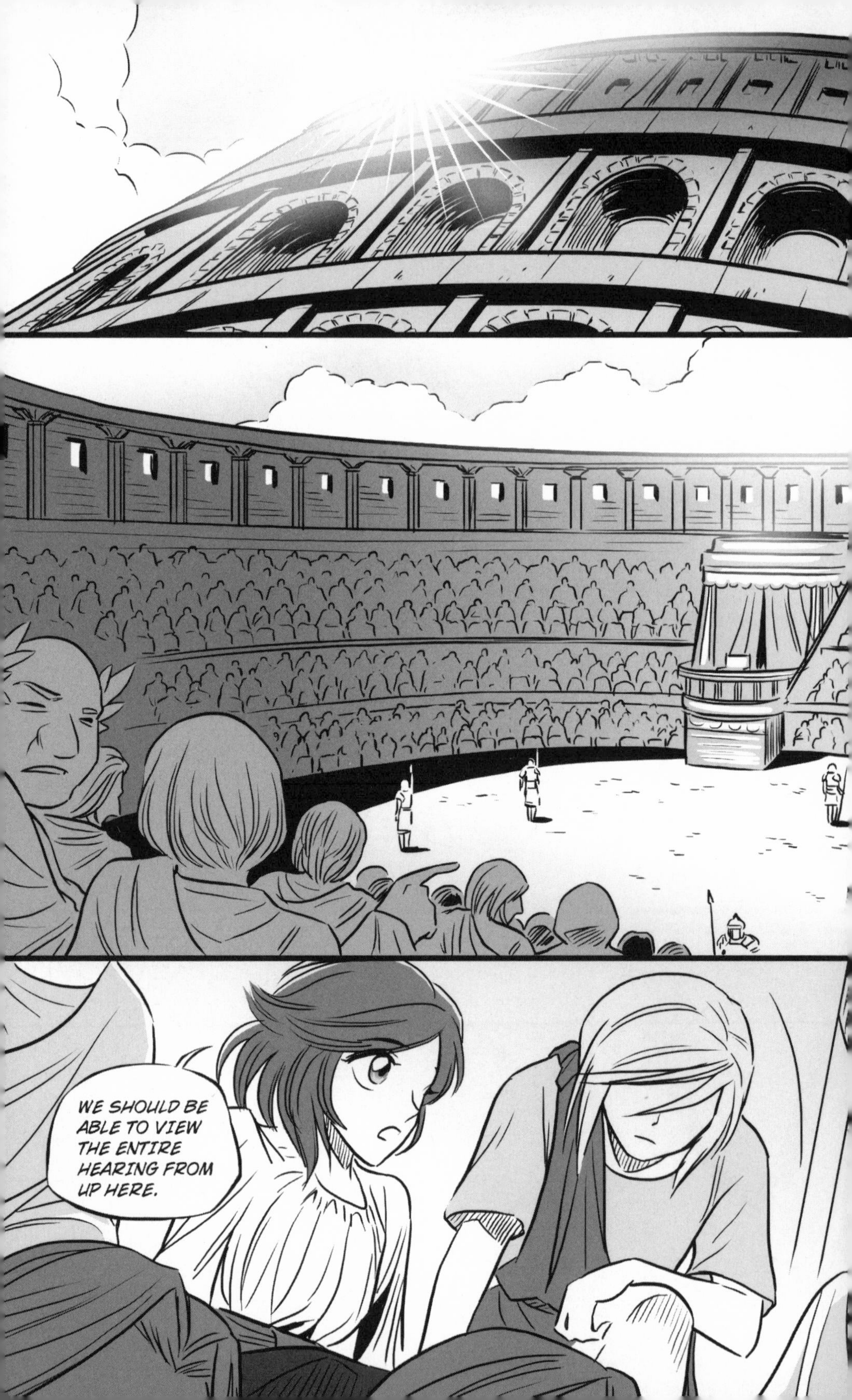
WE SHOULD BE ABLE TO VIEW THE ENTIRE HEARING FROM UP HERE.

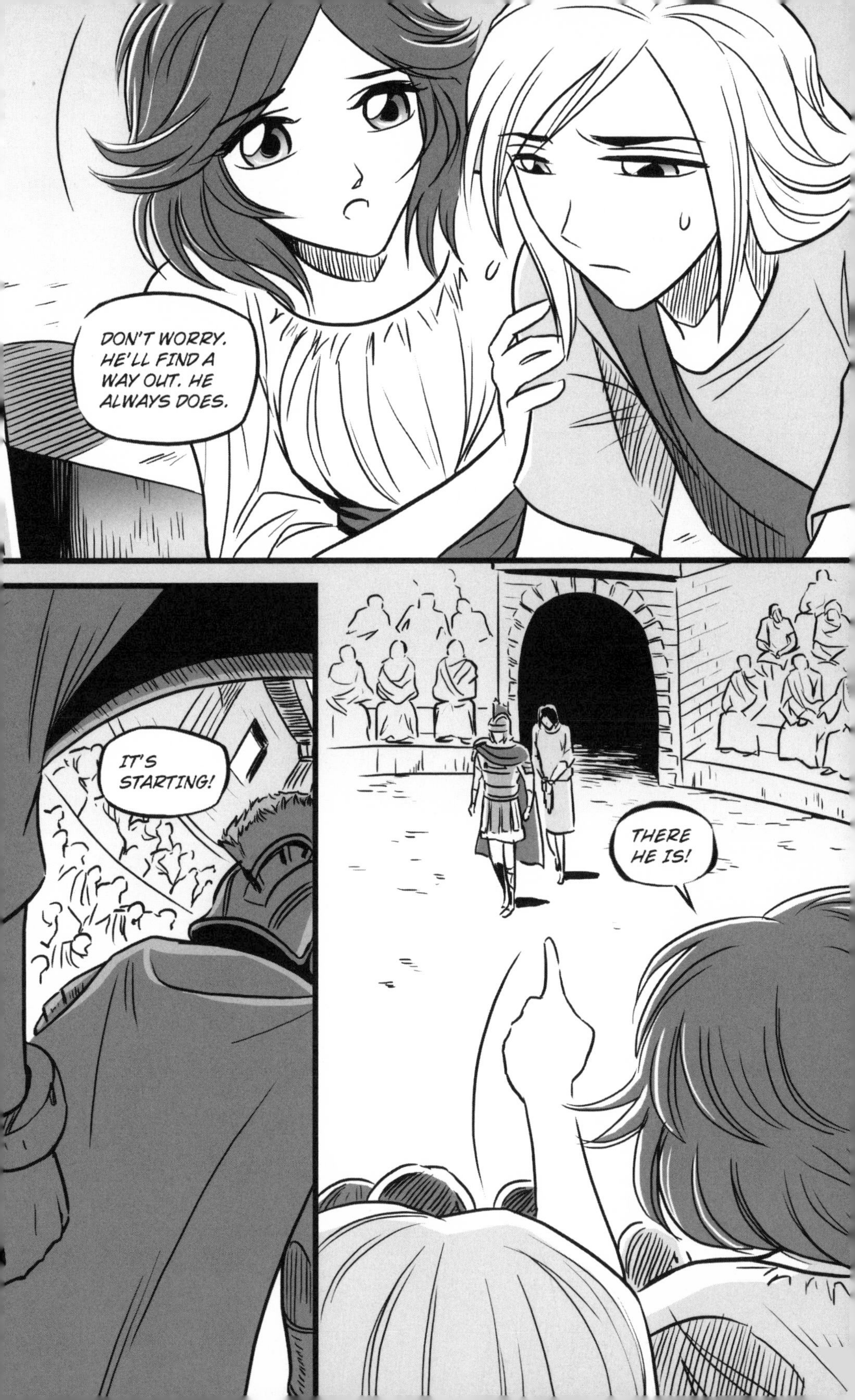
DON'T WORRY. HE'LL FIND A WAY OUT. HE ALWAYS DOES.
IT'S STARTING!
THERE HE IS!

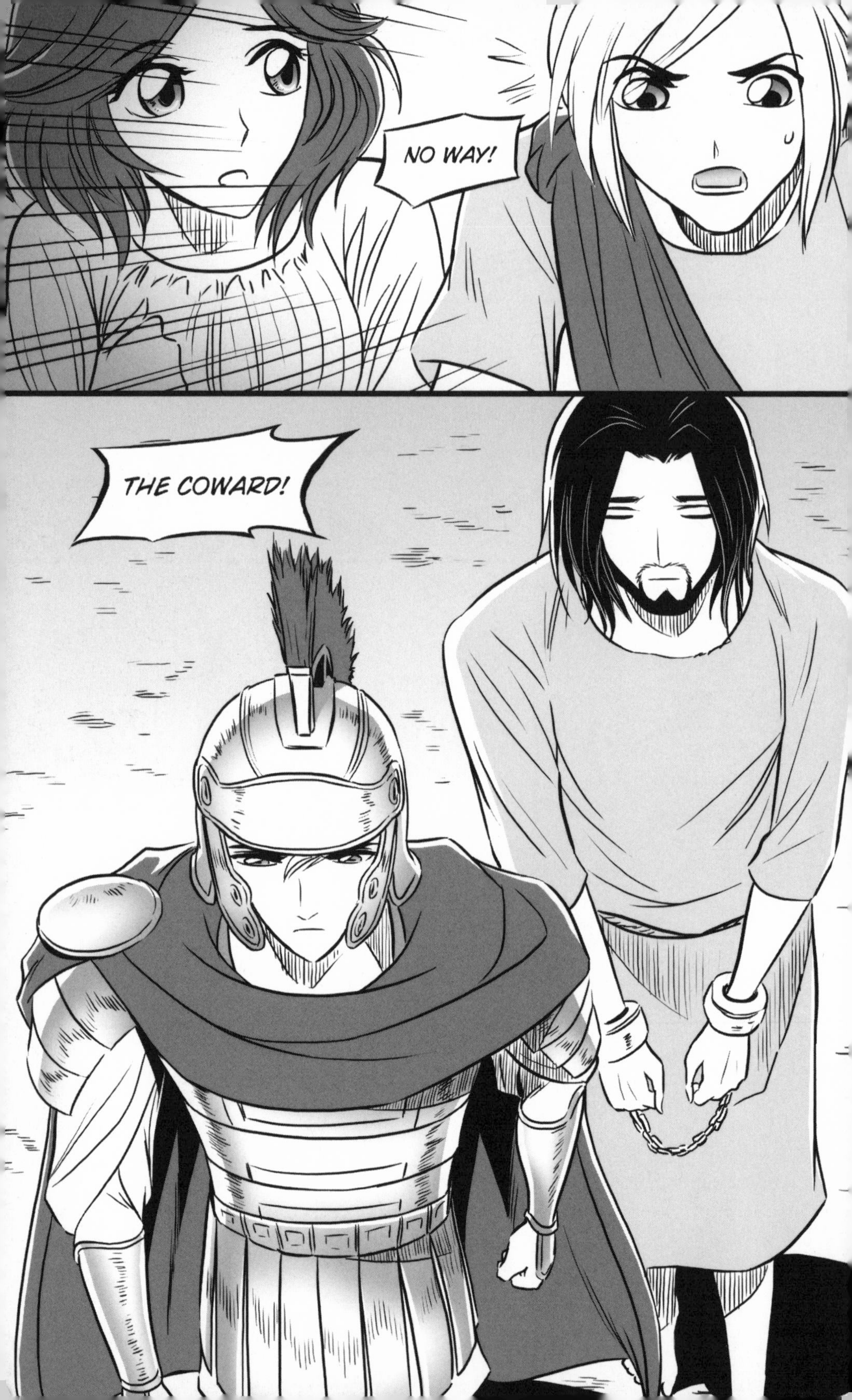
NO WAY!
THE COWARD!

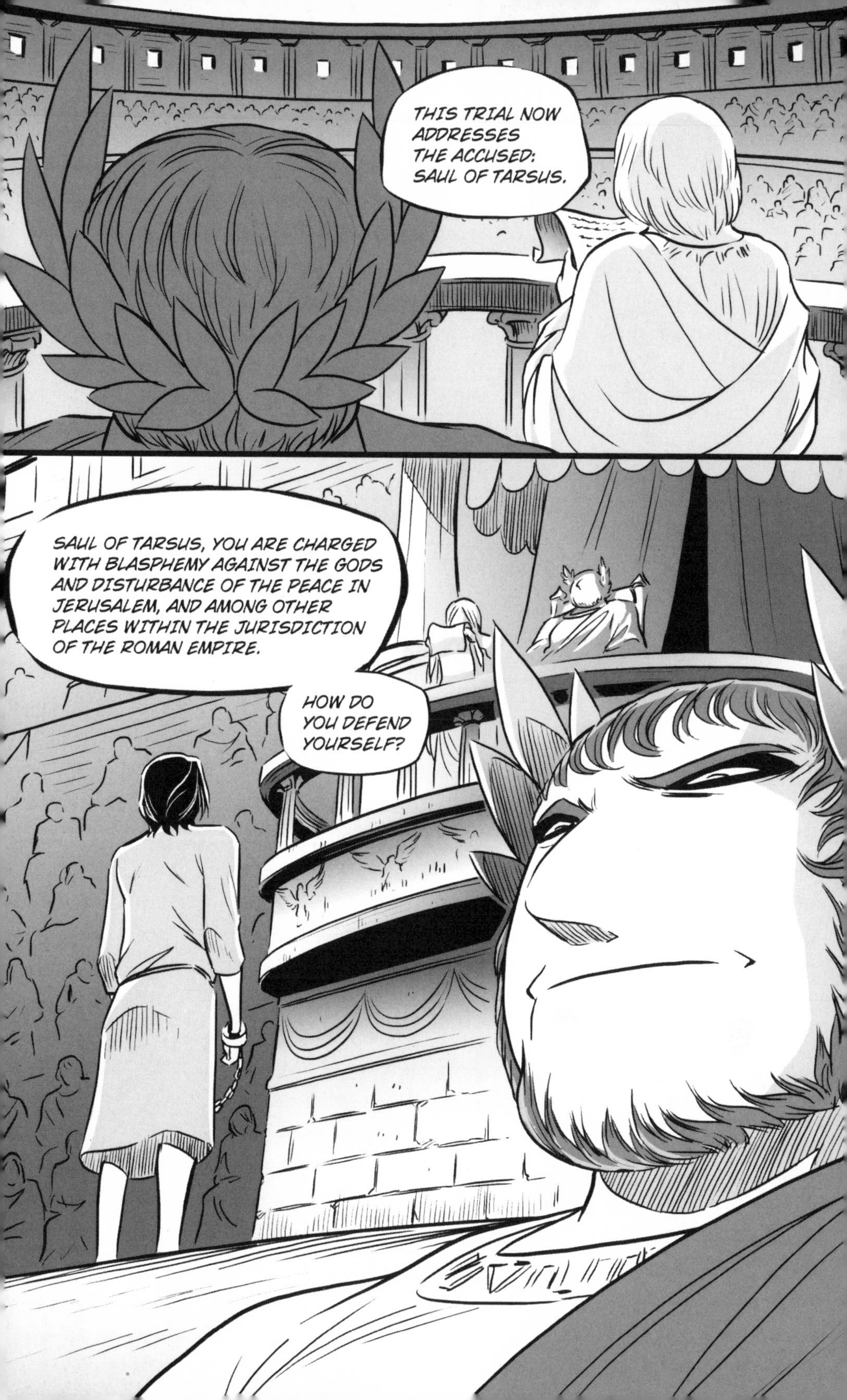
THIS TRIAL NOW ADDRESSES THE ACCUSED: SAUL OF TARSUS.
SAUL OF TARSUS, YOU ARE CHARGED WITH BLASPHEMY AGAINST THE GODS AND DISTURBANCE OF THE PEACE IN JERUSALEM, AND AMONG OTHER PLACES WITHIN THE JURISDICTION OF THE ROMAN EMPIRE.
HOW DO YOU DEFEND YOURSELF?

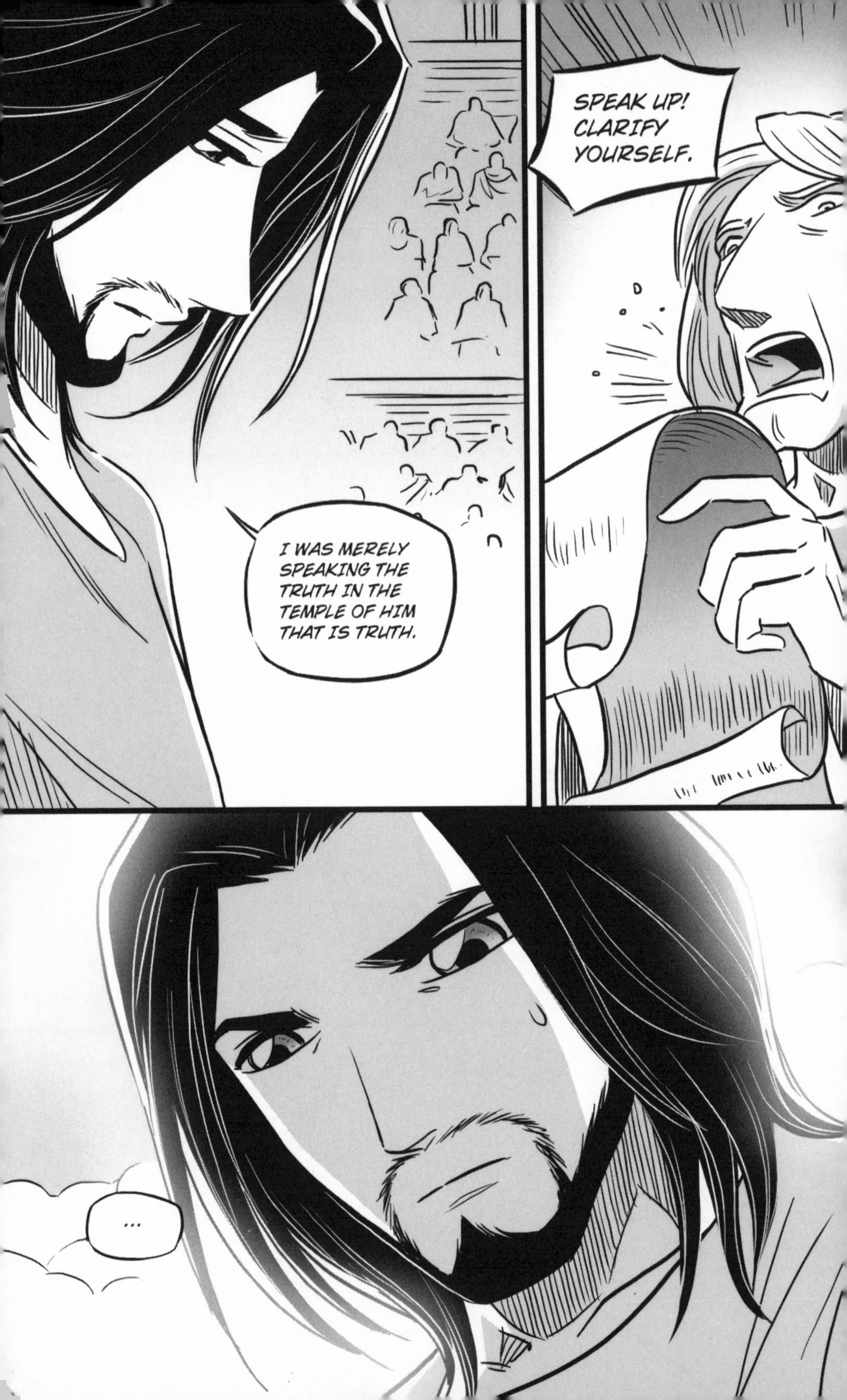
I WAS MERELY SPEAKING THE TRUTH IN THE TEMPLE OF HIM THAT IS TRUTH.
SPEAK UP! CLARIFY YOURSELF.
...

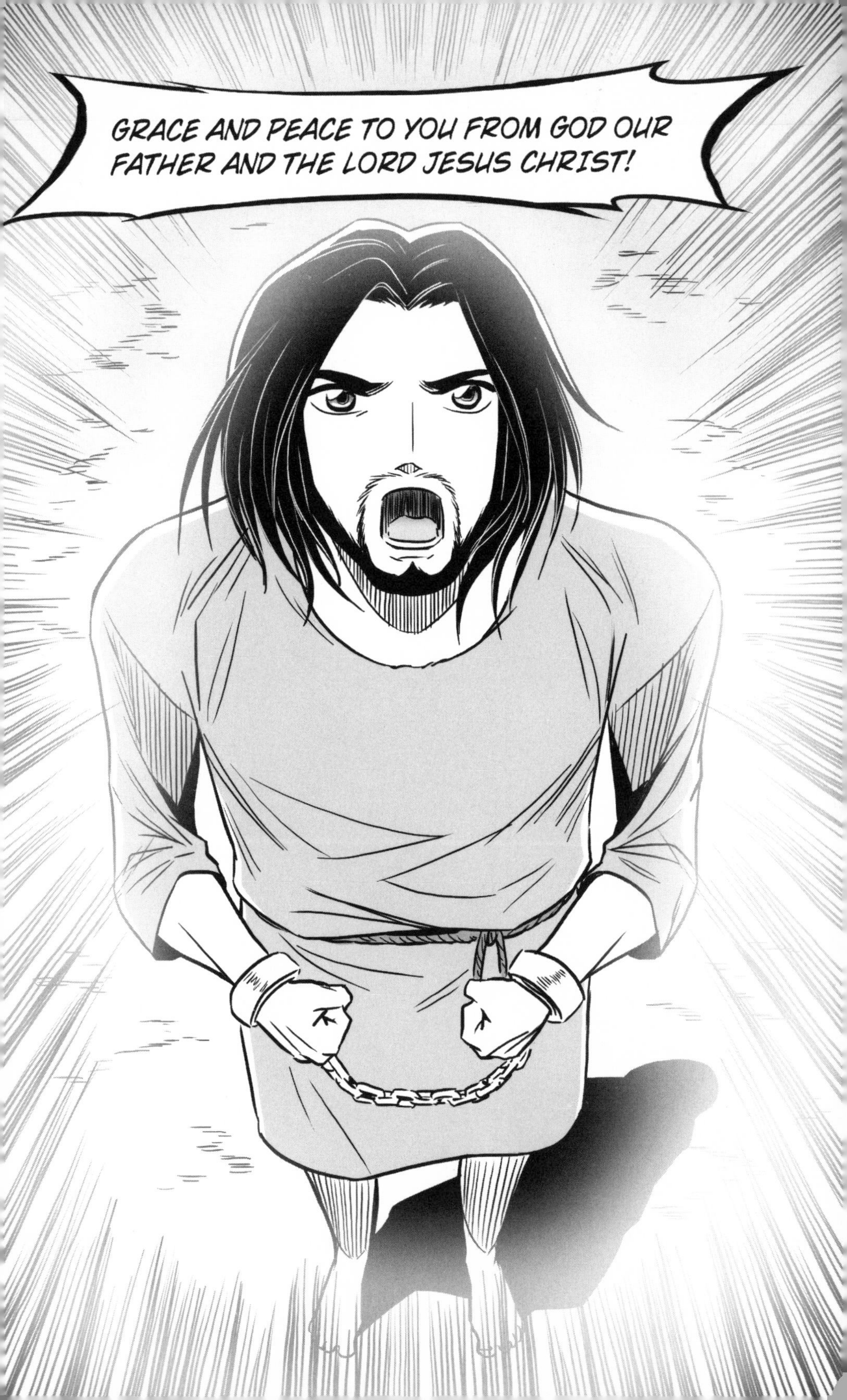
GRACE AND PEACE TO YOU FROM GOD OUR FATHER AND THE LORD JESUS CHRIST!

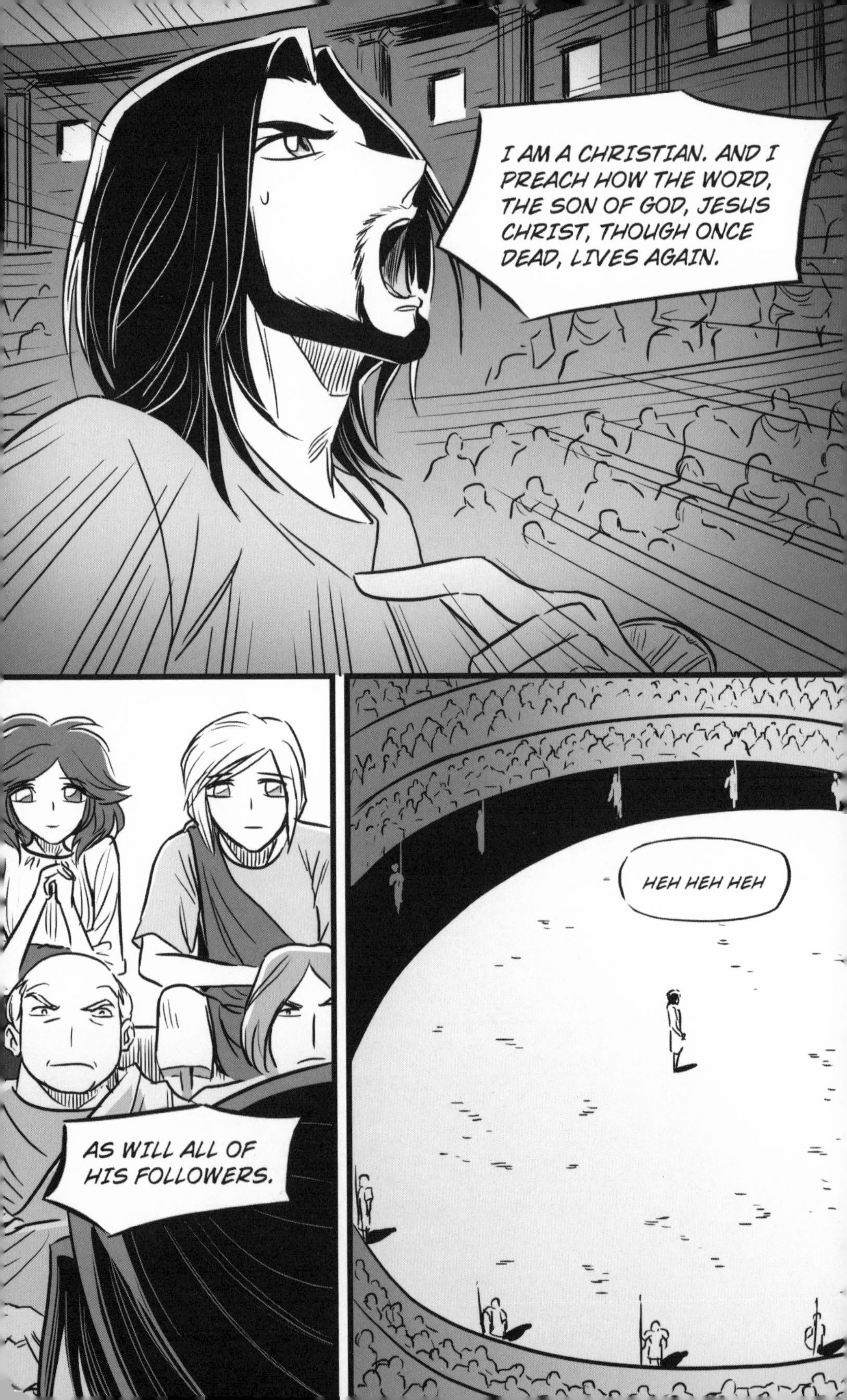
I AM A CHRISTIAN. AND I PREACH HOW THE WORD, THE SON OF GOD, JESUS CHRIST, THOUGH ONCE DEAD, LIVES AGAIN.
AS WILL ALL OF HIS FOLLOWERS.
HEH HEH HEH

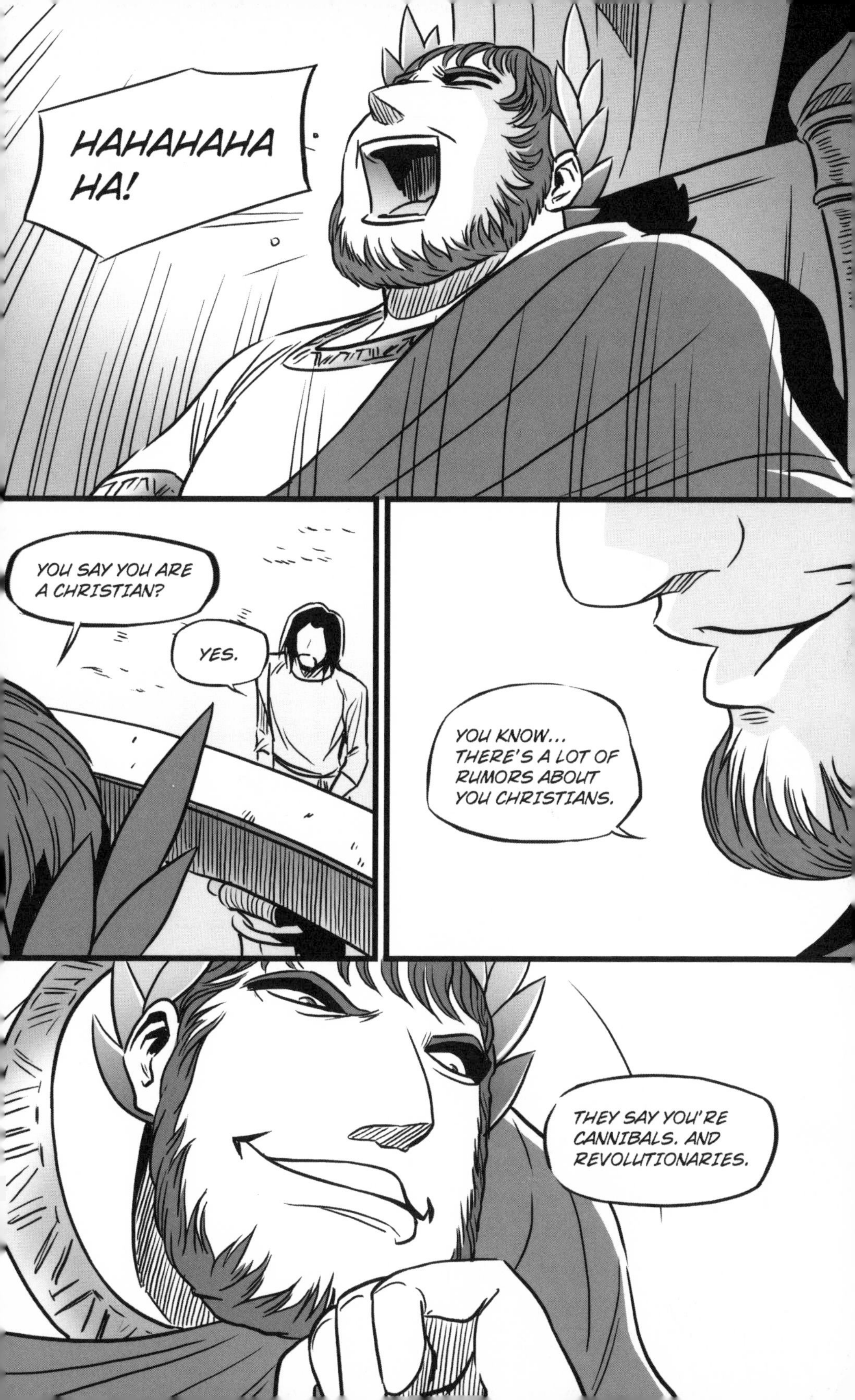
HAHAHAHA HA!
YOU SAY YOU ARE A CHRISTIAN?
YES.
YOU KNOW... THERE'S A LOT OF RUMORS ABOUT YOU CHRISTIANS.
THEY SAY YOU'RE CANNIBALS. AND REVOLUTIONARIES.

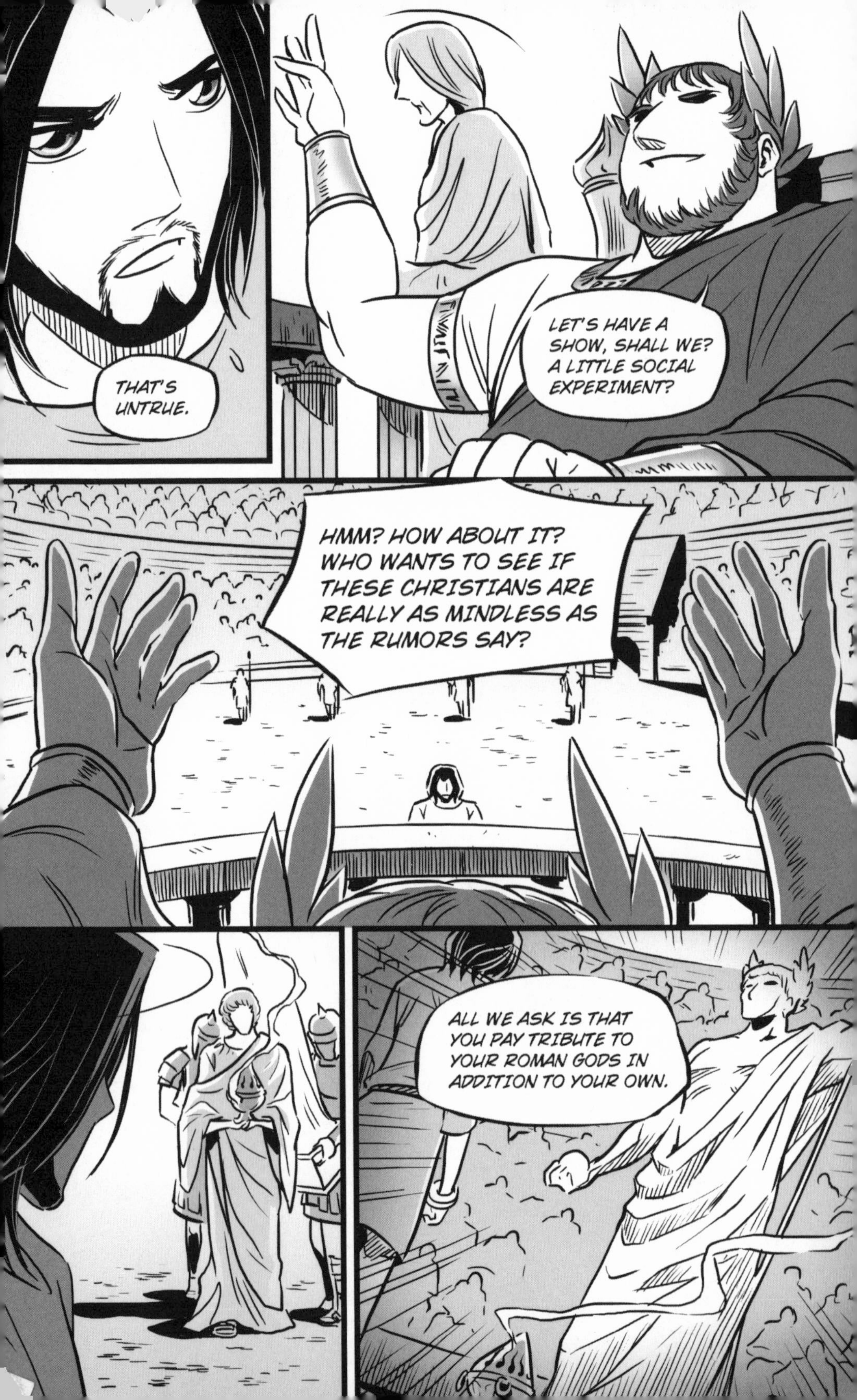
THAT'S UNTRUE.
LET'S HAVE A SHOW, SHALL WE? A LITTLE SOCIAL EXPERIMENT?
HMM? HOW ABOUT IT? WHO WANTS TO SEE IF THESE CHRISTIANS ARE REALLY AS MINDLESS AS THE RUMORS SAY?
ALL WE ASK IS THAT YOU PAY TRIBUTE TO YOUR ROMAN GODS IN ADDITION TO YOUR OWN.

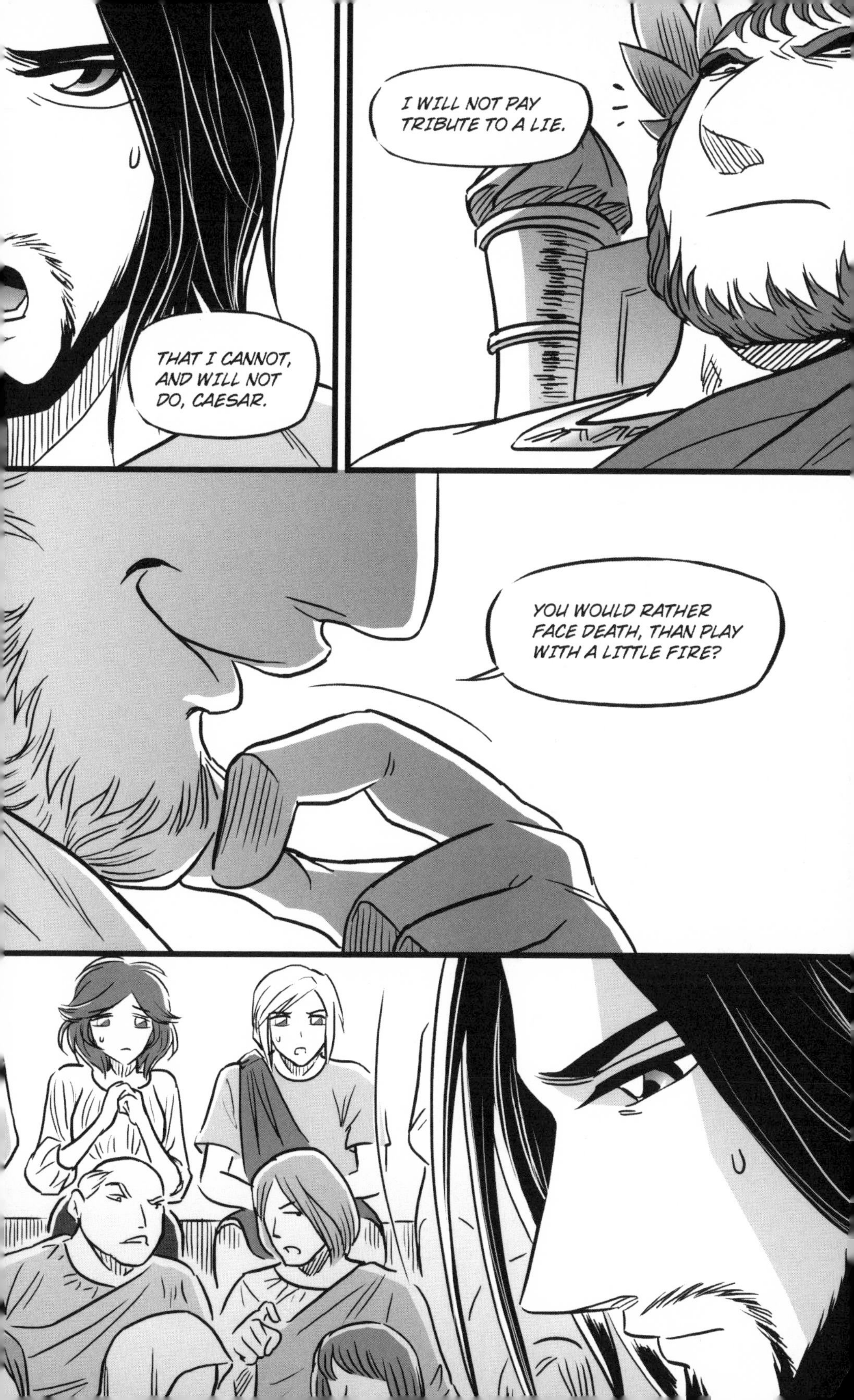
THAT I CANNOT, AND WILL NOT DO, CAESAR.
I WILL NOT PAY TRIBUTE TO A LIE.
YOU WOULD RATHER FACE DEATH, THAN PLAY WITH A LITTLE FIRE?

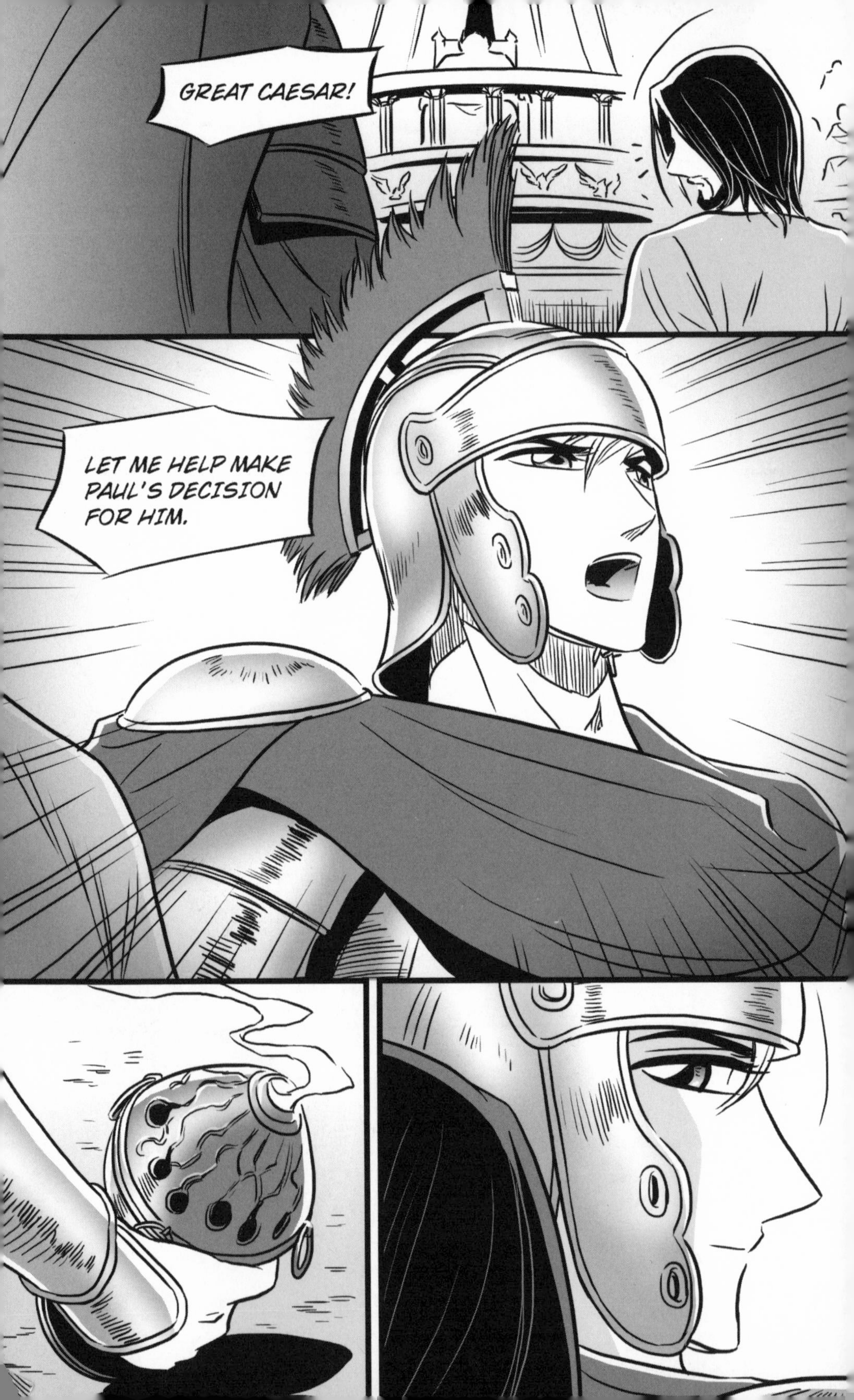
GREAT CAESAR!
LET ME HELP MAKE PAUL'S DECISION FOR HIM.

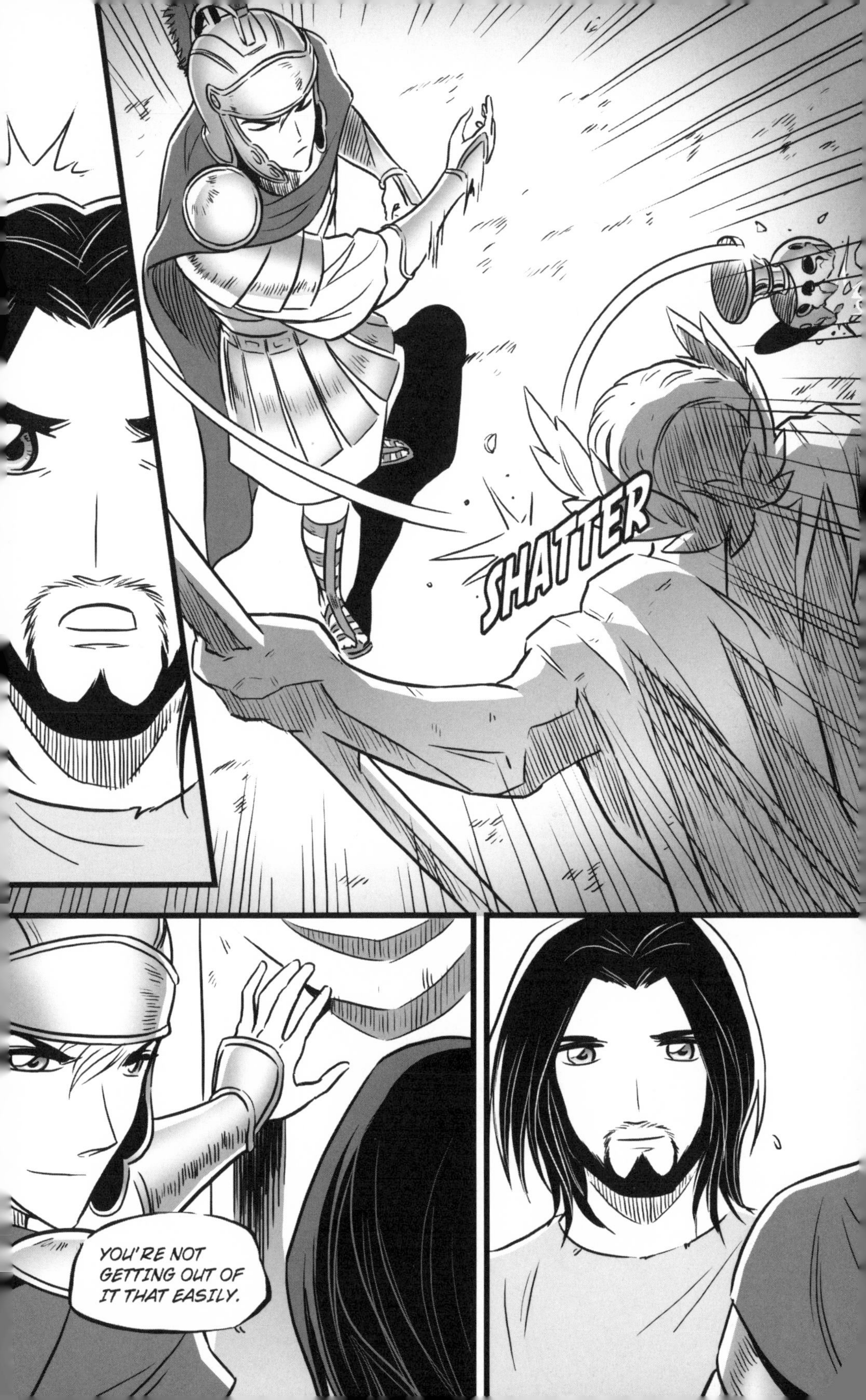
SHATTER
YOU'RE NOT GETTING OUT OF IT THAT EASILY.

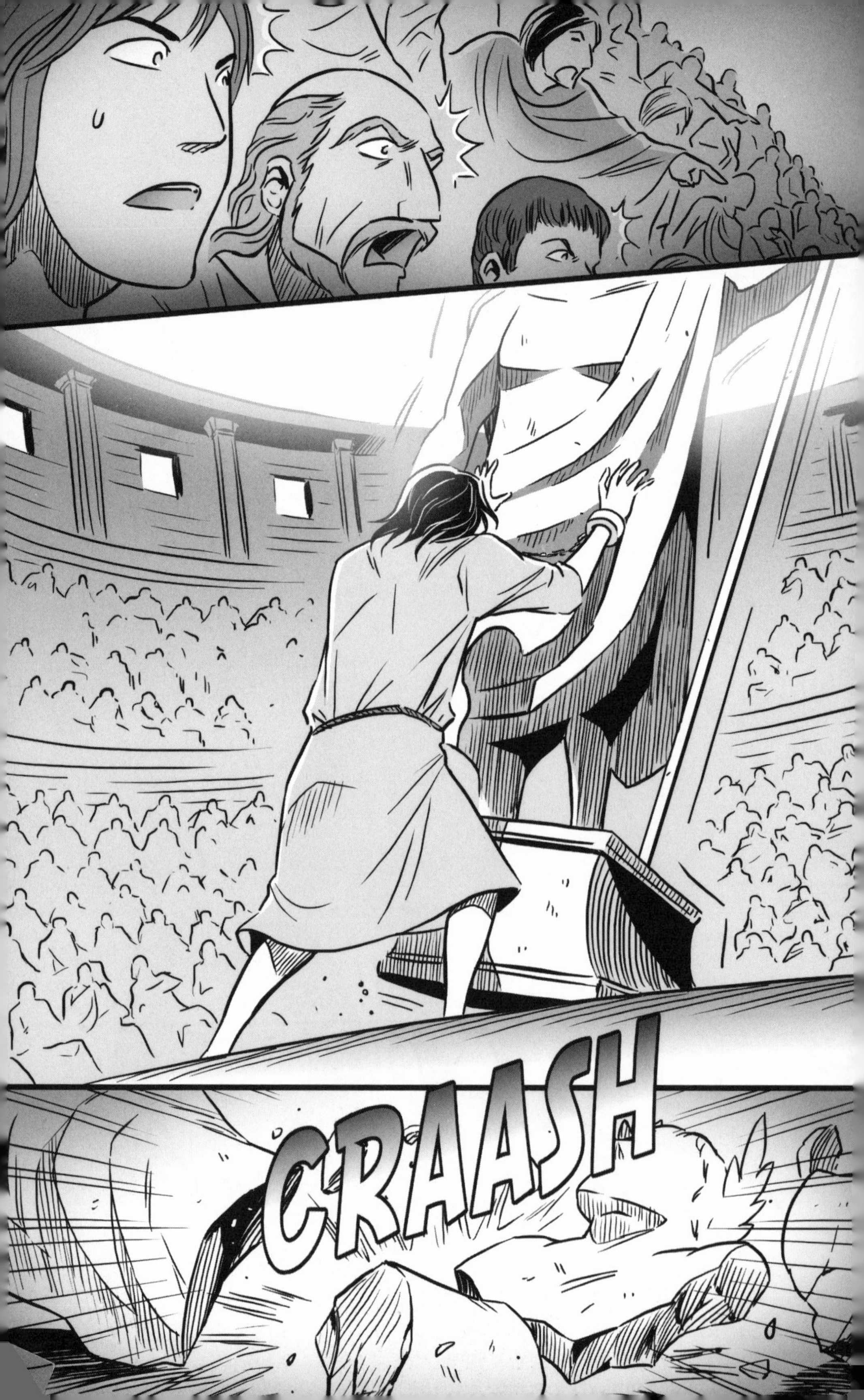
CRAASH

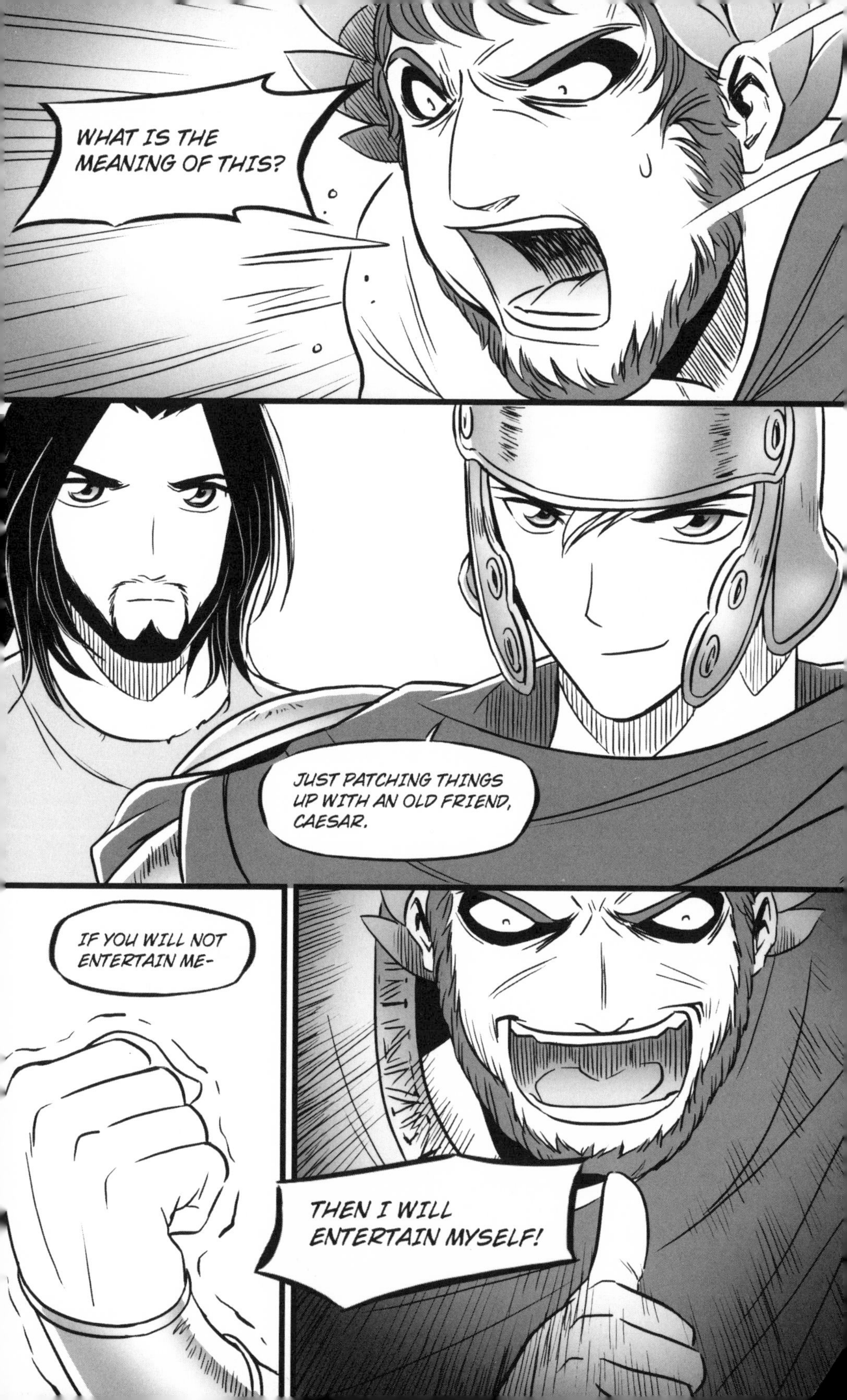
WHAT IS THE MEANING OF THIS?
JUST PATCHING THINGS UP WITH AN OLD FRIEND, CAESAR.
IF YOU WILL NOT ENTERTAIN ME-
THEN I WILL ENTERTAIN MYSELF!

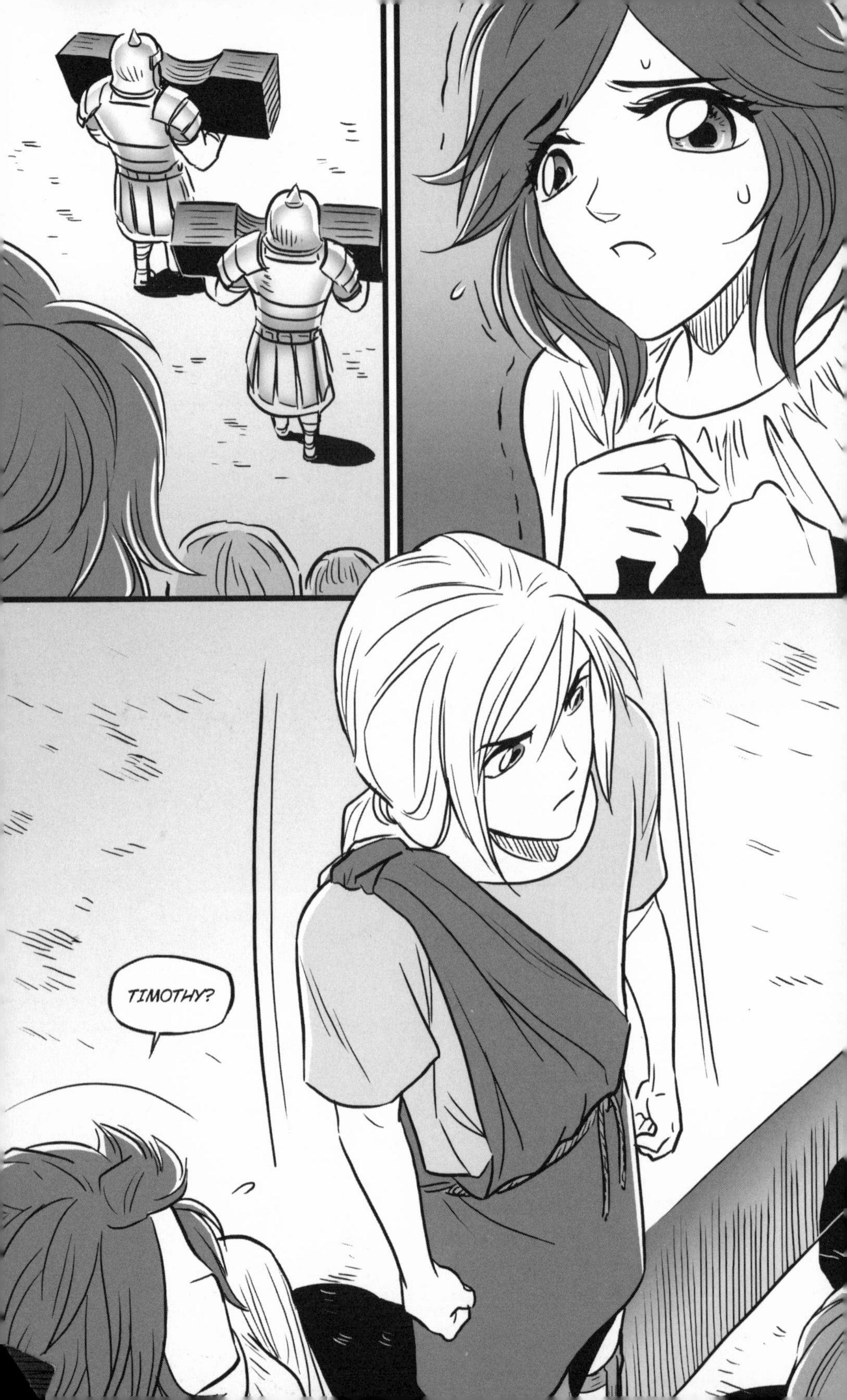
TIMOTHY?

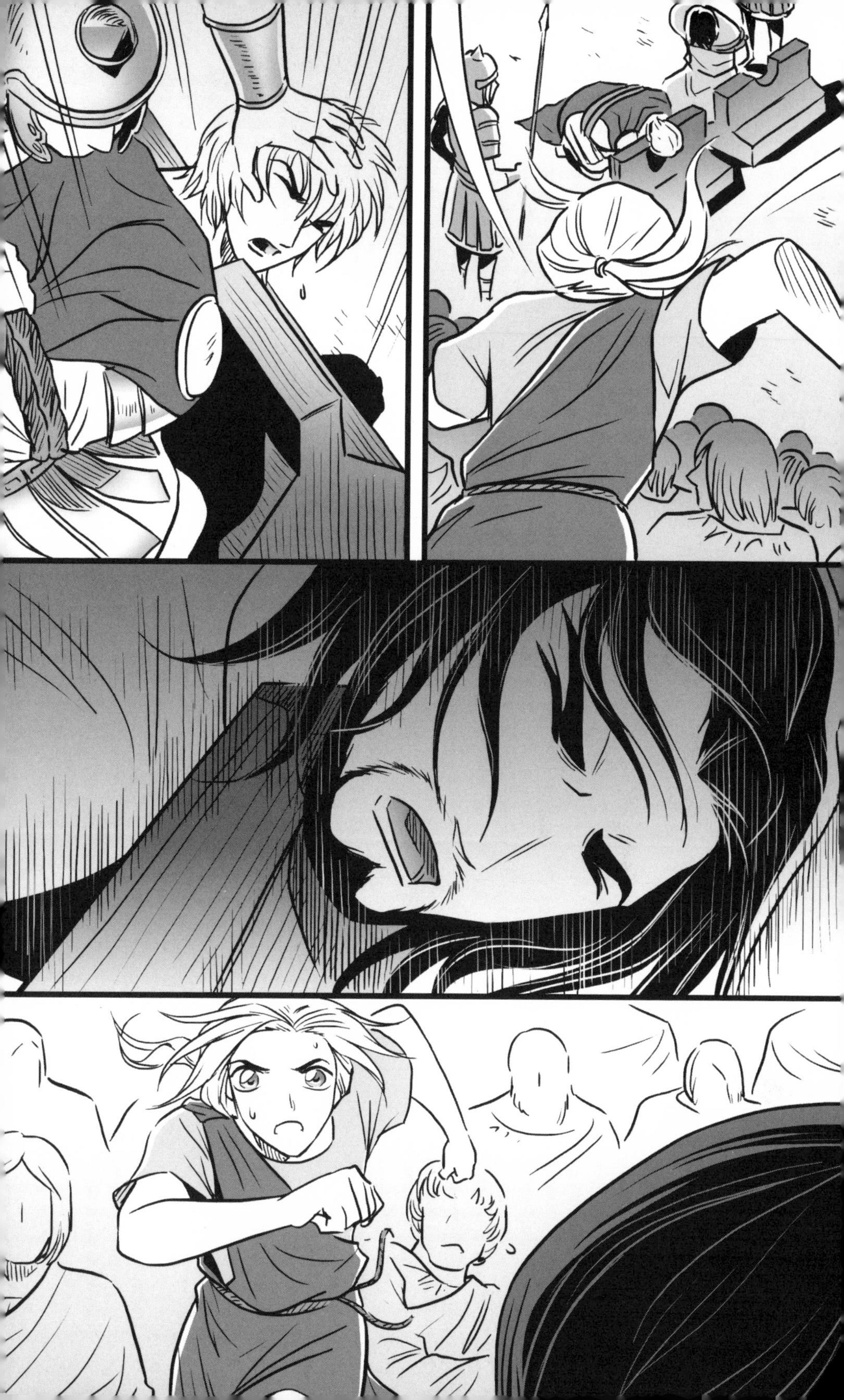

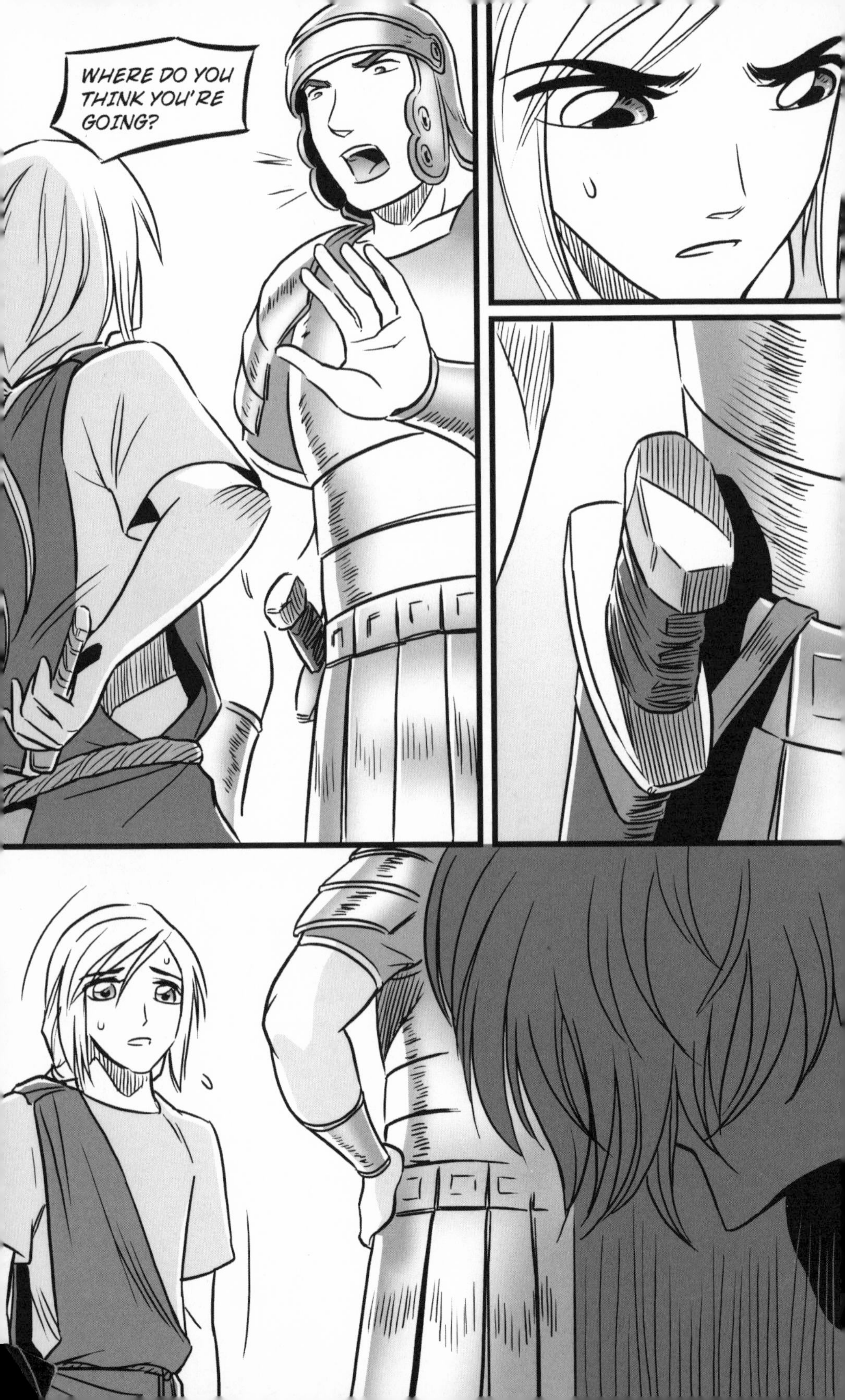
WHERE DO YOU THINK YOU'RE GOING?

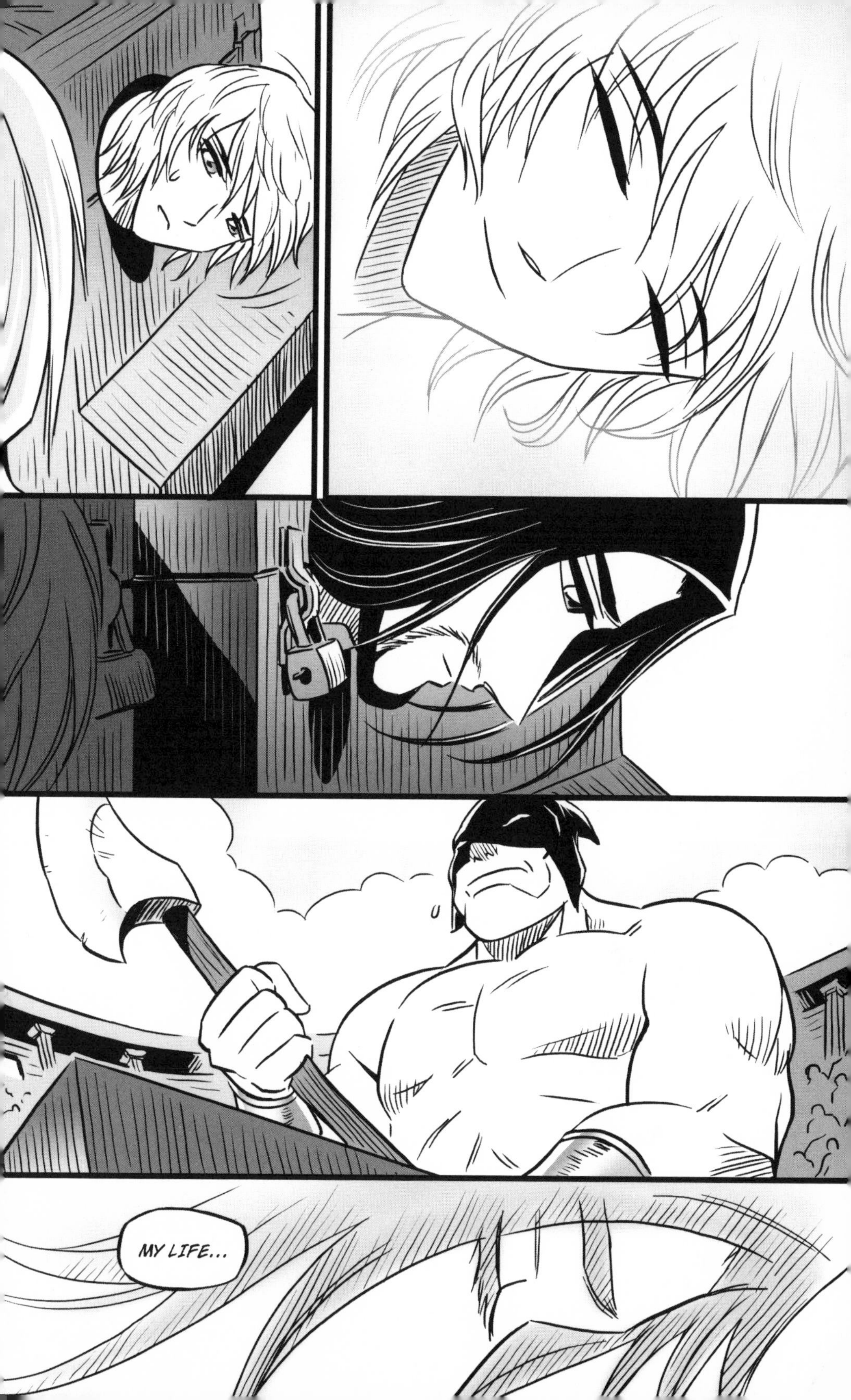
MY LIFE...

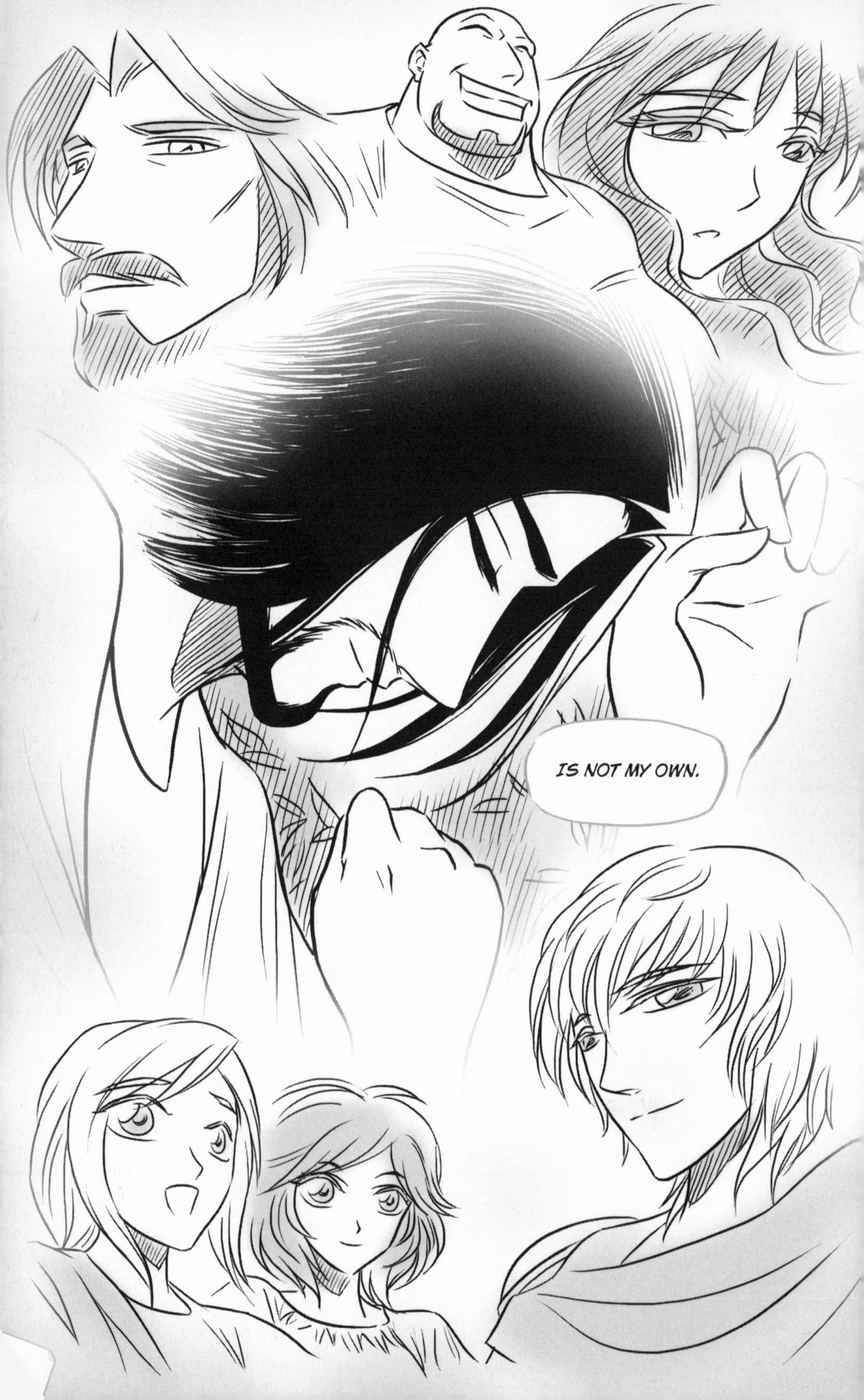
IS NOT MY OWN.

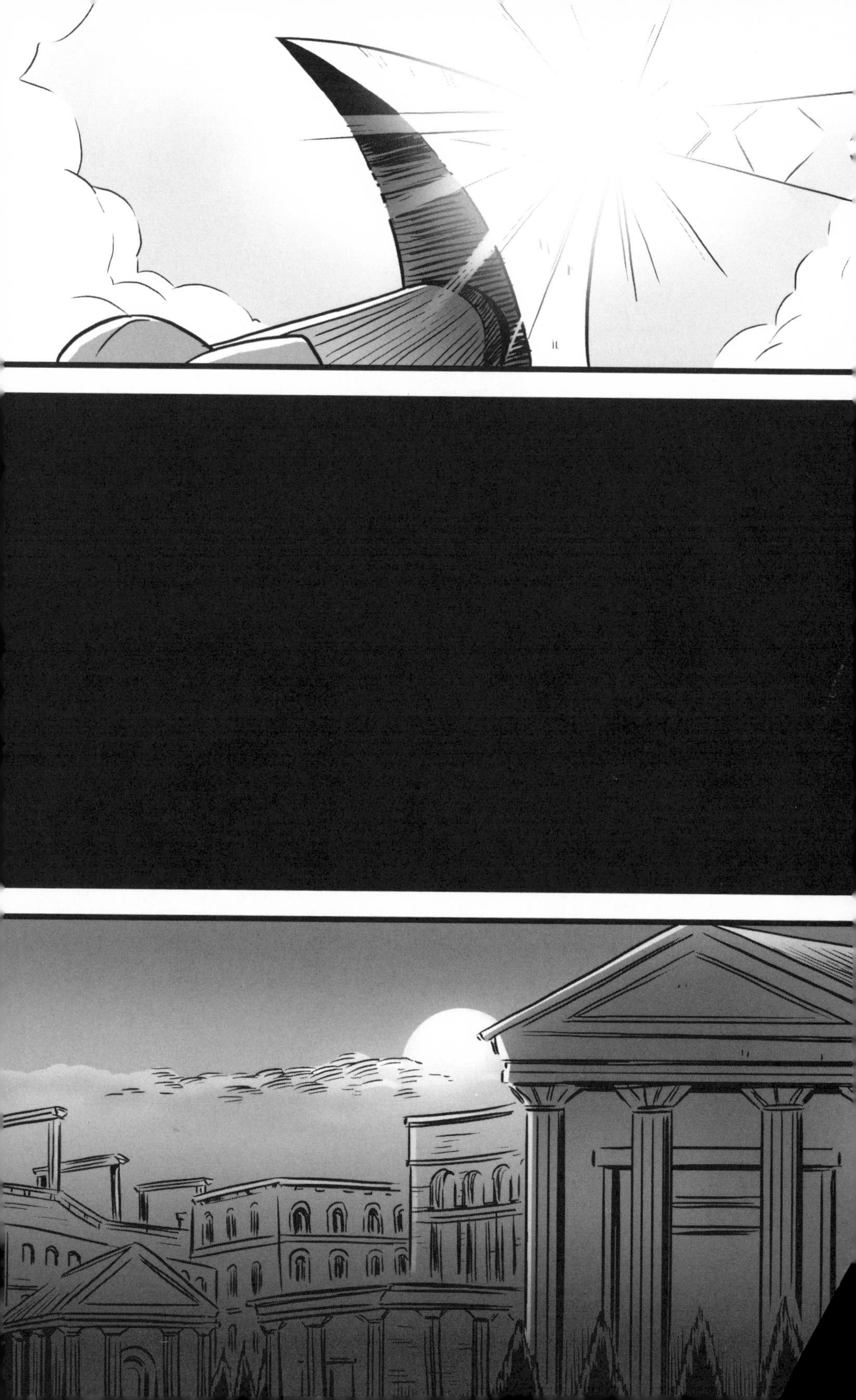

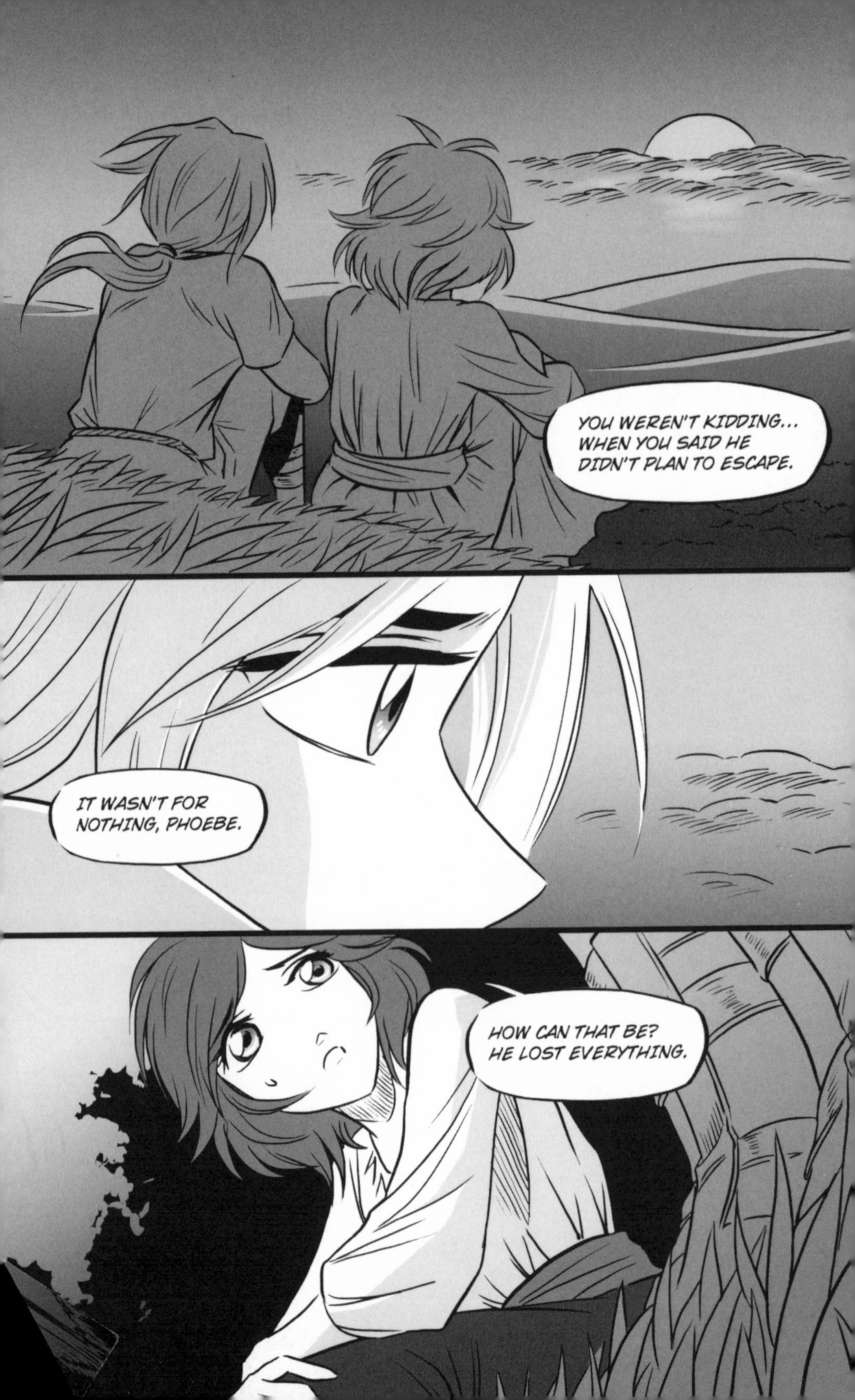
YOU WEREN'T KIDDING... WHEN YOU SAID HE DIDN'T PLAN TO ESCAPE.
IT WASN'T FOR NOTHING, PHOEBE.
HOW CAN THAT BE? HE LOST EVERYTHING.

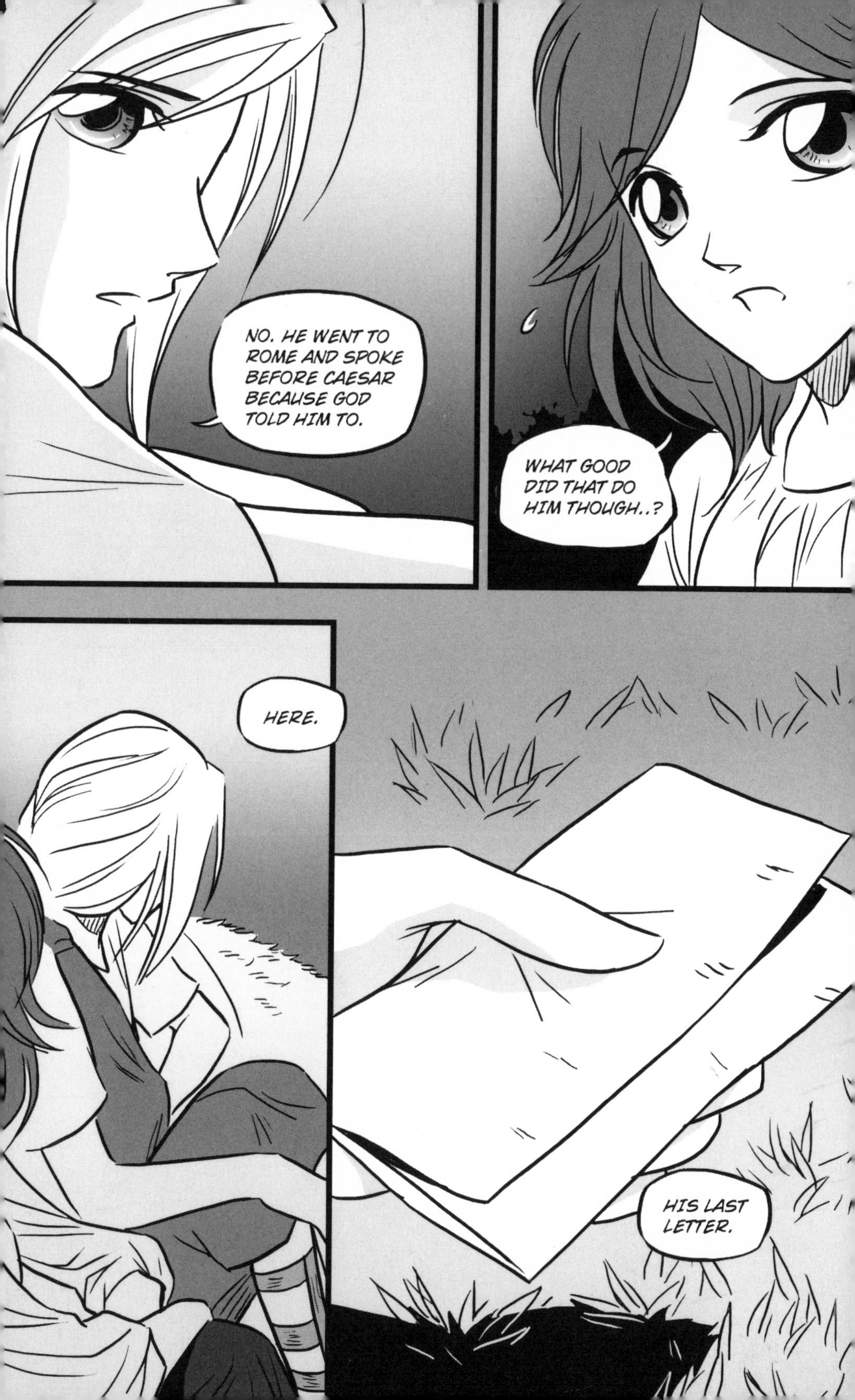
NO. HE WENT TO ROME AND SPOKE BEFORE CAESAR BECAUSE GOD TOLD HIM TO.
WHAT GOOD DID THAT DO HIM THOUGH..?
HERE.
HIS LAST LETTER.

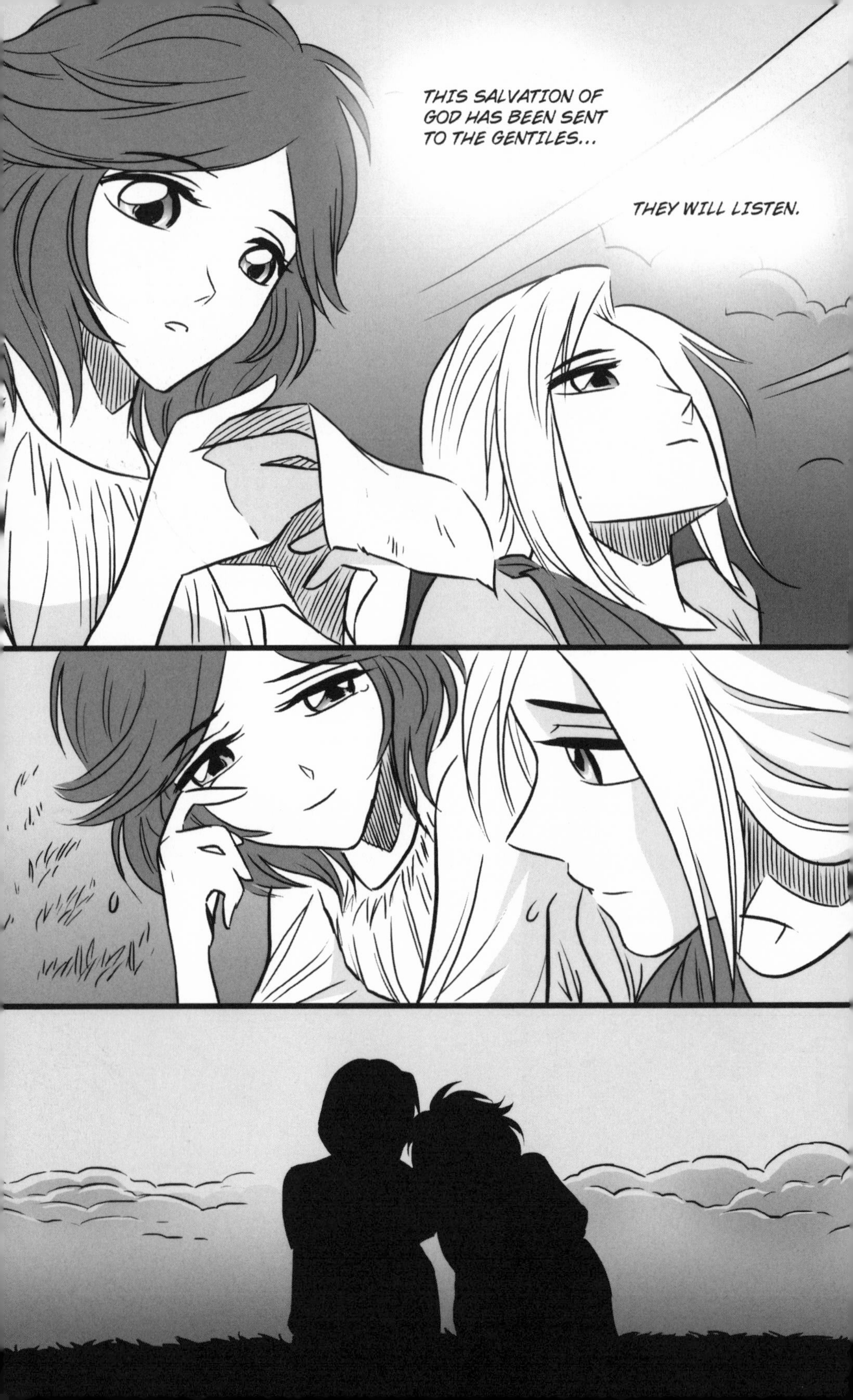
THIS SALVATION OF GOD HAS BEEN SENT TO THE GENTILES...
THEY WILL LISTEN.

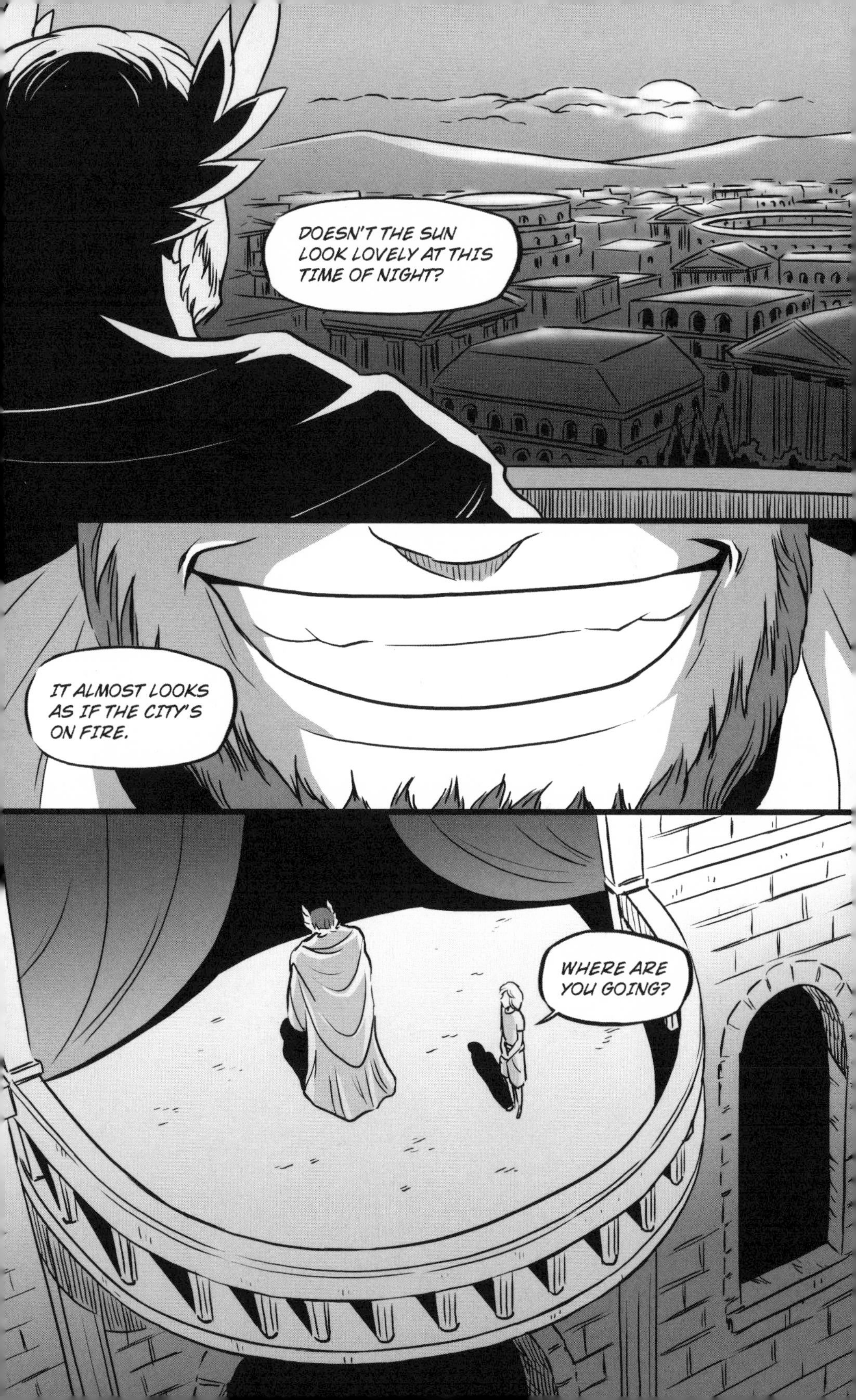
DOESN'T THE SUN LOOK LOVELY AT THIS TIME OF NIGHT?
IT ALMOST LOOKS AS IF THE CITY'S ON FIRE.
WHERE ARE YOU GOING?

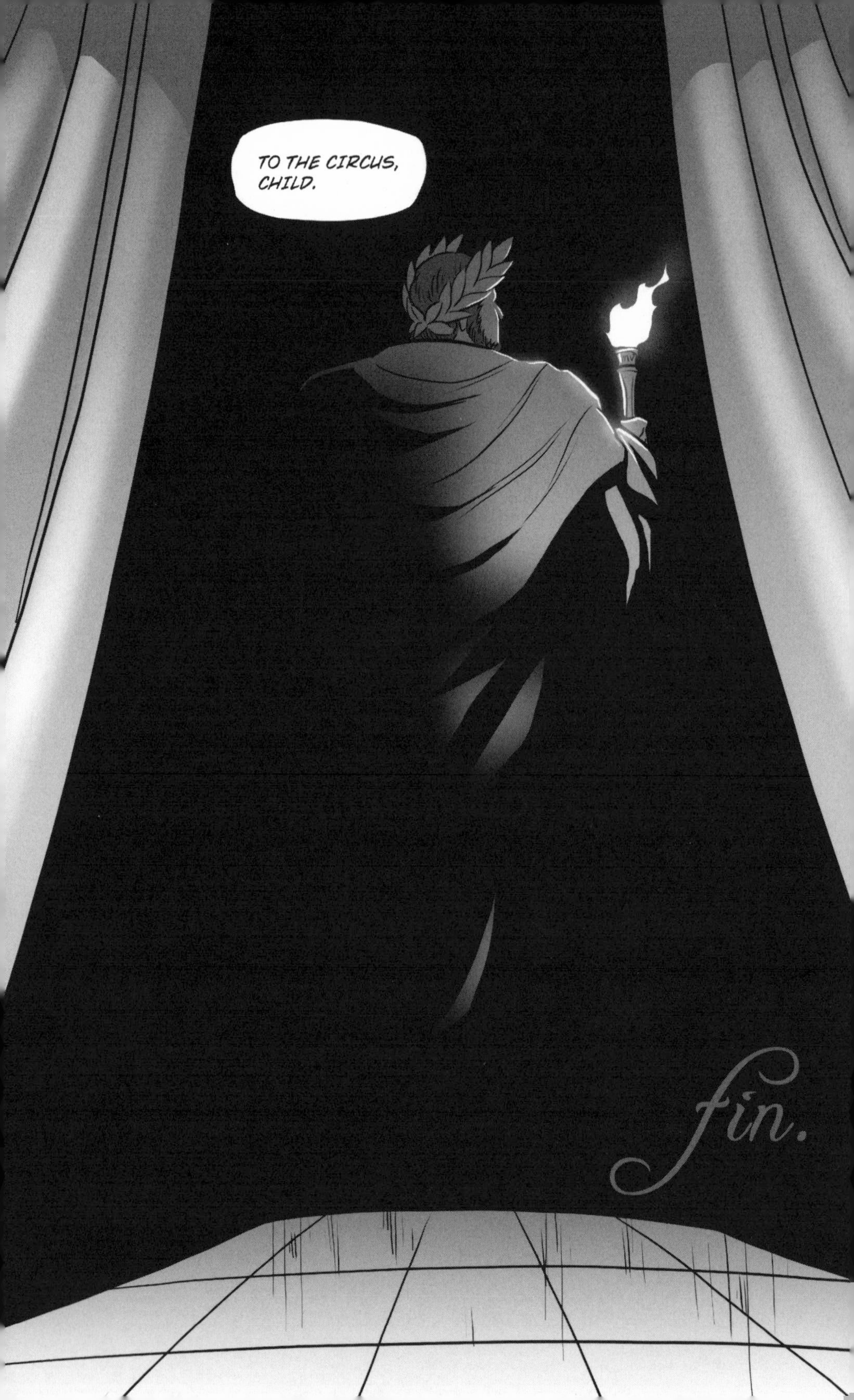
TO THE CIRCUS, CHILD.
fin.

What defines the heroes and heroines in our manga?
Honor, sacrifice, courage, faith, love, or wisdom?
Read the new manga series by ATIQTUQ.
Got it? Say "ah tick took" to get it!

PAUL
TARSUS TO REDEMPTION
VOLUMES 1, 2 & 3

www.paultarsustoredemption.com

JUDITH
CAPTIVE TO CONQUEROR
VOLUMES 1 & 2

www.judithcaptivetoconqueror.com

Want to hear about our new releases?

Find us on Facebook @ *Manga Hero*